W9-AGX-974

Thorough-Bass Accompaniment according to Johann David Heinichen

REVISED EDITION

Studies in Musicology, No. 84

George J. Buelow, Series Editor

Professor of Music
Indiana University

Other Titles in This Series

Thorough-Bass Accompaniment according to Johann David Heinichen

REVISED EDITION

George J. Buelow

UMI RESEARCH PRESS

Ann Arbor, Michigan

Produced and distributed by
UMI Research Press
an imprint of
University Microfilms, Inc.
Ann Arbor, Michigan 48106

Library of Congress Cataloging in Publication Data

Buelow, George J.
Thorough-bass accompaniment according to
Johann David Heinichen.

(Studies in musicology ; no. 84)
Bibliography: p.
Includes index.
1. Thorough bass.   I. Heinichen, Johann David,
1683-1729.   II. Title.   III. Series.
MT49.B84   1986   781.3'2   85-21005
ISBN 0-8357-1648-1 (alk. paper)

To my parents

Johann David Heinichen (Standing in the Midst of the Instrumentalists) Conducts
the Dresden *Hofkapelle* in His *Serenata fatta sulla Elba.*
This was part of the marriage festivities for the Prince-Elector of Saxony in
September 1719. This illustration was preserved in the Staatliche
Kupferstichkabinett Dresden (Sax. Top. Ca. 200), and has been published by
Gerhard Pietzsche in "Dresdner Hoffeste von 16.–18. Jahrhundert," in *Musik und
Bild: Festschrift Max Seiffert* (Kassel, 1938), plate 26, and also in *MGG* 3, plate 18.
(Photograph by courtesy of Bärenreiter Archive.)

Contents

Figures

Preface to the First Edition

The impetus resulting in this book was generated a number of years ago when, as a graduate student at New York University, I was first attracted to the music of the Baroque era. More specifically, it was a course, "The Music of Johann Sebastian Bach," taught by Professor Martin Bernstein, that largely determined the nature of the work in hand. In this course I met Johann David Heinichen and his unique treatise. After a tentative acquaintance with the formidable bulk of book and its complex language, a friendship grew steadily as I made by way through page after page of obviously authoritative instructions for the complex art of thorough-bass accompanying. In a search through existing research for the thorough-bass, I was surprised to discover that Heinichen had been neglected, the only exception being the passages from Heinichen's treatise used by F. T. Arnold in his important survey of thorough-bass treatises.

Since the great bulk of Baroque music is inseparable from the thorough-bass practice, it is difficult to understand why our current enthusiasm for reviving Baroque music has not stimulated major research related to the practice. Often one meets discouragement rather than assistance, for example William J. Mitchell's comment in the introduction to his translation of C. P. E. Bach's *Versuch über die wahre Art das Clavier zu spielen*: "The extemporaneous realization of a figured bass is a dead art. We have left behind us the period of the basso continuo and with it all the unwritten law, the axioms, the things that were taken for granted; in a word, the spirit of the time."

Such a statement (written in 1949) was too pessimistic. Although one cannot deny that the practice of accompanying from thorough-basses was lost during the nineteenth century, this loss does not preclude rediscovery. Musicologists tend to be somewhat defeatist in their attitude concerning the many problems related to the thorough-bass, and the previous lack of accessibility to Heinichen's treatise as well as the many other Baroque thorough-bass treatises indicates some of the disinterest of musicians in the art of thorough-bass accompaniment. One sign of encouragement, however, is the increasing number of university curriculums offering a special course in thorough-bass accompanying.

The present book gives a detailed study of late Baroque thorough-bass practices based primarily on one of the great Baroque treatises. The clarity of Heinichen's instructions coupled with the many practical musical illustrations makes this book a manual of self-instruction for keyboard performers or a suitable text for a course in thorough-bass practices of the late Baroque. Similar studies are long overdue for other major thorough-bass treatises written during the lengthy history of the Baroque. Only when this is achieved shall we be capable of assimilating the multitude of facts for the thorough-bass practice and of applying them accurately to Baroque music. Then we shall have the information to distinguish between kinds of thorough-bass accompaniment; for there must be, in the era of style-consciousness that is the Baroque, distinctions between accompaniments for sacred, operatic, chamber, and orchestral styles, as well as differences in accompanying affected by national temperaments. Most importantly, we shall be able to appreciate better the changes wrought in the character of thorough-bass realizations by the advancing age of the Baroque. And the problems of the thorough-bass do not stop at the borders of the Baroque age, for despite what some music historians have said, the thorough-bass practice does not suddenly disappear when music styles shift to Classicism. But what do we know about the thorough-bass practice in early Classical music, such as the symphony?

This book was written originally (though in somewhat different form) as partial fulfillment for the Ph.D. degree from New York University. In that endeavor I had frequent assistance and encouragement from the Music Department, Graduate School of Arts and Science. I should like to acknowledge my thanks to Professor Gustave Reese and Professor Martin Bernstein for their many invaluable suggestions during the development of my research. The entire project, however, owes its greatest debt of gratitude to Professor Jan LaRue, whose continuous good counsel over a lengthy period enabled me to avoid innumerable pitfalls of method, and whose advice on matters of form and style continues to stand out from every page of this considerably revised version. I should also like to thank here the several libraries and their staffs for giving me so much help: the Music Division of the Library of Congress, the Music Library of Northwestern University, the Newberry Library, the Music Library of the University of Chicago, the Kongelige Bibliotek (Copenhagen), the Staats- und Universitäts-Bibliothek Hamburg, and the Bibliothèque Nationale (Paris). Special thanks are due to the cordial staff of the Music Library of the University of California (Berkeley), particularly Professor Vincent Duckles and Mr. John Emerson.

The entire revision of the dissertation was made possible through generous research grants received from the University of California. Lastly, this book would not have reached completion without the aid of my assistant at the University of California, Riverside, Mr. Robert Morin, and without the patience and coöperation of the staff of the University of California Press.

George J. Buelow
Riverside, California

Preface to the Revised Edition

During some two decades since this book first appeared, achievements in historical performance of Baroque as well as earlier music have accumulated at an astonishing rate. Performance practice has become a concept of second nature to the scholar as well as the amateur music lover. As a descriptive label it is often used to promote sound recordings in conjunction with other key phrases as "original instruments" or "authentic style of performance." Those doubts once expressed about recovering lost traditions of performance — like that of thorough-bass accompaniment (doubts prevalent at the time of this book's first publication) — now fade in significance. A revised edition of this book, which illuminates explanations of the art of accompanying from a thorough-bass, based on late Italian Baroque practices, seems timely.

One can only regret that in the intervening decades all too little additional scholarship has contributed to this particular aspect of historical performance. We still lack translations into English of most of the other major thorough-bass treatises from the Baroque, and very few new studies of continuo accompaniment have been published.

Even though Italian Baroque music — for opera as well as solo, ensemble, and orchestral performance — has become exceedingly popular, Italian concepts of historical performance, whether related to continuo practice, ornamentation, or instrumental performance styles, still seem overshadowed by German theories and ideals. And though Heinichen was German, his musical training was essentially Italian, and his career at the court of Dresden developed in a largely Italian milieu. But his remarkable treatise has as yet to take its pre-eminent place among the most important documents of the Italian musical Baroque in theory and practice. The shadows of German musicology, German Baroque music, and especially Johann Sebastian Bach still loom large.*

This revised edition retains the text of the first edition except where factual and typographical errors needed correction or adjustment. I am grateful to many colleagues who over the past decades have taken the time to assist me in locating these errors that marred the original text.

Two new appendices expand the scope of the book and clarify more completely Heinichen's contributions. Appendix B gives a complete English translation of the *Einleitung* to *Der General-Bass in der Composition*, in which Heinichen offers an extensive discussion about various aspects of the composer's métier and other views on his art. Most valuable, and frequently cited in the musicological literature, is his lengthy analysis of the affections and how they can be realized in vocal music for which a text offers little or no inspirational content. Appendix C offers an analysis of Heinichen's theory of dissonance resolution in the theatrical style.†

This new edition thus provides a more comprehensive consideration of Heinichen's importance in the study of Baroque performance practice. It is hoped that this volume will prove useful and instructive to scholar and performer alike.

Bloomington, Indiana
May 1986

---

*For example, in his article "continuo," in *The New Grove Dictionary of Music*, Peter Williams devotes almost half of his extensive remarks about the history of continuo practices to how Bach's music should be realized, as if this exposition summed up all of Baroque continuo practice at the turn of the eighteenth century.

†This originally appeared as an article in the Yale *Journal of Music Theory* 6 (1962): 216–73.

Abbreviations

AmZ	*Allgemeine Musikalische Zeitung*
AfMw	*Archiv für Musikwissenschaft*
DDT	*Denkmäler deutscher Tonkunst*
GroveD	*Grove's Dictionary of Music, 5th edition*
JAMS	*Journal of the American Musicological Society*
JMT	*Journal of Music Theory*
Kgr. Ber.	Kongress-Bericht
Mf	*Die Musikforschung*
MGG	*Die Musik in Geschichte und Gegenwart*
ML	*Music and Letters*
MQ	*Musical Quarterly*
SIMG	*Sammelbände der Internationalen Musikgesellschaft*
VfMw	*Vierteljahresschrift für Musikwissenschaft*

1

Biography

"The Rameau of Germany," "Nature guides his every note." He "does not just compose, he contemplates and thinks . . . and shows the world what knowledge is." These quotations are typical of the praise bestowed upon Johann David Heinichen by mid-eighteenth-century writers on music, and represent the opinions of Charles Burney, Johann Scheibe, and Johann Mattheson.[1] Heinichen was the author of the first comprehensive treatise on the thorough-bass, one of the most instructive works for musical composition written in Germany in the first half of the eighteenth century. In addition he was a distinguished composer as well as capellmeister at the court of Augustus I (the Strong) in Dresden. During the less than fifty-year span of Heinichen's life, from 1683 to 1729, German culture in most of its aspects experienced the great onslaught of Italian artists, especially in connection with the rise of opera. Throughout these years German music achieved a synthesis of many conflicting national trends and crosscurrents of music that is particularly evident in the works of Johann Sebastian Bach.

Indeed, Bach's preponderant influence is one reason for the almost complete obscurity of Heinichen's name in present-day knowledge of German Baroque music. Bach's music, like a massive shadow, has concealed the creative efforts of many lesser masters working in his and preceding epochs. Nevertheless, our understanding of one of the Baroque's greatest composers and of eighteenth-century German music in general remains incomplete until we search more deeply into the musical thinking of Bach's predecessors and contemporaries. Another reason for the almost total neglect of Heinichen's theoretical and musical output lies in the indifference to the thorough-bass exhibited by writers on music in all nations at the beginning of the nineteenth century, a condition resulting from the new musical styles that had brought the Baroque to an end.

In 1913 Gustav Adolph Seibel[2] published the first biography of Heinichen to reëxamine the composer's life and music with modern musicological methods. Only two other major studies of Heinichen exist: the works of Richard Tanner[3] (concerning Heinichen's dramatic music) and Günter Hausswald[4] (for the instrumental works).

A review of Heinichen's life brings one into close contact with three of the great cities of the Baroque, focal points for many of the distinguished musical events of that era: Leipzig, Venice, and Dresden. Lines drawn between these cities on a map of Europe form a triangle that encompasses symbolically the musical mainstream of the German Baroque.

In the eighteenth century Leipzig had reached a peak of musical productivity that it never surpassed. The richly inventive genius of native-born musicians and those coming from neighboring Saxon and Thuringian towns[5] brought a remarkable array of musical talent to the city. Numerous opportunities existed for a musician in Leipzig: the many churches, the new opera house that opened in 1693, the several groups of collegia that gathered at local coffee houses to play for patrons (and for themselves). The university in itself attracted musicians to Leipzig; here they could prepare themselves for court and church positions demanding a scholar as well as a trained musician.

Unlike Leipzig, which was only sporadically important as a musical center, Dresden, where Heinichen lived during the last twelve years of his life, had been of special musical significance since the sixteenth century when the Saxon Elector moved his court there from Torgau. Its musical fame continued into modern times, though in no period did the city enjoy as much cultural splendor and political importance as it did during the first half of the eighteenth century. Before its destruction during World War II, Dresden stood as an architectural monument to the era of Augustus the Strong, who dreamed of building the center of his political system to rival any other European court, including Versailles. Significantly, this Dresden built along the east bank of the Elbe was both musically and architecturally Italian in origin.

It was in Italy that the roots of much of the German Baroque were anchored. Major German courts and cities imported Italian opera composers, singers, instrumentalists, architects, and painters; German musicians traveled south of the Alps to experience firsthand the sources of Italian musical inspiration, to refine their own styles, and especially to learn to write Italian opera. Heinichen gave one reason for the arduous journey to Italy in *Der General-Bass*: "Why do we go through effort, danger, and expense to travel around from nation to nation . . . ? Simply and solely to develop our good taste [*Goût*]."[6]

This Italian musical magnetism affected many generations of German musicians. Hans Leo Hassler (1565–1612) was the first great German composer to study in Italy, and among the many following him were Johann Jakob Froberger (1616–67) and Heinrich Schütz (1585–1672). In the first years of the eighteenth century Handel preceded Heinichen to Italy, and after the latter had been appointed capellmeister to the court at Dresden, Johann Adolf Hasse (1699–1783) joined the steady flow of Germans to Italian soil seeking what they thought to be the musical truths. Handel, Hasse, and Heinichen, each having served his musical apprenticeship in Italy, were later dubbed the "three important H's of German music" by Johann Mattheson,[7] a musical triumvirate forgotten long before Hans von Bülow created the more enduring symbol of the three B's.

The earliest biographical reference to Heinichen is found in Walther's *Musicalisches Lexicon* (1732). Walther's biographical entry is significantly long (more than two full columns, while Johann Sebastian Bach and Francesco Gasparini each are allotted only two-thirds of a column) and indicates Heinichen's prominence during the middle of the eighteenth century. Walther begins: "[Heinichen] . . . the son of a pastor, born the 17th of April, 1683 in Crössuln, a place two hours from Weissenfels, close to Teuchern, studied in Leipzig, made a trip to Italy around 1710, and was appointed Capellmeister in 1715 by His Royal Highness, the Prince-Elector of Saxony. . . ."[8]

The Heinichen family line originates in Anhalt-Sachsen, a region approximately fifty miles southwest of Leipzig. The church records at Pegau, birthplace of Johann David's father, list the family name of Heinichen back to the mid-sixteenth century. They were middle-class workers, tanners, needle-makers, and soap-makers, although a Michael Heinichen, born in 1632, studied at the Thomasschule in Leipzig and became cantor in Pegau.[9]

Heinichen's father, David, an alumnus of the Thomasschule and the university at Leipzig, moved to Crössuln in 1674 to begin his lifelong career as pastor of the village church. Crössuln borders the larger town of Teuchern, though it is too small to appear on most maps of the region. The source of young Heinichen's education before going to Leipzig is unknown, but he probably studied with his father or another musically trained teacher or perhaps at a school in neighboring Teuchern. We learn from Heinichen himself of his early musical talent: "Already in my thirteenth year, [I had] composed and personally conducted numerous church compositions in small villages."[10]

Following his father's example, Heinichen enrolled in the Leipzig

Thomasschule on March 30, 1696.[11] The church boarding school connected with the Thomaskirche had been founded during the Reformation to provide young musicians for services and it was well known for its emphasis on musical training. At the turn of the eighteenth century the students of the Thomasschule came largely from the homes of Saxon theologians, organists, and well-to-do burghers; they came to a school in which "thought and action, one certainly can say, were arranged by the hour to music."[12] Weddings, burials, or Sunday services all demanded the performance of vocal music by the students. Often, in the case of special festivals, regular studies might be suspended for days to make music rehearsals possible. The four upper classes received seven hours of music instruction each week from the school's cantor, who not only taught in the school but was responsible as well for the music in the churches of St. Thomas and St. Nicholas.[13]

The cantors of the Thomaskirche have included many outstanding German composers: Georg Rhaw (1488–1548), Seth Calvisius (1556–1615), Johann Hermann Schein (1586–1630), Johann Kuhnau (1660–1722) and, of course, Johann Sebastian Bach. Johann Schelle (1648–1701), cantor at the time Heinichen began his studies, was installed as director of the Thomasschule in 1677 and retained this position until his death in 1701.[14] Heinichen, however, studied organ not with Schelle but with Kuhnau, organist at the Thomaskirche until he became cantor upon Schelle's death. In light of Heinichen's comment on his own musical abilities before coming to Leipzig, it is not difficult to imagine that his talents interested Kuhnau enough for the latter to give him private organ and harpsichord lessons. Christoph Graupner (1683–1760), also a private student of Kuhnau's, was taught composition by the teen-age Heinichen,[15] another substantiation of Heinichen's early mastery of music.

Johann Kuhnau became cantor in 1701 after seventeen years as church organist. One of the great names in pre-Bach music history, Kuhnau belongs more to the spirit of the seventeenth than to the eighteenth century, even though his music often spanned the style gap between the two centuries. He was, in Schering's words, one of the last great cantors "in whom an element of medieval universality was evident, who mastered music, law theology, oratory, poetry, mathematics, and foreign languages."[16]

Heinichen was among the fortunate few at the Thomasschule, for he gained special attention from Kuhnau as his assistant, and was made responsible for copying and correcting his manuscripts.[17] These duties were not only an honor, but enabled Heinichen to copy considerable amounts of music, an instructional method often used by teachers of the time. Heinichen was the first student with a superior musical gift for composition to come to Kuhnau. Heinichen's own words, "while I was a student of counterpoint . . . (for at that time I was so enthusiastic about counterpoint that I hardly ate, drank, or slept),"[18] describe his extraordinary application to study. He had a resourceful mind and was apparently interested in theoretical matters from his youth. He indicates in his treatise[19] that the concept of a "musical circle" for relating all major and minor tonalities originated while he was a harpsichord student with Kuhnau. Kuhnau must have found considerable solace in Heinichen's musical enthusiasm, which was in sharp contrast to the attitudes of other students who were poorly disciplined and avid champions of the new operatic music. "For most of the students . . . as soon as they have attained, through the painstaking efforts of the cantor, some training and could be useful, seek out the company of opera singers, and from then on do little good and seek dismissal before their time, often with impudence and defiance. . . ."[20]

Heinichen became a law student at Leipzig's university in 1702, eventually qualifying for the profession of lawyer, a preparation often favored by eighteenth-century musicians. Music was not a separate university curriculum but was bound together in the humanistic concept of *artes liberales*. The seven liberal arts — the *trivium* including grammar, dialectics, and rhetoric, and the *quadrivium*, arithmetic, music, geometry, and astronomy — made up the two levels of university preparation that were somewhat analogous to our educational system in which the general training required for a Bachelor's degree leads the student into more specific studies for the Master's degree. At Leipzig this old tradition of intellectual development remained in force for a longer period in the Baroque than it did in many other European universities where music became a subject for dilettantes and unsuitable for scientific study. Dissertations written at the University of Leipzig during this time often connected music to non-musical subjects such as physics, mathematics, history, and particularly theology, a good indication that music was stressed frequently in the lectures given in these subjects.[21]

The accent on music in academic life resulted at least partially from the important role music held in the daily lives of Leipzig's citizens. Heinichen undoubtedly learned much from assisting in frequent performances of church music and by hearing a variety of compositions in coffee houses, on the streets, and at the new opera house. Leipzig enjoyed the distinction of being one of the few German cities to have an opera house before 1700, and no small amount of Leipzig's success in its operatic venture can be attributed to the versatile assistance of university students who, as singers and orchestral players, contributed to every performance.

To establish opera in a city without operatic traditions or the patronage of a royal court required the unremitting efforts of Nikolaus Adam Strungk (1640–1700), capellmeister at Dresden and a composer with impressive operatic successes in Hamburg, Hanover, and Venice.[22] The Elector of Saxony granted him an opera privilege for Leipzig, possibly in the hope that an opera company under Strungk would become a training school for local talent on which the court at Dresden could draw for musical activities. Strungk retained the directorship until his death in 1700, although his actual musical duties were not heavy since operas could be performed only during the three annual fairs. With few exceptions lesser roles were sung by university students, including Telemann, Petzold, Grünewald, Graupner, Schieferdecker, Fasch, and even Heinichen.[23] From these experiences Heinichen first discovered the "theatrical style," which he described in detail in the *General-Bass*.

At this same time the university's Collegium musicum, founded some time in the mid-seventeenth century, shared with church and opera an important part in Leipzig's musical life. Kuhnau became its director in 1682 while he was a law student. Another law student, Georg Philipp Telemann (1681–1767), reorganized the Collegium in 1701 and also served as organist and music director of the Neukirche. Gathering in coffee houses, the students explored new instrumental music as well as cantatas and opera arias.[24] Heinichen directed the Collegium in 1709, which met at that time in the *Lehmannische Kaffeehaus am Markte*.[25]

Heinichen completed requirements for the law degree in the winter semester of 1705–6 and began a short-lived practice in Weissenfels, a center of provincial German culture and the residence of the Elector of Saxe-Weissenfels. Why did Heinichen move to Weissenfels? The city's proximity to Crössuln, Heinichen's home, might have drawn him there. More important perhaps was the attraction of an active music center under the artistically enthusiastic Duke Johann Georg, who imported student musicians from Leipzig to his court, either for guest performances or permanent positions. The court capellmeister was Johann Philipp Krieger (1649–1725), his assistant, Gottfried Grünewald (1675–1739), and the court organist, Christian Schieferdecker (1679–1732). Krieger's presence in Weissenfels had unquestioned significance for Heinichen's musical growth, although we can only guess at the extent to which the older musician influenced the young lawyer from Leipzig. Krieger, one of the great composers of the period, wrote in a wide variety of forms, but he succeeded with particular brilliance in his operas and cantatas. These works display a considerable Italian influence, not an unexpected characteristic since Krieger had studied in Italy. He knew Heinichen's music and apparently found it interesting, for he conducted a cantata by Heinichen in Weissenfels on St. Michael's Day, 1711.[26]

Reinhard Keiser (1674–1739) was another important German composer whom Heinichen met more than once during the years 1707 and 1708. Keiser, Hamburg's most brilliant opera director, spent the year as a guest in the home of his former teacher, Christian Schieferdecker.[27] In 1711, when Keiser returned to Hamburg, he supposedly performed Heinichen's opera, *Der Carneval von Venedig*.[28] Considering the musical forces at work around him, it is hardly surprising that Heinichen soon discarded all plans for a law profession; he had too much talent, and destiny insisted on bringing him into contact with three of the most dynamic composers of the time, first Kuhnau and then Krieger and Keiser.

At Leipzig the fledgling opera, after enduring several years of financial insecurity, underwent a series of managerial crises. Following Strungk's death his heirs, his business partner, Hieronimo Sartorio (architect of the opera house who also managed the staging of each opera), Sartorio's son, and the lessee on whose land the theatre was built all fought bitterly among themselves.[29] The ultimate victory of Samuel Ernst Döbricht, Strungk's son-in-law, who was an opera singer from Weissenfels, made Heinichen's return to Leipzig possible; for as opera director Döbricht invited Heinichen in 1709 to abandon his law career and to write operas.[30]

Although involved in his responsibilities as opera composer and as director of the Collegium musicum, Heinichen also found time to write his *Neu erfundene und gründliche Anweisung . . . zu vollkommener Erlernung des General-Basses*, published in Hamburg in 1711, and later to be revised and greatly enlarged as *Der General-Bass in der Composition*. His many musical activities brought him to the attention of Duke Moritz Wilhelm, who appointed him court composer at Zeitz and opera composer for Naumburg.

On July 9, 1710, Heinichen wrote to his patron at his summer residence, Moritzburg on the Elbe, for recommendations as an opera composer to other German courts that he planned to visit. In the letter[31] he speaks of the good fortune enabling him to serve the Duke "*mit meiner wenigen Composition bey denen Naumburgischen Opern.*" It was Heinichen's plan to make the trip at the end of the summer of 1710. Apparently hoping for

quick action, Heinichen wrote to the most influential member of the
Duke's household, Duchess Maria Amalia, requesting that she urge her
husband to dictate the letters he needed.[32] With remarkable swiftness, the
Duke wrote to his cousin, Duke Anthon Ulrich of Braunschweig and
Lüneburg, the following day:

> Johann David Heinichen previously has composed several operas for us of a kind
> with which one can be satisfied. Now he desires to visit some of the important
> German courts and their orchestras for the greater perfecting of himself in music.
> Since he hopes particularly to profit at your court and, to better achieve this, has
> discreetly sought a petition of recommendation, we have not, therefore, refused
> him. Rather we commend him to your favor with the assurance that he is pre-
> pared to carry out all the agreeable duties of my friend and cousin.
> Mortizburg on the Elbe
> 10 July 1710.[33]

No evidence exists, however, that Heinichen carried this letter to the court
of Braunschweig for, not long after it was written, Heinichen changed his
plans radically and set out for Italy.

According to Walther,[34] our oldest source, Heinichen reached Italy
about 1710, after an expensive and time-consuming journey that Hiller[35]
believes resulted from the intervention of Councillor Buchta of Zeitz, who
acted as a patron of the arts and offered to take Heinichen to Venice,
paying all expenses.

It is symptomatic of German musical thought in the mid-Baroque
that a composer of Heinichen's tested abilities and proven pedagogical
interest should make the traditional pilgrimage to Venice. Venetian music
had been important to the Baroque from its beginnings. Monteverdi
(1567–1643), Cavalli (1602–76), Cesti (1623–69), Legrenzi (1626–90),
and Stradella (1644–82) are only a few of many names in the musical
history of the city known for their contributions to the development of the
opera and cantata. Heinichen had many opportunities to hear Italian
opera in Leipzig and Weissenfels. Generally speaking, Germans have
always been attracted to Italy; and Heinichen, who believed strongly in
the role of "good taste" in music, must have rejoiced in the opportunity to
learn the Italian theatrical style firsthand.

Soon after Heinichen's arrival in Venice, he was commissioned by the
impresario of the Sant' Angelo Opera House to write two operas. The
director-impresario, perhaps influenced by pressures from Italian composers who resented foreign competition, refused to stage the works once
Heinichen had completed them, and the composer was forced to sue for
the money owed him. At this time Heinichen met a German cooper named

Kühnlein living in the same hotel, Alla Scudo di Francia, who offered to represent Heinichen at the pending trial and to advance the necessary court costs. (The Councillor Buchta, supposedly responsible for bringing Heinichen to Venice, mysteriously evaporates from the picture at this point.) Thus in 1712, relieved of his legal obligation, Heinichen left for Rome where he was well enough known to be sought out by Prince Leopold of Anhalt-Cöthen (later the patron of Johann Sebastian Bach). The musically inclined young prince studied with Heinichen, who traveled with him on certain trips in Italy.[36]

Heinichen did not remain long in Prince Leopold's services, and before the end of 1712 he returned to Venice, perhaps drawn back by the news that he had won his lawsuit against the impresario: in addition to the original sum promised for the two operas commissioned, he was awarded sixteen hundred Venetian ducats for damages.[37] Two of Heinichen's operas were produced in 1713 at the Sant' Angelo Opera House, bringing to their composer considerable success and fame. Both were given during the carnival season, and they were entitled *Mario*[38] and *Le passioni per troppo amore.*[39] *Mario* was to be staged again in Hamburg[40] in 1716 with the German title, *Calpurnia, oder die römische Grossmut.* Heinichen's success was so great that the Venetian public demanded more performances of his operas than almost any other composer of the period,[41] making him the second German thus honored in Venice—sharing this distinction with Handel alone.

These operatic successes prove vividly how fully Heinichen was able to assimilate Italian elements of music into his style. His contacts with such important Italian composers as Gasparini (1668–1727), Pollaroli (1653–1723), Lotti (ca. 1667–1740), and probably Vivaldi (1678–1741) facilitated his absorption of Italian music.[42] Heinichen was a frequent visitor in the home of the wealthy Venetian merchant Bianchi whose wife Angioletta was famous in musical circles as a singer, harpsichordist, and patroness of the arts. A number of Heinichen's cantatas were performed in Bianchi's home with Angioletta as soloist; and it was she who brought Heinichen's music to the attention of the Prince-Elector of Saxony, who had come to Venice in 1716.[43] In his honor, Angioletta arranged for Heinichen to compose a special cantata that was performed in front of the Prince's apartment facing the Grand Canal on October 17, 1716, the morning of his birthday. This event occasioned Hiller's picturesque description:

> [Heinichen's music] was performed from the water before the home (of the merchant), which stood . . . on the Grand Canal. Crowds of people gathered on the

bridge and along the canal. As the first aria was sung, however, the clocks of the city began to strike, preventing the people from hearing. They commenced to indicate their vexation over this by stirring up such a loud noise that one no longer could hear the music. Madame Angioletta immediately asked them politely to be quiet to permit the music to continue. All became quiet again, though a repetition of the first aria was asked for, after which a tremendous cry of approval arose from the crowd; and the remainder of the serenade was received with no less approval.[44]

The Prince-Elector was undoubtedly impressed as much as the citizens of Venice, for on August 28, 1716 he had already engaged Heinichen as capellmeister to serve his father and the royal court at Dresden.[45] Heinichen left Venice for his new post early in 1717.

Dresden had not been without important musical significance in the sixteenth and seventeenth centuries. It became the residence of Saxon nobility in the sixteenth century, and at that time Johann Walther (1496–1570) was appointed capellmeister. In 1568, Scandello (1517–80), an Italian, became capellmeister,[46] succeeding the Netherlander, LeMaistre (1505–77). Foreign musicians dominated music in Dresden until 1617, when a native Saxon, Heinrich Schütz, was made director of court music.

The ascent in 1693 of Elector Friedrich August to the Saxon throne marks the event that revitalized Dresden politically as well as culturally. In 1697 Poland joined Saxony's political orbit, and the Elector became Augustus I, King of Poland. He sought to make his court the center of a great European power; and he tried to establish proof of these ambitions through cultural display.[47] Augustus the Strong[48] had been impressed as a young man by the richness of Italian court life, and immediately upon succession to the electoral title he began importing Italian musicians to Dresden. In 1717, the year of Heinichen's arrival in the city, the son of August I had engaged an entire Italian opera company under the direction of Antonio Lotti to move to Dresden. They opened the new Dresden Opera House on September 3, 1719, with Lotti conducting his own *Giove in Argo*.[49] This performance initiated four weeks of splendid celebrations in honor of the marriage of the Prince-Elector to Maria Josepha, daughter of Joseph I of Austria.[50] Heinichen's part in the festivities included the performance of his cantata *La gara degli dei* in the garden of the Japanese Palace on the 10th, and his *Diana sul'Elba*, given in connection with a festival of Diana held at the Elbe River Bridge on the 18th (see frontispiece).[51] The composer pleased his royal employer so much that he was granted in the same month a salary increase of three hundred talers.[2] On October 6, a royal hunt and festival took place at the country estate, Moritzburg Palace, and again Heinichen presented a new cantata, *Serenata di Moritzburg.* Telemann mentions attending this performance in an autobiographical sketch written for Mattheson's *Ehrenpforte.*[53]

For the carnival season of 1720, Heinichen composed a new opera, *Flavio Crispo.*[54] It was never staged because a violent quarrel broke out during rehearsal between Heinichen and the Italian singers Senesino and Berselli. When Heinichen reported the disagreement to the king, he issued a royal decree commanding the immediate dissolution of the opera company.[55]

Heinichen devoted much of the last nine years of his life to writing cantatas for court entertainment, in addition to a considerable amount of church music. In 1721 he married in Weissenfels,[56] and the birth of his only child was recorded in January 1723.[57] Little has been uncovered about his professional life, though he must have had time for the rewriting of his thorough-bass treatise.

In 1728 Heinichen published at his own expense *Der General-Bass in der Composition*; in 1729 tuberculosis, which had attacked him several years earlier, brought his life to a premature end. On July 16, around one o'clock in the afternoon, he died;[58] he was buried in St. John's cemetery, reserved for those in the court's employ. Even this honor was eclipsed, for the cemetery has long since vanished, covered over by an expanding city.

Heinichen has often suffered unjust criticism during the last century. Early historians have pictured him as a pedantic and overly critical theoretician whose music displayed more "the thinking artist than the invention-rich mind,"[59] and he has even been accused of lacking an understanding of the practical use of counterpoint.[60] As a theorist, his name seldom appears in historical and analytical literature. Most of his manuscripts were easily accessible in Dresden libraries (unfortunately his church music was partly destroyed in World War II), but few of his composition have been published in modern editions, despite the complete editions of lesser musical luminaries printed with such regularity, particularly in Germany.

Every study of Baroque music stresses the importance of the thorough-bass; Riemann did not hesitate to label the years between 1600 and 1750 the "era of the thorough-bass."[61] Even though such an all-inclusive generalization overlooks the use of the thorough-bass in music well after the mid-eighteenth century, there can be no doubt that the greatest portion of Baroque music shares the thorough-bass as a common denominator. Yet research concerning the thorough-bass has failed to produce a true picture of stylistic variances in accompanying from a *continuo* for different countries and in different epochs. A major error, particularly in many practical editions of Baroque music, is the undue dependence on

Carl Philipp Emanuel Bach's *Versuch über die wahre Art das Clavier zu spielen*, almost universally considered the single authority on the entire problem of performing from a thorough-bass for all periods and nations, despite its publication in 1762 (the first part, examining other aspects of keyboard performance, appeared separately in 1753). This distinguished son of Johann Sebastian Bach became the leading exponent of the *emfindsamer Stil*; his music typifies neither the late Baroque of his father nor the early Classicism of his brother, Johann Christian Bach (1735–82). C. P. E. Bach's treatise, like his music, reflects the transitional age in which he lived and his special position in that age; its relevance to the late Baroque is as incomplete as its application to the Classicism of Mozart.

As a comprehensive source of the thorough-bass techniques of late Baroque masters, Heinichen's *Der General-Bass in der Composition* merits a detailed study. Heinichen was a student of Kuhnau; he also knew intimately and wrote Italian operas. Although firmly rooted in the German scholarly approach to music and plainly concerned with the many problems of German music as they existed around 1730, he discusses with preciseness and genuine enthusiasm the *stylo theatralis*, giving us our clearest picture of the Italian operatic style in the late Baroque.

Particularly for keyboardists today confronted with the complexities of late Baroque thorough-bass realizations, Heinichen's *Der General-Bass in der Composition* is a source of inestimable value.

Notes

1. Charles Burney, *A General History of Music* (London, 1776–1789). New ed. Frank Mercer (London, 1935; repr. New York, 1957) II, 459; Johann Scheibe, *Der critische Musikus* (Leipzig, 1737), 764; Johann Mattheson's *Ode auf des S.[alvo] T.[itulo] Hrn. Capellmeister Heinichen[s] schönes neues Werck von General-Bass*, printed as an introduction to Heinichen's treatise, *Der General-Bass in der Composition* (Dresden, 1728).

2. G. A. Seibel, *Das Leben des königl. polnischen und kurfürstl. sächs. Hofkapellmeisters Johann David Heinichen . . .* (Leipzig, 1913).

3. Richard Tanner, *Heinichen als dramatischer Komponist* (Leipzig, 1916).

4. Günter Hausswald, *Johann David Heinichens Instrumentalwerke* (Leipzig, 1937). This author contributed the article on Heinichen for *Die Musik in Geschichte und Gegenwart*.

5. The number of Baroque musicians born in Saxony and neighboring Thuringia, other than Heinichen, was prodigious. Among the better known were: J. S. Bach (Eisenach), Demantius (Reichenberg), Froberger (Stuttgart), Fasch (Buttelstädt, near Weimar), the Graun brothers (Wahrenbrück), Graupner (Reichenbach,

near Kirchberg), Handel (Halle), Hebenstreit (Eisleben), Keiser (Teuchern), Reiche (Weissenfels), Scheibe (Leipzig), and Zachow (Leipzig). See also Arno Werner, "Sachsen-Thüringen in der Musikgeschichte," *AfMw* 4 (1922), 322–35.

6. Heinichen, *General-Bass*, 23.

7. Johann Mattheson, *Der vollkommene Capellmeister* (Hamburg, 1739). Facs. ed. M. Reimann (Kassel, 1954), 1–36.

8. J. G. Walther, *Musicalisches Lexicon* (Leipzig, 1732). Facs. ed. R. Schaal (Kassel, 1953), 306.

9. Seibel, *Heinichen*, 2.

10. Heinichen, *General-Bass*, 840.

11. According to the enrollment list of the school. See Seibel, *Heinichen*, 6.

12. Arnold Schering, *Musikgeschichte Leipzigs, von 1650 bis 1723* (Leipzig, 1926), 50. For additional information concerning the musical history of Leipzig see the article in *MGG* 8, col. 540–72.

13. In addition to Schering's valuable account of the Thomasschule (*Musikgeschichte Leipzigs*, 43–67), see also Philipp Spitta, *Johann Sebastian Bach*, English tr. Clara Bell and J. A. Fuller-Maitland (London, 1899; repr. New York, 1951) II, 189.

14. Richard Münnich, "Kuhnaus Leben," *SIMG* 3 (1901–2), 517.

15. Johann Mattheson, *Grundlage einer Ehrenpforte* (Hamburg, 1740). New ed. M. Schneider (Berlin 1910), 411.

16. Schering, *Musikgeschichte Leipzigs*, 191.

17. Seibel, *Heinichen*, 7.

18. Heinichen, *General-Bass*, 935.

19. Ibid., 840.

20. From Kuhnau's letter of complaint to the Leipzig Council, reprinted in Spitta, *J. S. Bach* II (original edition only, not included in English translation), 856–60.

21. Schering, *Musikgeschichte Leipzigs*, 308–12.

22. Strungk's career and his music are the subject of a monograph by Fritz Berend, *Nicolaus Adam Strungk, sein Leben und seine Werke* (Hanover, 1913).

23. See Schering, *Musikgeschichte Leipzigs*, 437–71 for additional information regarding the early history of the Leipzig opera.

24. Ibid., 334–40.

25. E. L. Gerber, *Neues Historisch-biographisches Lexikon der Tonkünstler* . . . (2d ed. Leipzig, 1812), col. 614. The first edition (1790) omits any biographical reference to Heinichen, even though there is an entry under "Heynenghen" in which Gerber proudly asserts that this is but an Italian form of none other than "*unser brave Kapellmeister Heinichen*."

14 Biography

26. Recorded in Krieger's list of compositions he performed while capellmeister at Weissenfels. The list is reproduced in *DDT* 53, LVI.

27. F. A. Voigt, "Reinhard Keiser," *VfMw* 6(1890), 178.

28. The only reference to this performance appears in J. C. Gottsched's *Nötiger Vorrat zur Geschichte der deutschen dramatischen Dichtkunst* (Leipzig, 1765) I, 285.

29. See Berend, *Strungk*, 82–110 for a detailed account of the trials Strungk encountered in erecting the opera house, his financial tribulations inflicted by the Leipzig Council, the infidelity of the Saxon court, and the persistence of the demands for rent by Frau Siegfried, the landowner.

30. Not, however, to become director of the opera as stated in Schering, *Musikgeschichte Leipzigs*, 462. Schering probably took this incorrect information from Bernhard Engelke's unpublished dissertation on J. F. Fasch (Halle, 1908), a portion of which appeared as: "J. F. Fasch, Versuch einer Biographie," *SIMG* 10(1909), 267.

31. This letter is reprinted in La Mara [Ida Maria Lipsius], *Musikerbriefe aus fünf Jahrhunderten* (Leipzig, 1886), 155; also in Seibel, *Heinichen*, 12.

32. Seibel, *Heinichen*, 13.

33. Ibid., 14 reproduces this document with numerous misspellings and errors in punctuation. The following is reprinted from the original in the Sächsische Landesbibliothek Dresden (loc. 8590 fol. 25): "E.[ure]E.[xcellence]. Es hat bey Uns Johann David Heinichen et[liche] Opern zeithero dergestallt, dass man darmit satisfait seyn könne, componiret, und ist nunmehro gesonnen, zu desto besserer Excolirung der Music einig vornehme Teutsche Hoffe und deren Capellen zu besuchen. Wie non von E.[ure] Ld.[Liebden] Hoffe er insonderheit zu profitiren, sich Hoffnung machet, und zu Erlangung desto besserer adresse umb Recommendation unterth[unterthäniglich] angesuchet; allso haben Wir ihm darmit nicht entstehen; vielmehr Dero Gnade emphfehlen; und E.[ure] Ld.[Liebden] zu allen angenehmen freundvetter[lichen] Diensten stets bereith zu verharren, versichern wollen. Dat [Datum] Mb [Moritzburg] an der Elster den 10. July 1710."

34. Walther, *Lexicon*, 306.

35. J. A. Hiller, *Lebensbeschreibungen berühmter Musikgelehrten und Tonkünstler . . .* (Leipzig, 1784), 132.

36. Gerber, *Lexikon der Tonkünstler* (2d ed.) II, col. 615.

37. Hiller, *Lebensbeschreibungen*, 136.

38. Seibel, *Heinichen*, 33–34; Tanner, *Heinichen*, 40–53; Taddeo Wiel, *I teatri musicali veneziani del settecento . . .* (Venice, 1897), 35; Loewenberg, *Annals*, col. 128.

39. Seibel, *Heinichen*, 35; Hiller, *Lebensbeschreibungen*, 133; Robert Eitner, *Biographisch-bibliographisches Quellen-Lexikon . . .* (Leipzig, 1899–1904) V, 138 misleadingly lists this work under "Heyninghen," an Italian variant spelling, and not in the catalogue of Heinichen's compositions; Tanner, *Heinichen*, 55–73.

40. Johann Mattheson, *Der musicalische Patriot* (Hamburg, 1728), 189; Gottsched, *Nötiger Vorrat* I, 289.

41. Gerber, *Lexikon der Tonkünstler* (2d ed.) II, col. 615.

42. Moritz Fürstenau, *Zur Geschichte der Musik und des Theaters am Hofe zu Dresden* (Dresden, 1861) II, 105.

43. Seibel, *Heinichen*, 18. Angioletta Bianchi, it might be added, was no local dilettante; her well-established reputation as an opera singer led Walther to include her name in his *Lexicon*, 36.

44. Hiller, *Lebensbeschreibungen*, 137.

45. Seibel, *Heinichen*, 19 reprints the original document of appointment. Heinichen was not engaged, however, as director of the Italian opera company as is given in *Baker's Biographical Dictionary of Musicians*, ed. N. Slonimsky (5th ed. New York, 1958), 685.

46. Hans Schnoor, *Dresden. Vierhundert Jahre deutsche[r] Musikkultur* (Dresden, 1948), 29.

47. Ibid., 65–75 includes an excellent summary of this period in Dresden's cultural history. See also Irmgard Becker-Glauch, "Dresden I," *MGG* 3, col. 757–71; Fürstenau, *Musik . . . am Hofe zu Dresden* II, 97–179.

48. Irmgard Becker-Glauch, "August der Starke," *MGG* 1, col. 841–42.

49. Schnoor, *Dresden*, 69.

50. Fürstenau, *Musik . . . am Hofe zu Dresden* II, 142. See also Irmgard Becker-Glauch, *Die Bedeutung der Musik für Dresdener Hoffeste . . .* (Kassel, 1951), 98–112.

51. Seibel, *Heinichen*, 22.

52. Ibid., 22 quotes the state document notifying Heinichen of his salary raise, but omits the source.

53. Mattheson, *Ehrenpforte*, 354.

54. Tanner, *Heinichen*, 75–90.

55. Hiller, *Lebensbeschreibungen*, 138.

56. Seibel, *Heinichen*, 24.

57. Ibid., 24 (footnote 6).

58. Walther, *Lexicon*, 307.

59. Gerber, *Lexikon der Tonkünstler* (2d ed.) II, col. 618.

60. F. J. Fétis, *Biographie universelle des musiciens . . .* (Paris, 1860–65) IV, 280.

61. Hugo Riemann, *Handbuch der Musikgeschichte* II, pt. 2: *Das Generalbasszeitalter* (Leipzig, 1922).

2

The Thorough-Bass in Late Baroque Music: The Problem and the Sources

Our knowledge of the thorough-bass and its applications to eighteenth-century music comes from a wealth of sources. But in attempting to digest the contents of numerous treatises and less imposing practical manuals we quickly meet a dilemma: how to synthesize the great diversity of rules and conflicting advice into a single method of accompanying. The answer must be that any hopes we might entertain of deducing one set of principles applicable to all thorough-basses are illusory. Unfortunately, modern research has contributed little to help us reach this conclusion. It has shown almost no interest in those vital distinctions of the thorough-bass practice arising from the growth of Baroque music and the idiomatic modifications of the elements of this music that characterize French, German, or Italian musical style.

Much of our faulty perception regarding thorough-bass practices in the Baroque stems from hazy concepts of the Baroque itself. The year of Bach's death — 1750 — furnishes a more convenient than realistic date for ending the Baroque. The gradual supplanting of the Baroque in the arts had progressed far, even before Bach composed many of his greatest works. Yet the preponderance of present-day information for realizing a thorough-bass according to Baroque principles relies on treatises written after 1750.

At this point it would be well to review the achievements of F. T. Arnold and his pioneering *The Art of Accompaniment from a Thorough-bass*, published in 1931. Arnold, who began musical research as an enthusiastic amateur, demonstrated how much could be accomplished by a creative and indefatigable mind. If, some decades later, one finds parts of the work no longer completely definitive, these criticisms should not be interpreted as an attempt to minimize the importance of his original efforts.

Arnold faced the very dilemma outlined above: he sought to unify the art of accompanying from sources written over a span of almost two hundred years. In his *Art of Accompaniment*, after an admirable survey of many thorough-bass treatises, he devotes several hundred pages to details of accompanying. He produces an unreal, hybrid form of accompaniment embodying the ideas of writers separated not only by chronology, but by nationality, education, and musical milieu. The suggestions of Saint-Lambert, Heinichen, Mattheson, Marpurg, Schroeter, and the heavy influence of C. P. E. Bach are blended by Arnold[1] into a mélange that imposes unrealistic unity where diversity offers the only key to eventual understanding.

Equally serious was Arnold's oversimplification of the Baroque composer's harmonic understanding. Arnold freely applies terminology not only post-Baroque in origin but, one might say, anti-Baroque in conception. Much of the faulty terminology centers around the principle of chord inversions that Rameau championed in his *Traité de l'harmonie* (1722). Rameau's analysis of triads and their inversions and his system of fundamental basses that represented the roots of chords leave far behind the actual use of harmony in the Baroque, particularly the Baroque of Italy and Germany. Composers of this period constructed and organized chords on the actual bass, and not on a theoretical *basse fondamentale*; and throughout the baroque, intervals related to bass notes determined harmonic progression whereas dissonances followed the principles of linear counterpoint. Even as late as 1728, Heinichen explains dissonances in terms of counterpoint, though with some difficulty when he examines the aggressive verticality of Italian operatic music.

Heinichen, to be sure, recognized the chord of the sixth as an inverted triad; but with rare exception he speaks not of chord inversions but of inverted intervals. Without justification, therefore, Arnold[2] assumes that he could explain Baroque harmony in a terminology of inversions, dominant sevenths, and diminished triads, even though "the classification of a certain harmony as an 'inversion' does not necessarily imply the priority of its 'root position,' or, indeed, *its existence in actual practice.*" Despite this assurance, Arnold[3] boldly criticizes, for example, Heinichen's failure to recognize the second inversion of the dominant seventh and chides him because he did not apply the principle of inversion "with complete accuracy." Arnold, however, fell victim to the very error he apparently thought avoidable: as his criticism reveals, he did assume the priority of root positions and their inversions for music written in the early eighteenth century.

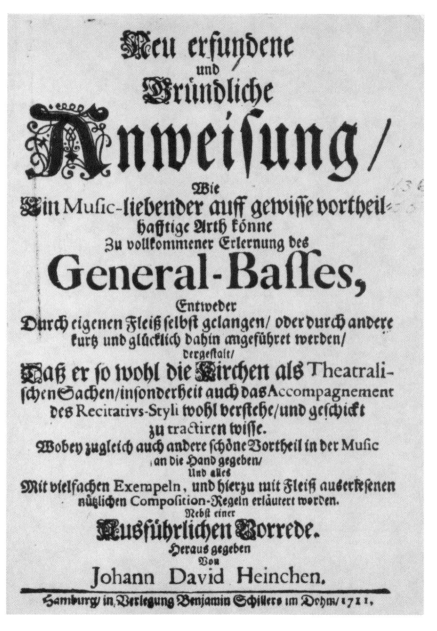

Figure 1. Title Page of the First Edition of Heinichen's Treatise.
Note the variant spelling of the author's name.

Der
GENERAL - BASS
in der
COMPOSITION,
Oder:

Neue und gründliche

Anweisung,

Wie
Ein Music-Liebender mit besonderm Vortheil, durch
die Principia der Composition, nicht allein den General-Baß
im Kirchen- Cammer- und Theatralischen Stylô vollkommen, & in altiori
Gradu erlernen; sondern auch zu gleicher Zeit in der Composition selbst, wichtige
Profectus machen könne.

Nebst einer Einleitung
Oder
Musicalischen Raisonnement
von der Music überhaupt, und vielen besondern
Materien der heutigen Praxeos.

Herausgegeben
von
Johann David Heinichen,
Königl. Pohln. und Churfl. Sächf. Capellmeister.

In Dresden bey dem Autore zu finden. 1728.

Figure 2.   Title Page of the Second Edition.
This was published at Heinichen's own expense
one year before his death.

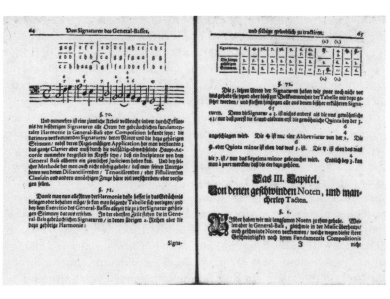

Figure 3.   Table of Thorough-Bass Figures (on p. 65) from
Heinichen's *Neu erfundene Anweisung* (1711).

Contemporary Sources for Comparisons

Heinichen's account of the art of accompanying, the most comprehensive available in the entire Baroque literature, offers the best tools for reconstructing thorough-bass accompaniments of music written in the German-Italian theatrical style after 1700. Thus, the material to follow centers on Heinichen's methods: comparisons with contemporary treatises are intended primarily as indications of important differences or as additions of materials omitted by Heinichen. The writings of four late Baroque theorists receive special attention, either for their completeness or their special popularity in the eighteenth century:

(1) *L'armonico pratico al cimbalo*, by Francesco Gasparini, was published in 1708 and reprinted six times. Born in 1668 near Lucca, Gasparini was closely associated with the musical life of Venice, Rome, and Vienna during various periods in his career; he died in Rome in 1727.[4] As musical director of the *Ospedale della pietà* in Venice, he held a post of prominent musical authority undoubtedly leading to an early meeting with Heinichen. The latter speaks of Gasparini's thorough-bass treatise more than once in the *General-Bass*, always with respect and admiration, even when disagreeing. Heinichen underscores his admiration for Gasparini by taking the entire section describing the *acciaccatura* from *L'armonico pratico al cimbalo* and freely admitting his indebtedness. Gasparini's treatise retained its popularity into the nineteenth century (6th ed., 1802), a rather surprising survival for instructions so brief and concerned mainly with unfigured basses. He realizes few of the many bass examples, and the major importance of the treatise lies in specific details to be cited as we proceed.

(2) The second comparison source, *Nouveau traité de l'accompagnement*, published in 1707 by Saint-Lambert is one of the most comprehensive thorough-bass sources from early eighteenth-century France. Despite this fact, however, the author remains an utterly mysterious personality. Tessier[5] writes that he doubts even the authenticity of Saint-Lambert's Christian name, Michel, since it appears in Fétis[6] only. In Walther[7] he is identified as a former *maître de la musique du chambre* at the French court, composer of a trio for various instruments, and author of *Principes du clavecin* (Paris, 1702) as well as a book on the thorough-bass. Fétis, unfortunately, errs by establishing the data of the *Nouveau Traité* as 1680 and by assuming the version of 1707 to be the second edition. A number of scholars followed Fétis, including Eitner and even Arnold, although Saint-Lambert himself offers sufficient evidence that an edition from 1680 could not exist: In the preface he alludes to the difficulty in finding a title that

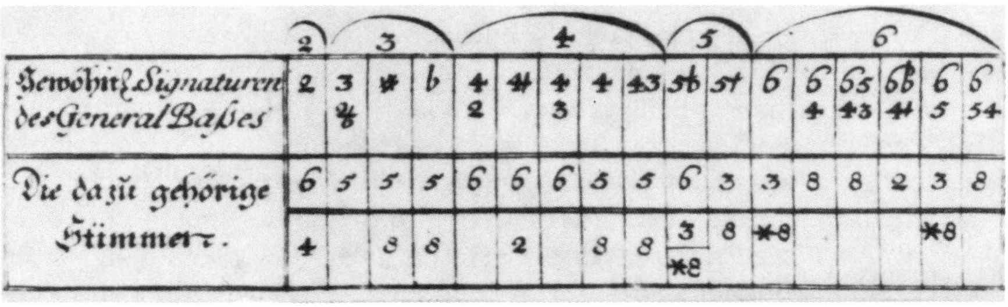

	2	3			4					5		6					
Gewöhnl. Signaturen des General Basses	2	3 4	#	b	4 2	4	4 3	4	43	5b	5t	6	6 4	65 43	6b 4	6 5	6 54
Die dazu gehörige Stimmen.	6	5	5	5	6	6	6	5	5	6	3	3	8	8	2	3	8
	4		8	8		2		8	8	3 *8	8	*8				*8	

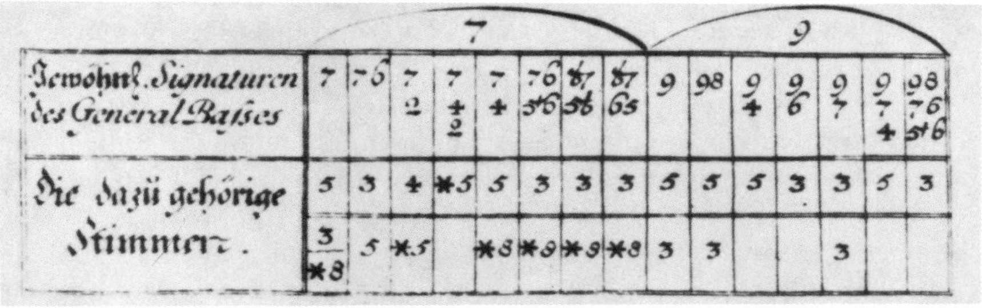

	7								9						
Gewöhnl. Signaturen des General Basses	7	76	7 2	7 4 2	7 4	76 56	87 56	87 65	9	98	9 4	9 6	9 7	9 7 4	98 76 56
Die dazu gehörige Stimmen.	5	3	4	*5	5	3	3	3	5	5	5	3	3	5	3
	3 *8	5	*5		*8	*9	*9	*8	3	3			3		

Figure 4. Table of Thorough-Bass Figures from Heinichen's *General-Bass* (1728).

would distinguish his new book from the earlier *Principes du clavecin*, first published in 1702.

Questions of chronology aside, Saint-Lambert's detailed and well-organized exposition of thorough-bass practices contains much that must have interested Heinichen. The *General-Bass* refers twice only to the French treatise, but this provides poor indication of Heinichen's obligation to Saint-Lambert. For example, much of Heinichen's discussion on good taste in music[8] comes directly from Saint-Lambert's ninth chapter, *De gout* [*sic*] *de l'accompagnement*.

(3) Another comparison source, *Treulicher Unterricht im General-Bass* (1732), was published by David Kellner (1670–1748) just four years after the *General-Bass*. Only the most meager information related to Kellner's life has been unearthed to date; it consists of his birth in Leipzig in 1670 and some evidence that his career centered in Stockholm. Elwyn Wienandt,[9] in a study of Kellner's *Lautenstücke*, summarizes the few available facts.

The first edition (1732) offers no clue to the author's name; the title-page to the 1737 edition gives only the initials D. K., although in the introduction Telemann spells out the name. The Swedish translation (1739), according to Wienandt,[10] served as that country's only thorough-bass manual for many years. A Dutch translation (1741) also was printed; and the last of several German editions appeared in 1797, an impressive indication of the book's popularity even after Kellner's death in 1748. His *Treulicher Unterricht* contains a fairly complete collection of instructions related directly to the thorough-bass, although frequently the content and manner of presentation seem to be copied from Heinichen's treatise.

(4) Finally, in regard to sources of comparison, no discussion of the thorough-bass in the late Baroque, or any other musical subject of that period, would be complete without consulting Mattheson's opinions. He wrote three books for performers of keyboard instruments: *Die Organisten-Probe* (1719), *Grosse General-Bass-Schule* (1731), and *Kleine General-Bass-Schule* (1735). The first two instruct organists mainly in the art of extemporizing solo pieces from given basses. Only in the *Kleine General-Bass-Schule* does Mattheson offer the beginner comprehensive instructions in the art of accompanying, from the first rudiments to the most complex figures.

Notes

1. F. T. Arnold, *The Art of Accompaniment from a Thorough-bass*, 290, indicates his partiality for C. P. E. Bach's treatise: "There is no single treatise on the art of accompaniment from a figured bass to which those who wish to recapture the

tradition owe a deeper debt than to the Second Part of Ph. Em. Bach's celebrated work on the Clavier. . . ."

2. Arnold, *Thorough-bass*, xi.

3. Ibid., 259.

4. Concerning Gasparini see *MGG* 4, col. 1414–18.

5. André Tessier, "Saint-Lambert," *GroveD*, ed. E. Blom (5th ed. London, 1954) VII, 364.

6. Fétis, *Biographie universelle* VII, 371–72.

7. Walther, *Lexicon*, 352.

8. Heinichen, *General-Bass*, 23–27.

9. Elwyn A. Wienandt, "David Kellner's Lautenstücke," *JAMS* 10 (1957), 29–38.

10. Wienandt, *Lautenstücke*, 29. Unfounded, however, is Wienandt's undocumented statement that Kellner's treatise was "the first theory book to be based entirely on major and minor keys." Any number of earlier treatises, including those by Delair, Campion, Saint-Lambert and, most important, Heinichen, use and refer expressly to major and minor keys only. This inaccurate statement is perpetuated in *MGG* 7, col. 819.

3

The Figures

When confronted with a *continuo*, the accompanist must know first the meaning of the figures. Only Heinichen, among all the theorists, attempts to summarize the varieties of figures used in different countries to express the same chord formations. He divides the figures into three basic systems for writing chromatic alterations of intervals:

♯2	♯3	♯4	♯5	♯6	♯7	♯9
2♯	3♯	4♯	5♯	6♯	7♯	9♯
2₊	⁺3	4₊	5⁺	6⁺	⁺7	₊9
♭2	♭3	♭4	♭5	♭6	♭7	♭9
2♭	3♭	4♭	5♭	6♭	7♭	9♭
2♭	♭3	4♭	5♭	6♭	♭7	♭9
♮2	♮3	♮4	♮5	♮6	♮7	♮9
2♮	3♮	4♮	5♮	6♮	7♮	9♮
2♮	♮3	4♮	5♮	6♮	♮7	♮9

Heinichen prefers the clarity of attaching accidentals to the numbers or, in the case of sharps, the stroke through the number. In other treatises and particularly in music, careless printing of figures frequently obscured the composer's harmony; for example, ♯6 printed above two adjacent bass notes could mean either a major triad on the first bass and a chord of the sixth on the second, or a chord with a major sixth on the second bass and a triad (no figure) on the first.

The form of figures that Heinichen chose, the simple yet ingenious method of attaching accidentals to numbers, seems to originate in German music toward the middle of the seventeenth century. Arnold[2] correctly surmised that the Germans were the first to place a stroke through the upper portion of a 6 (6⁺), when the sixth was major as the result of a chromatic alteration, and through the extended horizontal portion of a 4 (4+) for tritones; and examples abound in German music of the last decades in the seventeenth century.[3] Werckmeister published the earliest treatise[4] employing both symbols, while Delair[5] seems to be the first to use a stroke through a number in a printed treatise, though he limits the application to diminished fifths (5̸), a figure not found in Heinichen's list. Not until around 1700 do the 6⁺ and 4+ appear in French music, and François Couperin (1668–1733) still did not use them in his manuscript, *Règles pour l'accompagnement*,[6] written around 1698.

Even in the late Baroque most thorough-bass books conflict in their recommendations for placing accidentals with numbers. Delair, for example, uses accidentals after the number, but Boyvin shows less decisiveness in his treatise, placing them before and after numbers. Campion insists that accidentals must appear in front of the numbers, while Saint-Lambert maintains they belong after the numbers. Despite Heinichen's efforts on behalf of a far less ambiguous system, his contemporary Mattheson continued the well-rooted tradition of confusion by using 4+ , ♭4, ♭5, 5♭, ♭6, 6♭, and other equally inconsistent figures in the *Kleine General-Bass Schule*.

Before turning to the intricacies of Heinichen's instructions, it might be well to pause here for some words of encouragement from him:

> But how a beginner finds these practical figures with little effort over bass notes or on his keyboard (particularly when the key signature is well decorated with sharps and flats) may still cause many [students] some difficulties. It is, however, the easiest thing in the world in itself insofar as one (1) notes carefully the key signature or the scale degrees that are sharped or flatted; [and] (2) counts the steps of intervals correctly according to the lines [of the staff].[7]

Thorough-bass manuals written in the first decades of the eighteenth century range enormously in scope and include, in addition to treatises by authors cited previously, elementary though significant instruction books by Keller and Bayne[8] in England, Torres[9] in Spain, Fischer in the Netherlands, Telemann in Germany, Dandrieu[10] in France, and large numbers of smaller books having less importance. Regardless of size, however, these treatises usually follow a similar order in presenting the essential materials of accompanying: chords and their figures. Proceeding from the simple to the complex, each author first discusses the rudiments of music (scales, clefs, notation) and continues with triads, chords of the sixth, and each of the dissonant intervals. Heinichen orgainizes his work similarly, and his plan has been adopted for the following explanations of figures.

Triads

"In the beginning was the triad" describes succinctly not only the genesis of the thorough-bass but also each student's study of accompanying from a thorough-bass. The *Trias harmonica* — a bass note (*Fundamental-clave*), third, and fifth — becomes the *Trias harmonica aucta* by adding the bass octave, *welche sonst auch mit einem Worte zu nennen pfleget: einen Accord, oder ordinairen Satz und Griff.*[11] Heinichen suggests that students learn to play triads on every scale degree and to practice them repeatedly in the three distributions of chord tones, that is, with third, fifth, or bass octave as the upper part. These positions or *drey Haupt-Accorde* of each triad were so essential to Heinichen's teaching method that he printed every important example in the first part of the treatise in the three versions resulting from the rearrangement of chord tones.

These exercises contributed to the instinctive feeling an accompanist must posses for the keyboard and for the actual shapes of chords. Although Heinichen's reliance on this teaching device has no parallel in other sources, ample evidence exists to show that students of accompanying in the Baroque practiced the *drey Haupt-Accorde* just as piano students today practice triads and seventh chords as broken chords in all positions. Saint-Lambert, in defining *l'accord parfait ou naturel*, emphasizes its three positions: "All triads, except those that are doubled, have three different forms in the arrangement of their notes."[12] Similarly, Kellner comments: "The chords must be so rearranged that either the third, fifth, or octave appears on top."[13] Mattheson[14] devotes an entire chapter to *den dreien Ordnungen der Accorde insgemein*; his definition of the triad, in characteristic style, remains unrivaled for "completeness:" "Der vollkommene/gäntzlich wolklingende harmonische Drey-Klang oder Accord (*Trias harmonica*)."[15]

In distributing the tones of a triad between the two hands, the best four-part arrangement places the bass note in the left and the three remaining notes in the right. This arrangement of tones was essential for every student "because in this the beginner will need to learn at one time the essential parts of all harmonies, the indispensable resolutions of all dissonances, the regular movements of voice parts. With an overly full-voiced accompaniment . . . such skills would be partly inapplicable and partly could be treated only with disorder and incompleteness."[16]

Heinichen suggests no alternative to doubling the bass in four-part triads; and not until the middle of the eighteenth century or perhaps later did theorists generally advocate doubling the fifth or third of triads.[17] In

Germany this practice apparently first appeared in C. P. E. Bach's *Versuch* (part 2, 1762).[18] Arnold, in his chapter on triads, creates a misleading impression that doublings of fifths and thirds were generally recommended in all periods: he fails to distinguish between writers permitting such doublings and those allowing the doubled bass note only. Significantly, Arnold draws his examples of triads with doubled thirds and fifths solely from C. P. E. Bach and the even later treatise (1791) of Türk.[19]

Actually the principle of doubling only the bass of triads applies more to organ accompaniments than to harpsichord accompaniments of operatic works. Although the full-voiced style (see chapter 4) generally was used by harpsichordists in theatrical music, which required the doubling of as many chord tones as the hands could manage, the organist seldom abandoned four-part accompaniments. Heinichen and other contemporary writers warn the organist repeatedly to avoid the muddle of sound that results from full-voiced chords.

Chords of the Sixth

Heinichen fully understood the origin of chords of the sixth as inversions of triads: "That in the chord of the sixth the doubling of the third and sixth would be much more natural than the doubling of the bass, can be shown most easily in its origin, namely the inversion of the triad. . . ."[20] Although the third or sixth were the more natural tones to double, since they represent the fifth and fundamental of the original triad, Heinichen strongly urged the doubling of the bass as well: "The 6 indicated over the bass note usually has the third and octave for its harmony. One can, however, use this formerly ill-reputed octave in all kinds of parallel and contrary motion as long as no awkward progressions result from them. . . ."[21]

If, however, a series of chords moved in parallel sixths, the accompanist could omit the fourth part (ex. 1a, bar 8),[22] a conventional means of avoiding parallel octaves. The third or sixth could be doubled in place of the bass octave, although earlier theorists avoided doubling the major third, as Heinichen explains:

> Just as now, regularly and according to the opinion of all composers, the octave and fifth in triads can always be doubled before the third; so too with the inversion of such parts. The third and sixth will be naturally doubled before the octave, which is only an inverted [*superstruirte*] third and has nothing to do with the inversion in question. Here, however, one might ask if in good conscience one can

double the major third with the sixth, since theorists of the past accused the major third of harshness and for this reason forbade its doubling in few parts? To answer this requires a distinction. First, regarding the chord of a sixth, its major third (natural or chromatically altered), as long as it is accompanied by the major sixth, can for this reason be doubled in good conscience; because in this case it is never viewed as a major third but as an inverted fifth. For example: the natural third of the chord of the sixth $\overset{a}{\underset{c}{e}}$ is nothing other than the true fifth of the triad $\overset{e}{\underset{A}{c}}$ . . . . Thus, such doubling really cannot result in harshness if one . . . merely places the *Fundamental-Clavem A* . . . over the other two parts. For how can the simple inversion of these three innocent parts create a harshness that was not there previously?[23]

Heinichen concludes this footnote with two rules for doubling major thirds not joined to sixths:

1. Major thirds that are natural to the key can be doubled without hesitation.
2. Major thirds resulting from chromatic alterations should not be doubled since they produce a harsh sound.

To illustrate the latter, Heinichen refers to the triads on D and A in D major and minor. In major "the unprejudiced ear" will find nothing unpleasant in the doubling of the major thirds; but in minor he warns against doubling the major third in triads on D or A because the F♯ and C♯ both result from chromatic alterations.

The major triad on A in D major or minor contains the seventh degree or leading tone (which Heinichen calls the *semitonium modi*), and he seems to suggest that he approves doubling the seventh degree in major scales but not in minor. However, despite the apparent clarity of Heinichen's instructions, musical examples throughout the *General-Bass* fail to substantiate his words: four-part triads double the bass and not one chord of the sixth doubles the seventh degree.

Heinichen's purpose seems to be aimed at breaking down the old prejudice fostered by German theorists against doubling major thirds on keyboard instruments. Objection to doubling major thirds would in effect make full-voiced accompaniments impractical since no accompanist could double all notes of harmonies in the left hand without including major thirds. The outmoded restriction had grown principally from the unsatisfactory tuning of major thirds on keyboard instruments, a difficulty that Heinichen indicates no longer existed:

With the doubling of the accidental major third in music with few parts . . . indeed up to now I have not cared to have anything to do. Regarding the doubling of the natural major third, however, I avoid it in my latest works as little as do other composers of today. That in the past I had apprehension in doubling major thirds is, however, certainly true, because since my youth I had been so indoctrinated. In regard to which can be said: *consuetudo altera Natura* — one falls upon prejudices through long being so accustomed which one cannot quickly discard again. For this very reason I would sooner pardon the fear older composers of our time have for this doubling of the major third, which they have been accustomed to since their youth, and abhor all other instances of apparent harshness. But one really would not imagine the absurdity that there could also be newly experienced composers to whom the doubling of all major thirds, without distinction (they may be tuned as perfectly as possible), would be harsh and unbearable. . . .[24]

Returning to Heinichen's rules for chords of the sixth, certain chromatically altered thirds and sixths must not be doubled:

1. The chromatically raised major third joined to a minor sixth.
2. The chromatically raised sixth joined to a minor third.
3. Any chromatically raised bass figured with a minor sixth.[25]

These rules prevent the accompanist from doubling the raised seventh degree that exists in minor scales as: (1) a chromatically altered major third in triads on the fifth degree or joined with a minor sixth as the natural chord of the sixth on the fifth degree; (2) the chromatically raised sixth, but only when it is played with a minor third as the natural chord of the sixth on the second degree; (3) a chromatically raised bass note when it is played with a minor sixth as the natural chord of the sixth on the raised seventh degree.

The interval of a fourth could be added to chords of the sixth; but although the fourth was prepared it was not resolved, circumstances prompting Heinichen[26] to label the interval *Quarta irregolare* (ex. 1, bars 2, 3, 6). The upper tone of the fourth is repeated in the following chord. The augmented fourth could be introduced in chords of the sixth in a similar manner if the third were major. Most important, "with such sixths, however, this irregular 4 or 4+ will not be specifically indicated each time over bass notes, but it is left to the accompanist whether he can find and use them properly. If they are specifically indicated over a bass note, however, then a $\frac{4}{3}$ or $\frac{4+}{3}$ suffices to mark the complete chord, because then the natural major sixth is understood."[27]

Heinichen concludes with a general example for chords of the sixth. Three separate versions of the same realization show three distributions of the same chord tones. It would be difficult to overemphasize the practical value of these examples. Studying them at the keyboard gives one the best introduction to many facets of thorough-bass realization. The assimilation of this intricate art lies beyond the simple memorizing of rules and their exceptions; in addition, the student must train his fingers to react instantaneously as the eye travels along the thorough-bass. Just as an accomplished pianist never stops to remember which fingering he should use for scale passages, neither does the skilled accompanist consciously decide how his hands will realize each figure. This keyboard facility or tactile memory can be achieved only by a frequently repeated drill of typical progressions until the eye, mind, and fingers function together as a single reaction.

Example 1. *General-Bass*, 153–55.

a. *Octave on Top**

*Numerous printer's errors occur in these examples, particularly in the figures; editorial additions are indicated by brackets.

Heinichen's contemporaries agree almost completely with his definitions of chords of the sixth. In France a more specific terminology prevailed that made clearer the distinctions between the three forms of these chords. From Saint-Lambert[28] we learn the *accord simple* is the chord of the sixth with doubled bass, *accord doublez*, the chord of the sixth with either third or sixth doubled, and *petit accord*, the chord of the sixth with a perfect fourth (which Heinichen called *Quarta irregolare*) in place of the bass octave (as in ex. 1, bars 2, 3, 6).

The aforementioned form was a favorite harmony of the French; it appears in their treatises from the end of the seventeenth century and, in addition to Saint-Lambert, the *petit accord* is described in books by Delair, Campion, and Dandrieu.[29] Gasparini, on the contrary, does not mention this particular chord of the sixth; and Werckmeister[30] bans it by insisting that the perfect fourth must not be played unless indicated in the figure, and then the fourth must resolve.

Heinichen evidently was the first North German writer to recommend this mild harmonic license of apparent Italian origin.[31] Arnold[32] disregards Heinichen, however, by restricting the use of an optional fourth to a chord of the sixth on the supertonic or submediant. Although the various *règle de l'octave* methods for assigning chords to unfigured basses places a $^6_4$ on the supertonic and submediant, no Baroque theorist limits this chord to any particular scale degree. Telemann's rule[33] fully represents the Baroque practice: as often as a bass with a major sixth descends a whole or half step the following bass can take a fourth with the sixth and third, even though this fourth does not appear in the figure.

Consulting C. P. E. Bach's treatise, one finds additional reason to question the total validity of his instructions for late Baroque music. Bach[34] considers rare a chord of the sixth with doubled bass, yet Heinichen recommends the use of this "ill-reputed octave" in all kinds of parallel and contrary motion as long as consecutive octaves or fifths can be avoided. In addition, C. P. E. Bach[35] observes that should the bass octave become unavoidable, it should not be placed in the highest part of the right hand. Heinichen gives no restriction of this type, and his examples offer ample proof that he did not hesitate to place bass octaves on the top of a chord.

Dissonances: The Second $\left[2,\ \overset{5}{\underset{2}{2}},\ \overset{4}{\underset{}{2}},\ \overset{5}{\underset{2}{4}},\ 4\!+\!,\ \overset{6}{\underset{2}{4\!+}} \right]$

Seconds occur as regular vertical dissonances in the thorough-bass in two forms only: (1) as a bass suspension (*syncopatio*) or (2) as a passing tone (*transitus*). As a suspension, the bass requires preparation and resolves down by a whole or half step. The chords $\overset{5}{\underset{2}{2}}$, $\overset{5}{\underset{2}{4}}$, $\overset{6}{\underset{2}{4}}$, and their chromatic alterations may be played on a bass suspension. The three-part $\overset{5}{2}$ chord may be increased to four parts by doubling the second or fifth (ex. 3, bar 7; compare ex. 3a and ex. 3b).

The second and sixth in the $\overset{6}{\underset{2}{4}}$ chord may be major or minor;[36] the fourth, perfect or augmented. This harmony generally resolves to the chord of the sixth or to a $\overset{6}{5}$ or $\overset{6+}{\flat}$. In the movement of parts one retains the second as the third, the sixth moves to the octave, and the fourth either becomes a sixth or remains stationary as a perfect or diminished fifth. In the latter instance the sixth in the $\overset{6}{\underset{2}{4}}$ becomes the sixth of the $\overset{6}{5}$. When replacing a perfect fourth, the tritone may resolve to a sixth in a chord of the $\overset{6}{\text{sixth}}$ or may be repeated as the fifth of a major triad while the bass of the $\overset{6}{\underset{2}{4\!+}}$ descends a half step (ex. 3, bar 4). The figure $\overset{6}{\underset{2}{4}}$ frequently appears as $\overset{4}{2}$ or simply as 2, and the $\overset{6}{\underset{2}{4\!+}}$ as $\overset{4\!+}{2}$ or $4\!+$.[37]

As a passing tone (*2da in transitu*) the second occurs naturally as the second of three bass notes descending by step. The triad on the first bass is repeated and forms either the $\overset{6}{\underset{2}{4}}$ or $\overset{6}{\underset{2}{4\!+}}$ on the passing-tone bass, and these chords resolve to a chord of the sixth, $\overset{6}{5}$, or triad (ex. 3, bars 4–5, 6, 7–8).[38]

"3a syncopata" $\left[\overset{6}{\underset{3}{4}},\ \overset{6}{\underset{3}{4\!+}} \right]$

Since the suspension of a third over a suspended bass resembles the structure of chords with seconds, Heinichen[39] discusses these progressions together. Because the perfect or augmented fourth generates the dissonance, the outward appearance of these chords corresponds to the chord of the sixth with a *Quarta irregolare*. The distinction lies in the preparation and resolution of the bass and in the figure itself, for the bass of the *3a syncopata* resolves a whole or half step to a chord of the sixth (ex. 3, bar 3), $\frac{6}{5}$, $\frac{6}{\flat}$, or a major third. The fourth, which usually lacks preparation, remains stationary or ascends to a sixth in the chord of resolution.

Heinichen includes with the *3a syncopata* a group of irregular chords belonging mainly to the operatic style. As the following examples show, the basses lack regular resolutions and skip down a third, while the right hand chords anticipate the following bass note over which they continue to sound. "I do not value greatly the first four chords [see example below], but I want to include them so that a beginner in accompanying from thorough-basses would not remain unacquainted with such striking rarities."[40]

Example 2. *General-Bass*, 164–65.

A general example demonstrates the various chords with seconds as well as the *3a syncopata* and two examples of the irregular chords just examined (ex. 3, bars 10, 11).

Example 3. *General-Bass*, 166–68.

a. *Third on Top*

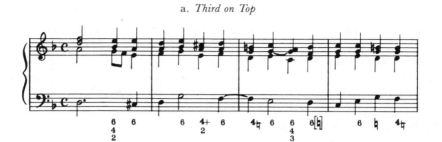

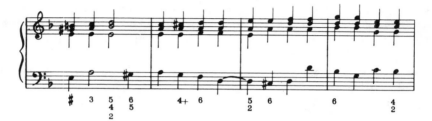

b. *Fifth on Top*

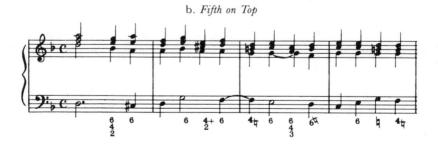

c. *Octave on Top*

Among the many treatises written in approximately the same period as Heinichen's, only Saint-Lambert's *Nouveau traité* has opposing suggestions for chords with a second. Drawing upon a decidedly conservative style of composition that seems more suited to music for the church than for the opera house, Saint-Lambert[41] would not accompany the figure 2 with the usual $\frac{6}{4}_2$ chord but prefers a $\frac{5}{2}$ with doubled second or the $\frac{5}{4}_2$. The latter chord, he recommends, should resolve to a diminished triad by means of a half step descending motion of the bass. For the double figure $\frac{4}{2}$, Saint-Lambert[42] favors the fifth and not the sixth as the third part, an opinion conflicting not only with Heinichen but also with earlier writers. Already in 1690 Delair implies that the use of a fifth with a second was old-fashioned: "One should note that older musicians usually place a fifth with the second instead of the sixth, as one can find in the works of Du Cauroy [Du Caurroy (1549–1609)] and other skilled composers: nevertheless one always meets the sixth in opera choruses."[43] Additional proof of the lack of popularity of the $\frac{5}{4}_2$ in the operatic style comes indirectly from Gasparini who ignores its very existence.[44]

In realizing the figure 2, as we have seen, one frequently employs a secondary dissonance in the chord, either a perfect or augmented fourth. Baroque music, both in theory and practice, distinguishes between two degrees of functional importance for dissonances: either as fundamental or auxiliary dissonances. In learning chords and their corresponding figures, the student practiced groups of harmonies classified together by the fundamental dissonance. Baroque thorough-bass manuals give instructions for the correct resolutions of fundamental dissonances and the several possible combinations of intervals that may be associated with them. Whether a treatise includes twenty or fifty figures, each one belongs to the five or six groups of chords having in common one of these fundamental dissonances: second, fourth, fifth, seventh, ninth, and — in late Baroque works — the *falsae* (see pages 55 ff.).

Although exceptions arise contrary to the general rules for each group of chords, this method of teaching had an over-all practicality and simplicity that was universally accepted in treatises. As soon as Rameau's principles of functional harmony replaced Baroque theory, however, chords lost their independence, and the knowledge of the figures gradually became an academic discipline and finally disintegrated into a system of symbols for harmonic analysis.

As yet unaffected by Rameau, Heinichen continued to group the $\frac{5}{2}$, $\frac{5}{4}_2$,

$\begin{smallmatrix}6\\4,\\2\end{smallmatrix}$ $\begin{smallmatrix}6\\4+\\2\end{smallmatrix}$ together as harmonic variations built on the dissonant second. To separate these chords into their respective harmonic functions according to post-Baroque theory and practice not only imposes on the music a foreign system of analysis, but complicates fruitlessly the essential thought processes of the student. This becomes clear, for example, when we examine Arnold's[45] lengthy chapter for the $\begin{smallmatrix}6\\4\\2\end{smallmatrix}$ chord, which he interprets only as the third inversion of a dominant seventh. Nowhere in the chapter does he discuss chords such as the $\begin{smallmatrix}5\\2\end{smallmatrix}$ or $\begin{smallmatrix}5\\4\\2\end{smallmatrix}$ because they did not result from the inversion of the dominant seventh. Instead they turn up in a special concluding section of his book entitled "Harmonies Due to the Retardation . . . of One or More Intervals."[46] If, however, the student must remember that the $\begin{smallmatrix}6\\4\\2\end{smallmatrix}$ derives its harmonic function from the inversion of a dominant chord and that two other chords employed exactly as the $\begin{smallmatrix}6\\4\\2\end{smallmatrix}$ in accompanying, except for the difference of one auxiliary part, have nonharmonic origins, then the barrier to realizing a thorough-bass grows appreciably. Even if the student can remember these facts, to what advantage? The thorough-bass figures are not supposed to give a harmonic analysis of the music nor are they to be limited by the later system.

The Fourth $\left[\, 4,\ 4+,\ \begin{smallmatrix}6\\4\end{smallmatrix},\ \begin{smallmatrix}6\\4+\end{smallmatrix}\,\right]$

The fourth, as a fundamental dissonance (*4ta dominanta* or *4ta sopra syncopata*), normally occurs as a suspension with a perfect fifth and bass octave as auxiliary parts. Neither the perfect nor the augmented fourth needs preparation when joined with a sixth, although generally they are resolved. A perfect or augmented fourth may ascend as a passing tone (ex. 4, bars 3, 5).[47]

Example 4. *General-Bass*, 174–77.

a. *Third on Top*

b. *Octave on Top*

c. *Fifth on Top*

The octave of the bass, according to Heinichen, is the only tone available as the fourth part to $^6_4$ chords, and his contemporaries concur with him. C. P. E. Bach,[48] on the contrary, suggests that the sixth may be doubled when the need arises. Examination of early eighteenth-century treatises, however, indicates that this practice was rare before 1750.

The Fifth $\left[\flat5, \, ^6_5, \, ^6_{\flat5}\right]$

A diminished fifth, as the fundamental dissonance of a chord, enjoys the relative freedom that permits its occurrence with or without preparation. According to Heinichen,[49] the resolution of a diminished fifth remains indispensable, and is formed by the upper part descending a step while the bass ascends either a whole or half step. The auxiliary parts usually are a sixth and a third. According to principles of resolution more characteristic of the operatic style, the bass of a diminished fifth may leap down a third (ex. 5, bar 7) or descend a half step to a $^6_4{}_2$ chord (ex. 5, bar 3).[50]

When used as part of a dissonance structure the perfect fifth (in Baroque terminology a "bound consonance") is prepared, suspended, or "bound" with a sixth, and resolves according to one of the three procedures already described for the $\frac{6}{5}$ chord. Frequently the $\frac{6}{5}$ forms part of a conventional cadence built over a bass note of long duration in which a four-part triad precedes the $\frac{6}{5}$ chord and the latter is followed by the $\frac{5}{4}$ or $\frac{6}{4}$ chord (ex. 5, bar 10). Heinichen[51] omits the third from a cadential $\frac{6}{5}$ to avoid a clash with the fourth in the $\frac{6}{4}$ chord; in place of the third he substitutes the doubled bass.

Example 5. *General-Bass*, 181–83.

a. *Third on Top*

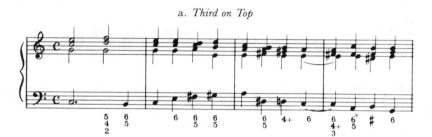

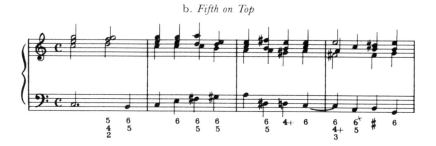

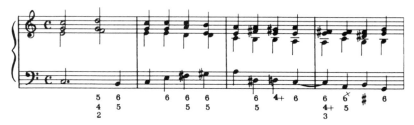

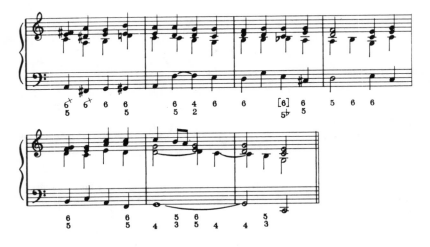

In one instance, Heinichen's account of the diminished fifth is incomplete when compared to other Baroque sources. He does not recognize the existence of a diminished triad, that is, a diminished fifth combined with a third and bass octave. This chord seems well established even as early as the end of the seventeenth century; Delair[52] recommends its use when the bass of the diminished fifth does not ascend by step, and Saint-Lambert[53] follows Delair's example. Kellner apparently follows Heinichen's example and omits this formation, while Mattheson,[54] the great encyclopedist among all theorists, gives both the $\frac{6}{3}$ and diminished triad with examples of each. Nevertheless, Mattheson says of the diminished fifth that the "regular auxiliary parts are . . . by no means the sixth and third, but rather the third and octave."

Mattheson must make the above statement, however, to support his peculiar declaration, issued a few years earlier,[55] that the diminished fifth was consonant because it required no preparation. As an extension of this idea, in *Der vollkommene Capellmeister* (1739)[56] he expands his catalogue of consonances to admit the augmented fifth, diminished and augmented octaves, diminished third, and augmented sixth. No other theorist, except Sorge,[57] supported Mattheson's extraordinary opinions that seemed based on the premise: once a consonance always a consonance, no matter how much the character of the interval becomes altered by chromatic inflection.

C. P. E. Bach,[58] who frequently favors greater harmonic conservatism than Heinichen, suggests that when the diminished fifth lacks preparation, the sixth instead should be played before the $\frac{6}{5}$ chord sounds in its entirety. A similar rule comes from Marpurg;[59] however, this idea appeared in thorough-bass sources only in the second half of the eighteenth century. Here, then, is another subtle though important distinction between the harmonic materials of Baroque and post-Baroque realizations.

The Seventh $\left[\; 7,\; \frac{7}{5},\; \begin{matrix}7\\5\\4\end{matrix},\; \begin{matrix}7\\4\\3\end{matrix},\; \begin{matrix}7\\4\\2\end{matrix},\; \begin{matrix}7\\5\\4\\2\end{matrix}\;\right]$

The seventh may be played either with or without preparation. The prepared seventh frequently resolves to a sixth on the same bass note; in this case the third and octave are the usual auxiliary parts. The octave may be omitted in lieu of doubling the third (ex. 6, bar 1), or the perfect fifth may be held until the sixth is played (ex. 6a, 6b, bar 2). Heinichen[60] advises the student to avoid the perfect fifth, since it frequently forms a false relation with the chord preceding the seventh; in other instances, no perfect fifth exists in the scale for the seventh chord (i.e., the seventh chord on the seventh degree of the major or minor scale). When the seventh does not resolve to a sixth on the same bass, the fifth and third furnish the auxiliary parts unless an awkward progression requires the substitution of the bass octave.

Heinichen[61] allows either a prepared or unprepared diminished fifth to become an auxiliary dissonance when it is the natural fifth to a bass figured with a seventh, and proposes further that the diminished fifth need not be resolved. He compares this use of a diminished fifth to the *Quarta irregolare* in a $\begin{smallmatrix}6\\4\\2\end{smallmatrix}$ chord, since both intervals function as an accessory part (*Hülffs-Stimme*) to the fundamental dissonance. He urges composers to indicate more carefully in the figures whenever they require a diminished fifth in a seventh chord. He believes, nevertheless, that no accompanist deserves criticism for playing diminished fifths natural to chords with sevenths when the $\flat\!5$ is omitted from the figures.

Unprepared sevenths, according to Heinichen,[62] may appear in accompaniments for any of the following reasons:

1. In the same manner as the prepared seventh; the seventh, accompanied by a third and fifth, usually resolves on the next bass (ex. 6, bar 4). Sometimes the seventh resolves to the adjacent sixth on the same bass (ex. 6, bar 5).
2. The seventh may be played against a prepared bass when accompanied

by a second and fourth or second and fifth. The bass resolves down a whole or half step while the seventh remains stationary (ex. 6, bars 4, 8).

3. Over a bass of long duration a triad may progress to a chord consisting of a major seventh, second, and fourth or fifth; this chord returns to the previous triad while the same bass continues to sound (ex. 6, bar 13).

4. The seventh is played to a suspended sixth. The fifth of the chord is omitted, and the sixth resolves on the same bass while the third is held. The fourth may be prepared and resolved with the sixth (ex. 6, bar 6).

5. The seventh may originate in the octave and serve as a passing tone (*8ve per transitum*).

Example 6. *General-Bass* 191–94.

a. *Fifth on Top*

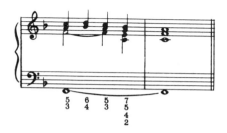

b. *Octave on Top*

c. *Third on Top*

Saint-Lambert[63] as late as 1707 contributes reactionary views for using the seventh that conflict with the instructions of every other late Baroque writer. He believes the third and fifth are the best auxiliary parts for a seventh resolving to a sixth on the same bass. He finds the substitution of the bass octave for the fifth less satisfactory, a license he would avoid unless no other means could be found to overcome faulty voice leading. Furthermore, he permits the fifth in each of these examples to leap somewhat awkwardly to the third of the same chord when the seventh descends to the sixth. This recommendation seems quite archaic, for even earlier writers such as Delair,[64] Boyvin,[65] and Werckmeister,[66] favored the octave and third for the figure 7 6.

These earlier sources as well as those more contemporary with the *General-Bass* oppose Heinichen's decidedly novel view that a diminished fifth need not resolve when combined with a seventh. In view of the weight of opinion against him, Heinichen's unkind criticism[67] of Gasparini seems unfounded (he accuses Gasparini of being narrow-minded simply because Gasparini insisted that all diminished fifths must resolve). One might expect Mattheson to confirm Heinichen's position. Despite Mattheson's proclamation that the diminished fifth was consonant,[68] with few exceptions his examples show the diminished fifth resolving down like any other dissonance; the few exceptions entail either the progression of the diminished fifth to another dissonance or show it ascending to a perfect fifth.

The Ninth $\left[9, \; 9, \; 9, \; 9, \; \begin{smallmatrix} 9 \\ 7 \\ 4 \end{smallmatrix} \right]$

The ninth, according to Heinichen,[69] must be prepared and resolved to the bass octave. The third and fifth serve as auxiliary parts, but the minor ninth prefers the major third and fifth or minor third and sixth.

The ninth frequently joins with either a seventh or fourth, or both; the latter dissonances are prepared and resolved with the ninth. The fifth accompanies the $\frac{9}{4}$ chord, and third the $\frac{9}{7}$.

Example 7. *General-Bass*, 196–98.

a. *Octave on Top*

b. *Third on Top*

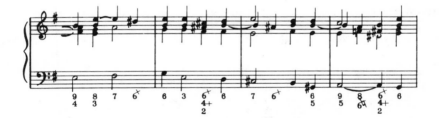

c. *Fifth on Top*

Heinichen disagree entirely with the instructions given by Gasparini and Saint-Lambert for chords with ninths. Neither author permitted perfect fifths with minor ninths because the resulting combination of intervals included a diminished fifth or augmented fourth that could not resolve properly. Gasparini[70] allows minor ninths to join only with sixths and thirds; Saint-Lambert[71] recommends the seventh in place of the sixth. Later theorists, including C. P. E. Bach,[72] use fifths with minor ninths, although Bach prefers to prepare diminished fifths, a practice Heinichen, Kellner, or Mattheson would have judged extraordinarily conservative.

Before concluding his first examination of the figures, Heinichen[73] makes three observations concerning liberties frequently taken by accompanists when playing dissonances. The importance of these statements far exceeds their brevity, since for the first time in the thorough-bass literature we receive some practical suggestions for circumventing the law that requires resolving every dissonance.

1. That the aforesaid dissonances do not always resolve on the immediately following bass note, but delay their resolution over several notes until finally the last note resolves for all the foregoing [dissonances]. For example:

Example 8.

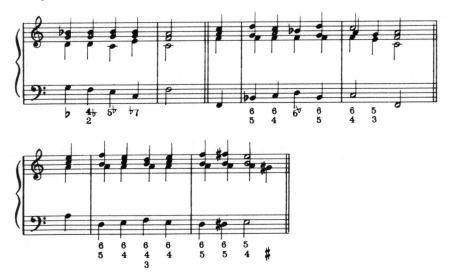

2. That dissonances frequently are disposed to resolve again to dissonances. Of this we have already seen two cases in which both the 4 and 5♭ resolve to the augmented fourth [see ex. 4, bar 3 and ex. 5, bar 3]. The following example, however, may illustrate the matter further:

Example 9.

3. That dissonances figured over bass notes and previously prepared are not always true *Syncopationes*, which require a resolution. They frequently result from a simple *Transitu[s]* in the bass, and require nothing more than that as with similar sevenths and ninths (at times in slow notes) the third accompanies them, when the contrary is not expressly figured, as the last two examples show. [These are] a type of *Transitus*, however, that is not always desirable in slow bass notes:[74]

Example 10.

Heinichen postpones discussion of chords with augmented and diminished intervals, with the exception of the commonly employed augmented fourth, diminished fifth, and diminished seventh, until the reader of the *General-Bass* has familiarized himself with the less difficult figures. He groups together all the remaining dissonances — augmented second, diminished third, diminished fourth, augmented fifth, augmented sixth, major seventh — into a special section entitled *falsae*. These dissonances, which Heinichen praises as the most beautiful materials of music, include "those intervals, which have either a semitone too little or too much in their appertaining [number of] steps, and produce, therefore (at times without the mediation of other parts), an exceptional harshness for the ear."[75] This harshness exists whether the *falsae* sound in the upper tones only of a chord or between the bass and an upper part. They can be divided into four groups:

I. Major, Minor, Augmented Chords of the Sixth

$$\left[6^{+}, \begin{matrix} 6^{+} \\ 5 \end{matrix}, \begin{matrix} 6^{+} \\ 4+ \\ 3 \end{matrix}, \begin{matrix} 6^{+} \\ 5\flat \end{matrix}, \begin{matrix} 6^{+} \\ \natural \end{matrix} \right]$$

Chords of the sixth may employ one of three forms of *falsae*.

1. An augmented sixth is accompanied by a doubled third; otherwise either a prepared perfect fifth (ex. 11, bar 1) or augmented fourth (ex. 11, bar 9) substitutes for the doubled third. In resolving the chord, the augmented fourth or perfect fifth remains stationary, the sixth usually rises (in ex. 11, bar 9, however, it descends to another dissonance), and the bass descends a semitone.
2. The diminished fifth joins with a major sixth to form an augmented second or diminished seventh between upper chord tones (ex. 11, bars 4, 6). The fourth part remains the same as for the regular $\begin{smallmatrix}6\\5\end{smallmatrix}$ chord: usually the third, occasionally the bass octave.
3. The major third joins with the minor sixth to form a diminished fourth or augmented fifth between upper chord tones (ex. 11, bars 2, 4). One doubles the bass as the fourth part.

Heinichen prefaces his general example for these dissonant chords of the sixth with the pertinent observation that "If one ever has need to practice any figures of the thorough-bass using the three positions of the triad, then it is certainly the *falsae*. For the interchanging of upper and middle parts of such extravagant chords gives a beginner new difficulties each time."[76]

Example 11. *General-Bass*, 230–33.

a. *Third on Top*

b. *Octave on Top*

c. *Fifth on Top*

II. Augmented Second, Diminished Third, Diminished Fourth $\begin{bmatrix} 6 & 5 & 6 & 6\flat \\ 4+ & \sharp & 4+ & 4+ \\ 2 & 2\flat & \flat 3 & 2 \end{bmatrix}$

This group, one of the richest in sound and perhaps the most important of the *falsae* for the music of early eighteenth-century Italy and Germany, involves primarily the augmented second. In general, the augmented form is used like the major and minor second, that is, it requires the preparation and resolution of a bass suspension. The augmented second, however, joins with a sixth and augmented fourth, although occasionally a prepared seventh may retard the sixth but resolves to it before the bass resolves.

Heinichen defines five specific applications of the augmented second:[77]

1. With a bass suspension. The augmented second and fourth either remain stationary while the bass resolves or they ascend to form a fourth and sixth.

Example 12.

2. With a bass moving as a passing tone. The chord with the augmented second can be viewed as an anticipation of the following chord.

Example 13.

3. With a prepared augmented fourth that does not resolve. In this exceptional usage, the preparation of the augmented second takes place in an upper part where it remains stationary together with the augmented fourth while the bass descends a tone. A prepared seventh may replace the sixth, as mentioned previously, but it must resolve before the bass moves to the next chord.

Example 14.

4. The preparation of the second also occurs in an upper part, but in this
   example it ascends a step while the bass remains stationary. This augmented second is a retardation of the third.

Example 15.

5. With a bass leaping up a minor third and then resolving down a tone.
   Heinichen considers the bass note that ascends by a minor third as the
   prepared minor third of the preceding chord; that is, the bass and part
   with the minor third interchange their parts. The augmented second,
   augmented fourth, and major sixth are played with this bass, which
   then resolves as if it were a bass suspension.

Example 16.

   Other harmonies with an augmented second or, in inversion, a
diminished seventh include chords with a major third and minor second.
The minor second results from a bass suspension; a perfect fifth forms the
fourth part.

Example 17.

Another combination of intervals producing an augmented second or diminished seventh is the minor third and augmented fourth. One adds a sixth as the fourth part. The minor third may be prepared and "syncopated" by an augmented fourth or may enter by step while the bass descends as a passing tone with the figure $\frac{6}{4+}$. Another example of a $\frac{6}{4+}$ chord results from a chromatic inflection of a simple chord of the sixth to which the dissonant chord returns in resolving (see ex. 18).

Example 18.

Despite the close similarity of the augmented second and diminished third, Heinichen[78] rejects the latter. He reports that certain learned and famous composers employ the diminished third for expressing the meaning of harsh words. In these cases this "unbearable interval" (Heinichen's words) arises by combining an augmented fourth and minor sixth. He attacks the excuse, given by some composers favoring the diminished third, that its sound is mollified by reason of its position in the upper tones of a chord. Heinichen retorts that if it sounds bad between a bass note and an upper part, it will sound just as bad between upper parts alone. Still, Heinichen had not fully resolved his own views. In the body of his text he suggests that if this interval must be used, he would prefer its inverted form, the augmented sixth. With the augmented fourth placed on top of the chord, he concludes that the spread of the tones will lessen the harshness. Either a second or minor third may be added as the fourth part.

Example 19.

The diminished third continues to trouble Heinichen, and for good reason, since his suggestion that the inversion sounds better than the uninverted form opposes an important principle he had established early in the treatise (see pages 30–31): if inverting an interval could not create a dissonance that had not existed previously, then an inversion also could not lessen the harshness possessed by an interval before inversion. In the Supplement to the *General-Bass*, written a number of years after the first part had been set in type, Heinichen admits his dissatisfaction with the preceding conclusion. In the following passage, a revealing glimpse into Heinichen's ceaselessly inquisitive mind, one detects no hint of the pedantry that nineteenth-century historians found in his writings. Quite to the contrary, he concedes that he has not found the answer to this important theoretical problem, an admission rare in any century for a prominent theorist:

> It [the greater distance between tones] seems to lessen the previous harshness, but this cannot be given out as a positive principle. And because I have more carefully pondered the matter, I would like to alter completely my opinion and retain without qualification my previously stated principle: That the inversion of parts cannot create any harshness that was not there previously and, therefore, cannot lessen any harshness that really existed beforehand. From this princip it follows that one must consider the two intervals of an augmented sixth and a diminished third either as endurable and permissible or both as unendurable and not permis-

sible. Most composers of the past agree with the latter, while only a very few novices agree with the former. The third forceful faction, however, holding the augmented sixth as more tolerable than the diminished third, now must either alter their opinion or defend it with other fundamentals. I shall give the matter further thought; anyone else may do likewise. But our accompanist will not err if he remains with the previous instructions, and he can take comfort that such harsh chords with $\frac{6^\flat}{4+}$ seldom occur in the music of today.[79]

The last chord listed in Heinichen's second class of *falsae* consists of a diminished fourth, viewed as a simple delaying of the third.

Example 20.

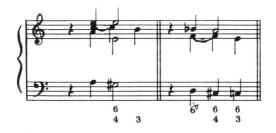

Further examples of the variety of chords with augmented seconds and diminished fourths appear in Heinichen's general example:

Example 21.

a. *Fifth on Top*

b. *Octave on Top*

c. *Third on Top*

III. The Augmented Fifth $\left[5^+, \frac{5^+}{2}, \frac{7}{5^+}, \frac{7}{5^+}, \frac{9}{4}, \frac{9}{7}, \frac{9}{5^+} \atop 3 \right]$

Chords with augmented fifths fall into two groups. In the first, the bass prepares a suspension of a second that occurs either with the augmented fifth alone (ex. 22, bar 3) or together with a seventh (ex. 22, bar 6). This $\frac{7}{5^+}$ chord resolves to a chord of the sixth or, according to Heinichen,[80] acts as a simple anticipation of the chord of the sixth.

In the second group, one prepares the augmented fifth in an upper part and resolves it to a sixth. This augmented fifth may be regarded, therefore, as a retardation of the sixth. A considerable variety of auxiliary parts may be employed, including the third and bass octave (ex. 22, bar 2), the fourth, the seventh (ex. 22, bar 4), the seventh and ninth (ex. 22, bar 8), or the fourth and ninth (ex. 22, bar 5).

IV. The Major Seventh $\left[{}^+7, \frac{{}^+7}{6^\flat}, \frac{{}^+7}{6^\flat}, \frac{{}^+7}{6^\flat} \atop 3, \quad 4, \quad 4 \atop 2 \right]$

The last group of *falsae* includes the major seventh as the fundamental dissonance. When joined with a minor third, the major seventh forms either an augmented fifth or a diminished fourth between the upper parts. The major seventh must be prepared and following the suspension ascends to the octave of the bass; the fifth usually forms the remaining part (ex. 22, bar 9).

A minor sixth combined with the major seventh produces either an augmented second or a diminished seventh between upper chord tones. The bass remains stationary before and after playing this chord, and auxiliary parts may include a third, a fourth (ex. 22, bar 1), or a second and fourth (ex. 22, bar 11). In less usual circumstances the bass may move by step to the chord of the minor sixth and major seventh.

Heinichen brings together both the third and fourth classes of *falsae* into one example serving a double purpose:

Example 22. *General-Bass*, 249–53.

a. *Third on Top*

b. *Octave on Top*

c. *Fifth on Top*

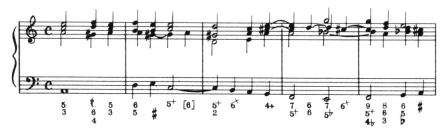

Heinichen's first treatise written in Leipzig does not mention the *falsae*; the prominence given to these exceptionally poignant intervals in the *General-Bass* affirms the powerful and growing influence of Italian operatic music. Conversely, the absence of the *falsae* from his earlier treatise emphasizes the independence of musical style that North German composers maintained into the first decade of the eighteenth century. It would be difficult to understand otherwise how, with his youthful enthusiasm for opera, Heinichen could fail to incorporate into his first publication the most recent Italian harmonic innovations, particularly when these harmonies served so well to express the affections. Heinichen[81] lists only eight chords (4+ , 5+ , 6, 6, 4, 7, 7, 4) in addition to triads as the total harmonic basis for theatrical recitatives, which disposes one to believe that he did not employ a larger variety of harmonies in his early operas written for Leipzig.

The early introduction of *falsae* in the *General-Bass*, where they belong to the basic instructions for realizing figures, emphasizes their importance. Heinichen was the first to insist that these dissonances, frequently deprecated by French and German writers as bizarre Italian harmonic excesses, were essential to the education of every professional and amateur accompanist. He undoubtedly learned from personal experience that an accompanist would suffer quick defeat when faced with a thorough-bass to an opera aria, cantata, or instrumental ensemble, if he were unfamiliar with figures including *falsae*.

Earlier writers mostly ignore the *falsae*, although Delair[82] again proves exceptional, listing all *falsae* except the minor second, diminished third, and augmented sixth. He stresses, however, that these intervals were preferred by Italian composers and implies that they found little favor with the French.

Gasparini, though intimately familiar with the sharp, affective dissonances of the Italian operatic style, nevertheless omits the minor second, diminished third, augmented fifth, and augmented sixth from his treatise. Even more surprising, he restricts the use of other dissonances to their least harsh combinations. He permits the augmented second to be accompanied with a tritone in exceptional instances when this second originates in a melodic skip. As his example demonstrates, they carry little harmonic weight (see ex. 23).

According to Gasparini,[83] augmented seconds were suited to preparing certain cadences and for expressing *di parole meste*. Except for the dissonances arising from acciaccaturas,[84] *L'armonico pratico al cimbalo* neglects those expressive dissonances prevalent in Italian operas of that period.

Example 23. *L'armonico pratico*, 57.

The lack of interest Saint-Lambert displayed for these same dissonances can be explained more easily, stemming as it did both from his antagonism toward Italian opera and from the prevailing French abhorrence for harmonic excesses of all kinds. In his *Nouveau traité*[85] he acknowledges the value of major seconds but casts aside the minor and augmented forms as useless. He ignores the almost commonplace accompaniment of an augmented second for tritones and substitutes the major second and sixth or the bass octave. Saint-Lambert does advance a step beyond Gasparini's elementary accompaniments by permitting the augmented fifth to join chords with a second and major seventh or major seventh and ninth. When a major seventh appears by itself, however, he limits the auxiliary parts to a third and fifth or third and bass octave.

Mattheson, in his *Kleine General-Bass-Schule*,[86] invents a new figure for the augmented sixth, 6^{++}, which he thinks accompanists require to avoid confusing major and augmented sixths. Actually a musical context rarely leads an accompanist to play a major sixth when the augmented interval is intended or vice versa; and this new figure had little practical value other than in those catalogues of thorough-bass figures that separate the symbols from the chords they represent. Even for this purpose, subsequent authors rejected Mattheson's proposed 6^{++}.

Unlike Heinichen, Mattheson does not question the usefulness of diminished thirds, though he confirms the irregularity of chords such as $\frac{6^{\flat}}{4+}$ and $\frac{6^{\flat}}{4+}{3}$ when he comments that they are probably the rarest chords in music, useful *zu solchen Ausdrücken die dergleichen rührenden Misklang* [*sic*] *erfordern.*[87]

C. P. E. Bach certainly would not have agreed with Mattheson. Nowhere in his *Versuch* does he so much as allude to a chord with a minor sixth, augmented fourth, and a second. The $\frac{6^{\flat}}{4+}{3}$ appears only once, in an example that Bach[88] says he included to please those who are fond of "strange chords."

Notes

1. Heinichen, *General-Bass*, 112–13.

2. Arnold, *Thorough-bass*, 868.

3. An extensive examination of German manuscripts and printed music would be required to determine the earliest use of a stroke in the thorough-bass figures. Johannes Wolf, *Handbuch der Notationskunde* pt. 2 (Leipzig, 1913), 318–19, believes Scheidt first introduced this type of figure in his *Concerti sacri* (1621–22); Wolf lists other earlier appearances of the 6^{+} in: Rosenmüller, *Kern-Sprüche, mehrentheils aus heiliger Schrifft* (1648–52); and Bernhard, *Geistlicher Harmonien* (1665). See the facsimile from the latter source in *MGG* 1, col. 1787.

4. Werckmeister, *Die nothwendigsten Anmerckungen und Regeln wie der Bassus Continuus oder General-Bass wohl könne tractiret werden* (Aschersleben, 1698). Thus Arnold's reference to the first use of the $4+$ in Niedt's *Musicalische Handleitung* (1700) overlooks this slightly earlier example in a German treatise.

5. Etienne Denis Delair, *Traité d'acompagnement* [*sic*] *pour le théorbe et le clavessin* (Paris, 1690), 29.

6. Reprinted by Paul Brunold (ed.) in the *Oeuvres complètes* 1 (Paris, 1933), 13–17. A facsimile from this manuscript appears in *MGG* 2, col. 1721–22, where the ♯6 is clearly evident. Louis Clérambault (1676-1749), in a manuscript dated 1706, places a stroke through the 5, corresponding to Delair's usage, but retains the sharp with a 6; see facsimile in *MGG* 2, col. 1497–98.

7. Heinichen, *General-Bass*, 116–17.

8. Godfry Keller, *A Compleat Method, for Attaining to Play a Thorough Bass* (London, 1707); A.[lexander] B.[ayne], *An Introduction to the Knowledge and Practice of the Thoro' Bass* (Edinburgh, 1717). Although the latter treatise is ascribed generally to Alexander Baillie, eighteenth-century Scotch music engraver, *GroveD* I, 355 gives as the author Alexander Bayne, "first governor (1728–31) of the Edinburgh Musical Society."

9. José de Torres, *Reglas generales de accompañar* (Madrid, 1702).

10. J. P. A. Fischer, *Korte en noodigste Grondregelen van de Bassus-Continuus* (Utrecht, 1731); G. P. Telemann, *Singe-, Spiel- und Generalbass-Übungen* (Hamburg, 1733); J. F. Dandrieu, *Principes de l'acompagnement* [*sic*] *du clavecin* (Paris, [1718]).

11. Heinichen, *General-Bass*, 120. Heinichen prefers *ordinaire Accorde* to *Triade harmonica*. The former words suggest the comparable English usage "common chord," but it should be remembered that *ordinaire*, from *ordinarius*, does not mean "common" in the usual sense. Rather *ordinaire* refers to being ordered or arranged. Werckmeister shows this most clearly when he describes *ordinaire Accorde* as forms existing as God and Nature created them, that is, as they occur in the series of natural harmonics (*Die nothwendigsten Anmerckungen*, 10).

12. Saint-Lambert, *Nouveau traité*, 71.

13. Kellner, *Treulicher Unterricht*, 9.

14. Mattheson, *Kleine General-Bass-Schule*, 137.

15. Ibid., 141.

16. Heinichen, *General-Bass*, 131 (footnote).

17. An exception to this general rule occurs in the MS *Regulae concentuum partiturae* (Vienna, 1699) by Georg Muffat and published in a new ed. by H. Federhofer as *An Essay on Thoroughbass* (Tübingen, 1961), in which Muffat states (39): "All three consonances [third, fifth, and octave] can be doubled in four as well as more parts." Nevertheless, in the four-part examples found throughout his treatise Muffat rarely doubles any tone other than the bass.

18. C. P. E. Bach, *Versuch über die wahre Art das Clavier zu spielen* (Berlin, 1753–62). English tr. & ed. W. J. Mitchell (New York, 1949), 199.

19. Daniel Türk, *Kurze Anweisung zum Generalbassspielen* (Halle & Leipzig, 1791).

20. Heinichen, *General-Bass*, 140 (footnote).

21. Ibid., 139.

22. Many of Heinichen's examples in this chapter are given in three versions or chord distributions. When a point is demonstrated equally well in all three, no reference is made to version a, b, or c.

23. Heinichen, *General-Bass*, 141–42 (footnote).

24. Heinichen, *General-Bass*, 940–41.

25. Ibid., 145–49. The first and third rules have been reworded to state positively Heinichen's negative phraseology.

26. Ibid., 151 (footnote g).

27. Ibid., 151.

28. Saint-Lambert, *Nouveau traité*, 30.

29. Delair, *Traité*, 28; François Campion, *Traité d'accompagnement et de composition selon la règle des octaves de musique* (Paris, 1716), 11; J. F. Dandrieu, *Principes de l'accompagnement* [*sic*] *du clavecin* (Paris, [1718]), [18].

30. Werckmeister, *Nothwendigsten Anmerckungen*, 16.

31. The Italian origin seems likely from Muffat, *Essay on Thoroughbass*, 48, who labels this chord "*Quarta Italica, die welsche oder irregular Quart.*"

32. Arnold, *Thorough-bass*, 810–14.

33. Telemann, *Generalbass-Übungen*, 6.

34. Bach-Mitchell, *Versuch*, 209.

35. Ibid., 211.

36. Heinichen devotes a special section to chords combining diminished and augmented intervals such as the augmented second and sixth; see pages 56–65.

37. Heinichen, *General-Bass*, 160–62.

38. Ibid., 163.

39. Ibid., 165.

40. Ibid., 165 (footnote).

41. Saint-Lambert, *Nouveau traité*, 22–23.

42. Ibid., 34.

43. Delair, *Traité*, 25.

44. Gasparini, *L'armonico pratico*, 54–57.

45. Arnold, *Thorough-bass*, 648–72.

46. Ibid., 708–9, 711–12.

47. Heinichen, *General-Bass*, 173.

48. Bach-Mitchell, *Versuch*, 226; see also Arnold, *Thorough-bass*, 536.

49. Heinichen, *General-Bass*, 177.

50. The resolution by a bass leaping down a third results from an interchange of parts; the resolution in which a bass descends a half step occurs according to the principle of the anticipation of passing tones. Concerning these types of resolutions in the operatic style see appendix C.

51. Heinichen, *General-Bass*, 180.

52. Delair, *Traité*, 27.

53. Saint-Lambert, *Nouveau traité*, 27.

54. Mattheson, *Kleine General-Bass-Schule*, 180.

55. In *Das forschende Orchestre* (Hamburg, 1721), 489, 773.

56. Mattheson, *Capellmeister*, 253.

57. G. A. Sorge, *Vorgemach der musicalischen Composition* (Lobenstein, 1745–47) III, 335, makes something of a compromise in his catalogue of consonances by calling these intervals, with the exception of altered octaves, *pseudo-consonantiae*.

58. Bach-Mitchell, *Versuch*, 244.

59. F. W. Marpurg, *Handbuch bey dem Generalbasse und der Composition* . . . (Berlin, 1757–62), 60.

60. Heinichen, *General-Bass*, 184 (footnote q).

61. Ibid., 186 (footnotes r and s).

62. Ibid., 188–90.

63. Saint-Lambert, *Nouveau traité*, 31–32.

64. Delair, *Traité*, 28, suggests that the third, fifth, or octave may be used with a seventh when the tempo is slow, but in a quick tempo, he adds, one hardly ever uses the fifth.

65. Boyvin's *Traité abrégé de l'accompagnement pour l'orgue et pour clavessin* (2d ed. Paris, 1705), 11–13.

66. Werckmeister, *Nothwendigsten Anmerckungen*, 11.

67. Heinichen, *General-Bass*, 186.

68. Mattheson, *Kleine General-Bass-Schule*, 183.

69. Heinichen, *General-Bass*, 194–95.

70. Gasparini, *L'armonico pratico*, 67–69.

71. Saint-Lambert, *Nouveau traité*, 33.

72. Bach-Mitchell, *Versuch*, 300.

73. Heinichen, *General-Bass*, 200–201.

74. Ibid.

75. Ibid., 225–26.

76. Ibid., 230–31 (footnote h).

77. Ibid., 236.

78. Ibid., 238–39.

79. Ibid., 945.

80. Ibid., 246.

81. Heinichen, *Neu erfundene Anweisung*, 215.

82. Delair, *Traité*, 25.

83. Gasparini, *L'armonico pratico*, 57.

84. See below.

85. Saint-Lambert, *Nouveau traité*, 6.

86. Mattheson, *Kleine General-Bass-Schule*, 153.

87. Ibid., 153.

88. Bach-Mitchell, *Versuch*, 251.

4

Basic Principles of Thorough-Bass
Accompanying

The multitude of thorough-bass figures in the previous chapter embodies the primary knowledge of thorough-bass realization. This information in itself, however, offers few clues to Heinichen's "art" of accompanying, a compilation of details rooted both in the principles of composition and in the actual performance practices of keyboard musicians. "First of all, the question arises here: who is qualified to begin the study of the thorough-bass and when? Answer: whoever wishes to learn only the thorough-bass without including keyboard *galanterie*, need not, as is often customary, delay one or more years learning numerous suites and preludes. For he can more profitably acquire [the knowledge of] these afterwards or even simultaneously."[1]

Thus Heinichen advocates that students of the harpsichord or organ begin to study the thorough-bass prior to acquiring any advanced degree of keyboard technique or independent theoretical study. Heinichen favored the thorough-bass as a means of learning how to compose; and clearly he also considered thorough-bass study an excellent beginning for performers of keyboard instruments. Yet most writers of the eighteenth century did not agree with him; Couperin,[2] for example, urged his students to wait two or three years before undertaking the study of accompanying. He considered the thorough-bass a hazardous knowledge, detrimental to a harpsichordist's technique because it forced the right hand to suffer a constant strain of chord repetitions, stiffening the muscles. To avoid misusing the hand, Couperin thought the performer must have a wide variety of solo pieces at his command; these could be interspersed between thorough-bass realizations, allowing their technical diversity to aid in relaxing the hand.

Two decades later, Mattheson[3] advocated similarly that before a student started to accompany he should devote a half year or more to the

practice of *Handsachen* (solo pieces) by Kuhnau, Handel, Graupner, Telemann, J. S. Bach, and Mattheson; and C. P. E. Bach[4] offered much the
same advice. Couperin, Mattheson, and Bach, however, were fully as
concerned with the technical virtuosity of the performer as they were with
the less challenging technical demands of the thorough-bass. Couperin
leaves no doubt concerning his attitude when he says:

> If there were a question of choosing between accompanying and [solo] pieces in
> order to bring the one or the other to perfection, I feel that self-esteem would
> make me choose pieces in preference to the accompaniment. I admit that there is
> nothing more entertaining in itself, and nothing that links one more closely with
> others, than to be a good accompanist. But what injustice! It is [the accompanist]
> whom one praises last at concerts. The accompaniment of the harpsichord on such
> occasions is considered merely the foundation of an edifice, which nevertheless
> upholds and supports the whole, and of which one hardly ever speaks. Whereas
> one who excels in [solo] pieces enjoys the undivided attention and the applause of
> his audience.[5]

Mattheson's recommendation to begin with solo pieces stems from his
preoccupation with the contemporary practice of improvising technically
brilliant pieces from a given bass. Before an organist could hope to develop
this special competence, he had to achieve considerable technical command over his instrument, normally gained from *Handsachen*. Heinichen,
on the contrary, approached the study of music from the opposite direction; he proposed that a student first acquire a general musical training by
assimilating the art of accompanying from a thorough-bass. Later he could
specialize in the technical virtuosity of an organist or harpsichordist, or
master the particular abilities required of a capellmeister or composer.

Elementary Concepts of Style

At the very core of the art of accompanying lie two basic rules that determine the correct joining of four-part chords. These rules are found at the
very beginning of the *General-Bass*.[6]

1. Two voice parts never should move in parallel fifths or octaves.
2. To avoid these faults as well as others, one never makes unnecessary
   leaps with the right hand, but seeks, as much as possible, the smoothest
   connection of parts between chords.

A simple example of triads illustrates these two vital principles, showing
(a) errors of parallel fifths and octaves and (b) errors contained in unnecessary skips between chords.

Example 24. *General-Bass*, 123–24.

The following version of the bass line given in Ex. 24 illustrates a correct joining together of triads:

Example 25. *General-Bass*, 124.

In explaining the familiar concepts of similar and contrary motion, Heinichen comments that *motus contrarius* offers "one of the greatest advantages" (*einer der grössten Vortheile*)[7] or safeguards for avoiding parallel fifths and octaves. In order to take advantage of this *Vortheil*, Heinichen insisted that students undergo an initial period of training in which they would drill themselves in realizing four-part harmonies at the keyboard, a prerequisite to becoming a good accompanist. Even though the smooth conjoining of chords without parallel fifths and octaves seems simple in principle, in practice it requires diligent cultivation. Today, as in the eighteenth century, the art of the thorough-bass remains unconquered until the keyboard performer can play four-part chords at sight from a bass line.

Even within the strict four-part style an accompanist had certain freedoms in the number of parts he might choose. He could subtract a part (in the case of three-part accompaniments for chords of the sixth) or add a fifth part, as many of the examples in the previous chapter have shown. The bass part could be played in octaves whenever its character did not make octaves technically impossible (i.e., when numerous quick notes occurred).

To prevent the right hand from colliding with the left, the accompanist was free to play bass notes an octave lower than written. Other practical means to keep the hands apart existed:

> [With the] numerous descending resolutions of dissonances, the right hand often comes down so low [on the keyboard] that it has no room left for resolutions, nor can the left hand (even if it takes the bass in the lowest octave) act freely. Therefore, a beginner . . . need only observe the two following suggestions with which he can again bring the right hand higher [on the keyboard], for example:
>
> (1) After the resolution of the dissonance occurs, or even on bass notes with no dissonances above them (particularly long notes), he seeks to halve the value and to break the chord so that the right hand, bit by bit, regains a higher position and wins a new place from which to bring about the resolution of the following dissonances. . . .
>
> (2) He can, now and then, take a full-voiced chord high up [on the keyboard], and on the following bass note can again omit the lower part. In this connection, examine the first and third bars of the following example:[8]

Example 26.

Range

Unlike earlier treatises, Heinichen's work contains no iron-clad rule limiting the keyboard area utilized for the accompaniment. In his sole reference to range, however, he does approve the use of the entire keyboard for two special forms of accompaniment. This is apparently the earliest sanction of the extreme upper notes of keyboard instruments found in the thorough-bass literature:

> When the old theorists gave the rule that one should not readily go higher than c″ with the right hand or, on any account, not above e″, they sought in this way to prevent too great a vacuum or empty space between both hands in the accompaniments of their time, which were both very thin and usually in three parts. And on this basis they had complete justification. Just as then, this rule still applies to a four- or five-part accompaniment in which one divides the parts equally between the hands and which would sound bad when one would, for example, take two voices in the uppermost range of the right hand and two in the deepest range of the left hand. This rule, however, invalidates itself naturally in two instances, namely: (1) In a very full-voiced accompaniment in which, in any case, both hands cannot easily leave a large vacuum in the middle; thus the right hand has all the more reason to move to higher notes; (2) in the . . . melodic form of accompaniment in which one seeks to execute with the right hand alone a melody, embellishments, arpeggios, and all kinds of variations, in which case the amateur may go right up to x‴ if in so doing he believes he can achieve something really fine.[9]

Although just prior to the turn of the century Werckmeister[10] still limited the right hand to c″, most writers of the eighteenth century generally agreed on e″ or f″ as the highest note of accompaniments. Saint-Lambert, Kellner, and Telemann[11] refer specifically to this range limit, as does C. P. E. Bach.[12] The latter suggests two exceptions permitting the right hand to move higher on the keyboard: (1) when the bass part exceeds its usual range by ascending into the area generally reserved for the right hand, or (2) for the sake of tonal variety within exact repetitions of phrases or longer musical periods, in which case both the left and right hands would play in a higher octave.

A significant aspect of Heinichen's previous remarks on range is his testimony that composers previously did not exceed e″ or f″ to prevent an excessive distance and a contingent thinness of sound in four-part realizations. The reason is so simple that it might easily be overlooked; yet the principle on which it is founded, the avoidance of an excessive distance between the hands, belongs with the other *Vortheile* enabling one to accompany with skill.

Full-Voiced Accompaniment

Among the wealth of facts Heinichen has recorded about eighteenth-century performance practices, we are particularly fortunate to possess his exhaustive description of the filled-in or (in a more literal translation of *vollstimmig*) full-voiced accompaniment. The essence of this style consists in doubling as many notes from right hand chords as the left hand can grasp. Although Heinichen errs in implying that no other author had written about full-voiced realizations, he is the only Baroque composer to develop these ideas systematically and exhaustively. The practical need for full-voiced realizations largely resulted from the general increase in size of instrumental forces required by composers at the beginning of the eighteenth century, particularly in Italian operatic music. The problem of seeing but not hearing the harpsichord quite clearly concerned late Baroque composers. Heinichen frequently refers to the impossibility of sustaining tones on the harpsichord, and he urges accompanists to consider the full-voiced style as the best means of strengthening the sound.

Quite early in the history of the thorough-bass, composers used an accompaniment fuller than the normal three- or four-part chords when the circumstances required more sound from the organ or harpsichord. Praetorius, in the *Syntagma musicum* 3 (Wolfenbüttel, 1619),[13] suggests that when only a few voices sing, three-part chords are sufficient for the organ to be heard; when the voices are increased in number, however, the organist needs to play a more full-voiced accompaniment. Another early reference to a fuller form of keyboard accompaniment occurs in *Li primi albori musicali* (Bologna, 1672) by the Carmelite monk Lorenzo Penna. In this instance, too, a fuller accompaniment is recommended for accompanying two, three, and four choruses.[14]

The first mention of a full-voiced style in French sources appears in the introduction to D'Anglebert's *Pièces de Clavecin* (Paris, 1689) and recurs one year later in Delair's *Traité d'acompagnement* (Paris, 1690). Both authors suggest that the left hand accompaniment may be filled in with consonances or even by doubling the second or tritone of the right hand chord. Delair specifically warns that one should never double the diminished fifth, the seventh, or the ninth.[15]

This advice must have seemed radical to conservative French contemporaries of these musicians, for even as late as 1707 Saint-Lambert advocates a much more limited application of the full-voiced style: "When . . . voices are numerous one may double in the left hand some of the parts played by the right hand; one may even double all of them if the voices are very numerous [i.e., in large choral works] and when one is not supported sufficiently by the other orchestral instruments. If one doubles one part only, it should be the octave. If one doubles two [parts], they are the octave and the fifth or the part held in place of the fifth; and if one doubles three, they are the same as those of the right hand."[16]

Saint-Lambert would not double any notes in the left hand other than the triad or interval of a second, but he suggests that a certain elegance results if the performer chooses another note for the left hand in place of a dissonance found in the right hand chord: "First, one must never double dissonances, except the second. Thus when a bass note bears some one [of the dissonances] one doubles for filling in only the consonances that serve to accompany it, or when possible one employs and doubles the consonance that the dissonance replaces. . . ."[17] He clarifies this explanation with the following example: If a bass note is figured with a seven, one would normally double the third and fifth of the seventh chord in the left hand. Since the seventh replaces the octave of the bass, this latter note may be taken in the left hand and even doubled in the right. Prudently, however, Saint-Lambert concludes that the seventh is practically the only dissonance allowing this form of doubling in the left hand.

A treatise contemporary with Saint-Lambert's, but far less conservative in its application of the full-voiced style is Georg Muffat's *Regulae concentuum partiturae*, dated 1699 in the single existing copy kept in the Minoritenkonvent in Vienna, which also contains a second part, apparently of the same manuscript, entitled *Exempla der vornehmbsten Greiffen der Partitur, wie selbe auffs cantabliste zu nehmen seynd.* Muffat's work is copiously illustrated with examples showing how to realize the various figures on the keyboard; most of these illustrations are given in three- and four-part as well as full-voiced versions. Although throughout the first part of the treatise Muffat forbids the doubling of dissonances in the left hand, in the second part, in his discussion of cadences, he does state that *auf den Instrument dupliert man auch zum Fillen bissweilen alles, obschon wider die Regl.*[18] The example of full-voiced, dissonant chords that illustrates this statement is labeled *in Cembalo erlaubt*, thus depriving the organ of this freedom. The same restriction occurs in Heinichen's treatise.

Francesco Gasparini's *L'armonico pratico al cimbalo* (Venice, 1708), although published after both Saint-Lambert's and Muffat's works, contains no details for full-voiced accompaniments. This is disappointing, because Gasparini's general reference to doubling chords in the left hand leads one to believe that he regarded the full-voiced style a regular aspect of thorough-bass accompanying. Among the few examples in his manual not appearing as simple figured basses is the following series of triads in full-voiced forms:

Example 27. *L'armonico pratico*, 24.

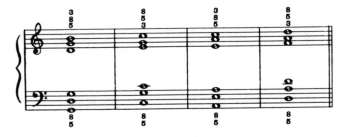

"When the player is experienced he must endeavor to include more notes, which he may do in order to bring out greater harmony."[19] According to Gasparini,[20] the consecutive octaves and fifths between inner parts of example 27 are "saved by the interchanging [*cambiamento*] of the parts as in compositions for 5, 6, or 8 voices," an explanation Heinichen adopts.

In general, Gasparini does not advocate doubling dissonances other than the perfect fourth and diminished seventh in the left hand; however, he does not say that other dissonances cannot be doubled. In the accompaniment of recitatives, possibly an exceptional circumstance, Gasparini[21] favors arpeggios played between the hands that double the second, tritone, and even the major seventh.

In turning to Heinichen's instructions we are told immediately that the full-voiced accompaniment is not well suited to the organ: "The more full-voiced one accompanies with both hands on the harpsichord, the more harmonious it will sound. Contrarily, on the organ one must not become too enamored with the all too full-voiced accompaniment in the left hand (particularly in music of few parts and except in tuttis), because the constant rumble of so many low notes is unpleasant to the ear and not infrequently burdens the solo singer or instrumentalist. Here judgment must do its best."[22]

To form a full-voiced accompaniment, Heinichen continues, is the simplest of procedures: One adds a top part free of parallel octaves and fifths to a bass part and fills up the space in between with as many chord tones as the fingers can reach, for example:

Example 28. *General-Bass*, 133.

When the bass notes of this example lie an octave lower, the full-voiced accompaniment may assume the following distribution of notes:

Example 29. *General-Bass*, 134.

The numerous parallel octaves and fifths between inner voices do not offend the ear, Heinichen believes, for the same reason offered by Gasparini: they sound as if they resulted from the crossing of parts. As further defense against pedantic criticism of these progressions Heinichen invokes a maxim borrowed from Saint-Lambert:[23] "Since music is made for the ear only, an error that does not offend it is not an error." Under no circumstance, however, should faulty progressions be permitted between the outer parts, for here parallel fifths and octaves are easily heard and cannot be excused as a by-product of crossing parts.

The full-voiced style frees the inner chord tones from the demands of good contrapuntal writing and makes superfluous many of the details required by four-part realizations. For example, in playing as many chord tones as possible with both hands, the accompanist can ignore the array of rules determining the correct tones to double for the various figures in four-part accompaniments. The full-voiced form of the chord of the sixth, for example, "requires far less skill than the previously practiced four-part accompaniment. For in the latter we have various accuracies we must observe as much for the distributions and doubling of essential parts belonging to the chord of the sixth as for the avoidance of bad progressions of the same. With a very full-voiced accompaniment, however, all of these rules naturally are as impossible as they are unnecessary to observe, because the number of parts hides all such errors from the ears."[24] Among the rules for chords of the sixth that the accompanist may ignore are those for doubling chromatically raised tones, though Heinichen reminds the student again to observe a difference between accompanying on the organ and on the harpsichord: "On the former such a doubled ♯ or ♮ (particularly with music in a few parts) sounds much harsher to sensitive ears than on the latter."[25] Since the accompanist must depend on his own judgment in deciding when these accidentals should be doubled in full-voiced accompaniments, Heinichen advises us that in his full-voiced examples he will avoid doubling any notes altered by accidentals, a point to be kept in mind when examining the full-voiced examples given below.

In the following example, Heinichen arranges a full-voiced version of the example previously given at the end of the explanations for chords of the sixth (see page 33 above).

Example 30. *General-Bass,* 157–58.

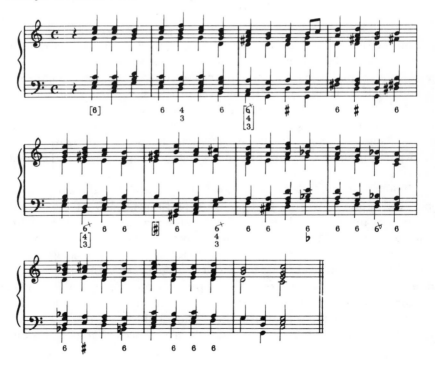

Note particularly the parallel fifths between the middle part of the right hand and the top part of the left hand beginning with the last chord of bar 7. Heinichen excuses them on the grounds that the closeness of the tones conceals the parallel motion; also, he contends that these fifths disturb the ear no more than the following chords, when played on an organ with four- and eight-foot registers:

Example 31. *General-Bass*, 159 (footnote).

The following realizations, however, are unacceptable.

Example 32. *General-Bass*, 159 (footnote).

In analyzing these examples, Heinichen tells us that one might question the steady flow of parallel fifths in the first two measures of the right hand, but a more critical error results from the parallel octaves between the outermost voices and their immediately adjacent parts. In the next two measures, the fault lies in the overly exposed parallel fifths in the right hand that are heard because of the distance between the lower note of the fifths and the bass part.

These simple examples omit the most controversial aspect of full-voiced accompaniments: the dissonances. "Indeed one can double [all sus-pended and resolving dissonances] in a full-voiced accompaniment (when these many doubled dissonances do not occur in music of a few parts or otherwise *mal à propos*)."[26] The resolution of dissonances in full-voiced accompaniments depends on whether they occur (1) in the outer or inner parts, (2) in the right or left hand chords. Dissonances struck by the right hand must proceed according to the general rules of preparation and resolution except, of course, in those instances when a dissonance requires no preparation. In contrast, the dissonances doubled in the left hand are handled with considerably more freedom, which Heinichen summarizes in three guiding principles:

(1) The left hand can also take hold of all the consonances and dissonances found in the right hand, preparing and forming suspension with the latter, also subsequently resolving with the latter in consecutive octaves.[27]

He warns the reader repeatedly to avoid a "vacuum" between the hands at all costs. In the first eight examples below, the consecutive octaves are hidden sufficiently by adjacent chord tones, but the remaining examples are *verdächtig* because the excessive space between the hands places undesirable emphasis on the exposed parallel octaves.

Example 33. *General-Bass*, 203.

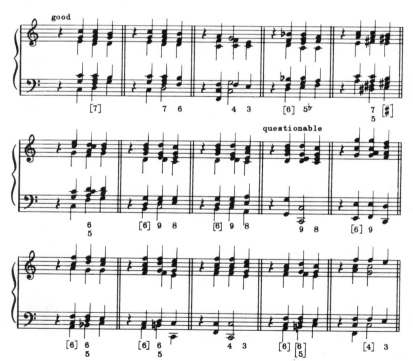

(2) The left hand also can resolve the dissonances borrowed from the right hand by ascending a degree or breaking off [the resolution] by leap where this is required for the convenience of the hand. It is enough if the

right hand (in which the important chord tones are more prominent) proceeds by rule. In order, however, that such freedoms do not turn out too coarsely, one seeks here again to avoid whenever possible the frequently mentioned vacuum between both hands.[28]

All the following examples are acceptable full-voiced realizations of dissonances. The dissonances of the left hand resolve upwards by step in the first four, break off without resolution in the next three, and occur without preparation but resolve in parallel octaves with the right hand in the final three.

Example 34. *General-Bass*, 205.

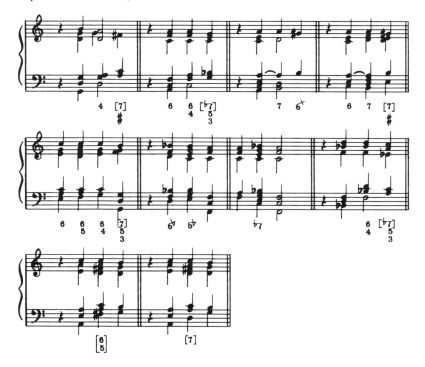

(3) In some cases the left hand may anticipate the resolutions of right hand dissonances in the same manner followed by some famous composers in full-voiced compositions. The matter requires a lengthy explanation, and it may well be skipped by beginners. To satisfy the experienced, however, we will describe it in detail.[29]

According to Heinichen a common practice in the full-voiced accompaniment of a 9 8 suspension was the anticipation of the ninth (*Anticipatio resolutionis nonae*) in the left hand before the ninth resolved in the upper part:

Example 35. *General-Bass*, 206.

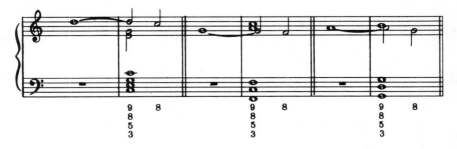

He proposes that if the ear could bear the sound of this anticipated resolution it could bear equally well several other anticipated resolutions formed by inverting the full-voiced ninth chord. First, an anticipated resolution of a 7 6 suspension results when the third of this ninth chord replaces the bass note:

Example 36. *General-Bass*, 207.

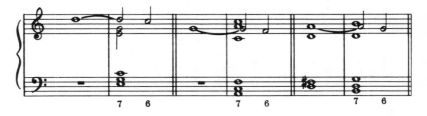

Heinichen interrupts himself at this point to caution: "In these examples the prepared seventh above against the anticipated sixth below forms the previous ninth; consequently all the rules must be observed for these parts that otherwise are observed with the ninth. E.g., the octave of the bass never descends to become a ninth; consequently the octave to this middle part also never descends to a ninth. Thus the following first example would be wrong, the second, however, correct."[30]

Example 37.

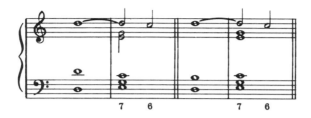

The second inversion of the 9 8 suspension places the fifth of the ninth chord in the bass and forms a $^6_{5\ 4}$ suspension. The fifth in the right hand and the anticipated fourth in the left hand are equivalent to the ninth of example 35.

Example 38. *General-Bass*, 208.

When the full-voiced 9 8 suspension substitutes a sixth for the fifth, that is, $^{9\,8}_{\ 8\ }_{\ 6}_{\ 3}$, the chord can be inverted so that the sixth replaces the bass. The suspended fourth of this inversion and the anticipated third in the left hand form the ninth of the chord before inversion.

Example 39. *General-Bass*, 209.

The *4tam irregularem* can be joined to a minor third, major sixth, and a ninth, that is, $\begin{smallmatrix}9\,8\\6^+\\4\\3\end{smallmatrix}$. When we exchange the bass with this fourth a suspension of a sixth against a seventh occurs (first example below). Omitting the seventh, the sixth alone can be anticipated (last three examples below). In all the following inversions the prepared sixth against the anticipated fifth in the left hand forms the ninth of the chord before inversion.

Example 40. *General-Bass*, 210–11.

Not infrequently the ninth appears with a seventh, that is, $\begin{smallmatrix}9\,8\\8\\7\,6\cdot\\3\end{smallmatrix}$. Exchanging the seventh for the bass of the chord, we form an *Anticipationem 3ae syncopatae*, which Heinichen[31] says "is more serviceable in full-voiced compositions [i.e., orchestral music] than in accompanying." The prepared third and the second in the lower part form the ninth of the chord before inversion.

Example 41. *General-Bass*, 211.

A double anticipated resolution concludes these examples. This rather harsh combination "should occur seldom and [then] with judgment so that the accumulated dissonances may not become unbearable to the ear."[32]

Example 42. *General-Bass*, 212.

To apply anticipated resolutions in the full-voiced style, the accompanist must follow two important principles:

(1) The *locus resolutionis*, or that individual key to which the prepared consonance and dissonance of the right hand should resolve, at all times must remain vacant and unused so that the ear can clearly distinguish the future resolution and [so that] the playing of many adjacent keys does not produce an abomination to the ear. With this in mind, the right hand prefers the assignment of correctly playing and resolving the consonances and dissonances; the left hand, however, contents itself with the anticipation of resolutions of the right hand. . . .

(2) Those *anticipationes resolutionum* are the best in which the resolving part descends a whole tone. If, on the other hand, it resolves by a half tone only and actually by a natural semitone, then the anticipated resolution becomes harsher because the prepared dissonance forms a minor ninth with the anticipated resolution, which naturally is more dissonant than the major ninth. But if the resolution descends by a chromatic semitone to a foreign (outside the scale given by the key signature), chromatically raised note [*ein fremdes ♯ und erhöhendes ♮*], then the anticipated resolution is absolutely forbidden because of its particular harshness. Rea-

son: The ear suffers doubly: (1) through the chromatic minor ninth that produces more harshness than the already harsh natural minor ninth; (2) through the immediately following doubling of a harsh accidental which, as was pointed out previously, is to be avoided assiduously. On these grounds then are all the previous [examples of] anticipated resolutions . . . fully correct. The first five that follow, however, are tolerable and can be used, with careful judgment, in the right opportunity. The last four, on the contrary, are unbearable and entirely forbidden:[33]

Example 43. *General-Bass*, 215–16.

Heinichen illustrates the whole of these preceding comments by repeating the general examples given earlier for the various dissonant figures in full-voiced arrangements. A careful comparison of the four-part versions with the corresponding full-voiced accompaniments entails the kind of mental discipline and training of the hands that harpsichordists today should find eminently instructive.

The analytical comments appended by Heinichen at the end of each full-voiced example below enable us to follow step by step as he points out .significant details.

Example 44. *General-Bass*, 217–18.*

*See example 4 for four-part version.

(NB. In this example the left hand employs the full-voiced fourth in the following way: Over the second bass note of the first bar this fourth resolves in consecutive octaves with the upper part. Over the first bass note of the third bar the resolution of the fourth is anticipated (actually the resolution of the augmented fourth. We shall also find below more examples of the anticipated resolution of the perfect fourth). Over the last bass note of this same third bar the prepared fourth resolves up by step, which also occurs on the last bass note of the fourth bar. On the last bass note of the ninth bar the fourth prepared in the lower part of the right hand again resolves up, and on the third bass note of the tenth bar the resolution proceeds in consecutive octaves with the upper part.)[34]

Example 45. *General-Bass*, 219–20.*

*See example 5 for four-part version.

(NB. The left hand in this example employs the full-voiced accompaniment of the diminished fifth and the suspension of a perfect fifth in the following way: The diminished fifth occurring over the fourth bass note of the second bar breaks off by leap on the following bass note in place of an obligatory resolution. However, the prepared diminished fifth over the second bass note of the third bar resolves up by step to the following bass note. The prepared [and] suspended fifth over the first bass note of the fifth bar also resolves up subsequently by step. The prepared diminished fifth over the third bass note of the seventh bar resolves with the upper part in consecutive octaves; the next following diminished fifth proceeds similarly. The prepared and suspended fifth over the fourth bass note of the ninth bar breaks off by leap on the following bass note; and finally on the second bass note of the tenth bar the resolution of the suspended fifth is anticipated.)[35]

Example 46. *General-Bass*, 221–22.*

*See example 6 for four-part version.

(NB. The left hand employs the full-voiced seventh in this example thus: Over the second bass note of the first bar the resolution of the seventh is anticipated. The seventh found over the second bass note of the second bar resolves with the upper part in consecutive octaves. The seventh over the third bass note of the third bar, instead of resolving, breaks off by leap down. The prepared seventh over the third bass note of the fourth bar again resolves with the upper part in consecutive octaves. Over the first bass note of the sixth bar the resolution of the suspended sixth is anticipated. Over the first bass note of the ninth bar the seventh again breaks off by leap down, and over the second bass note of the tenth bar the resolution of the suspended fifth is anticipated.)[36]

Example 47. *General-Bass*, 223–24.*

*See example 7 for four-part version.

(NB. In this example the left hand employs the full-voiced accompaniment in the following way: Over the first bass note of the second bar the seventh resolves in consecutive octaves with the upper part. Over the first bass note of the third bar, the well-known resolution of the ninth is anticipated by the playing of the octave. Over the first bass note of the fourth bar the anticipated resolution of the seventh and ninth are found together, the former really with justification since this bass note does not by nature permit a fifth over it. Over the first bass note of the fifth bar the resolution of the fourth is anticipated. The diminished fifth found over the last bass note of the seventh bar resolves with the upper part in consecutive octaves. Over the first bass note of the ninth bar the *Ambitus modi* permits a fifth;

therefore, no anticipated resolution of the seventh is allowable here, which, in contrast, on the following bass note is found with justification. Over the last bass note of the tenth bar the resolution of the fourth by a natural semitone is antici- pated, and over the next following bass note again an anticipated resolution of the fourth is found.)[37]

The full-voiced style of accompanying was very much part of the keyboard performance practice during Heinichen's lifetime. The detailed description of *Vollstimmigkeit* in his treatise and the numerous examples add imposingly to the size of the work. Knowing Heinichen's bent for practi- cality, we can be certain that he expended the extra money and effort only because he was convinced that this material was indispensable for training accompanists. Modern discussions, however, pay too little attention to this section of his treatise, and full-voiced accompaniments rarely are sug- gested for thorough-bass realizations published with modern editions of operas, cantatas with instrumental accompaniments, or purely instrumen- tal works of Baroque composers.

Arnold has contributed to this disregard for *Vollstimmigkeit*, possibly following C. P. E. Bach, who ignores the subject almost totally. Although quoting extensively from Heinichen's material for full-voiced realizations, Arnold brings his investigation to a vague and somewhat negative conclu- sion:

> Having carefully examined the rules laid down by Heinichen for a filled-in [i.e., full-voiced] accompaniment, the question suggests itself as to how far they are likely to have been in accord with the practice of the greatest exponents of the art of accompaniment among his approximate contemporaries. Unfortunately the question is very difficult to answer with any exactitude, owing to lack of informa- tion, since Heinichen is the only notable authority who enters into the matter in detail. There is, of course, no manner of doubt that a filled-in accompaniment was used, upon occasion, by the best masters.[38]

The words "upon occasion, by the best masters" give the substance of Arnold's viewpoint, but is this an accurate deduction? Certainly not when it is supported solely by C. P. E. Bach's treatise. However, the wide diver- gence between Bach and Heinichen in this matter, as in others, suggests again that they speak for two different musical climates, having as little in common as the climates of Hamburg, where Bach worked for the final twenty-one years of his career, and Venice, where Heinichen first discov- ered the full-voiced style of accompanying.

Objective evidence for our acceptance of Heinichen's advice may be found in frequent references to full-voiced accompaniments in the literature of the seventeenth and eighteenth centuries. Praetorius, Penna, Delair, Saint-Lambert, Gasparini, and especially Muffat have already been cited. Further proof exists in an anonymous manuscript, written around 1700, in the Corsiniana Library in Rome, in which a seventy-six measure arietta appears with an accompaniment realized in full-voiced style, including the doubling of numerous dissonances.[39] In Germany particularly, the full-voiced style of chords was discussed throughout the eighteenth century.

> There is more art to the perfect arrangement of parts in four-part accompanying than when one plays 5, 6, 7, and more parts together. Nevertheless, when it is required and particularly with music of many parts, one can strengthen his accompaniment by taking everything within the grasp of the two hands so that no overly large vacuum exists between both hands. And if it does not result in as pure a four-part accompaniment, the numerous parts nevertheless cover up the *vitia* in such a way as to satisfy the ear. One should see, however, that the outermost parts, namely the highest and the lowest, are not faulty between themselves. Such a full-voiced thorough-bass should be applied on stringed [keyboard] instruments, but not on the organ.[40]

These words of Kellner repeat almost exactly Heinichen's suggestions, and he also gives the substance of Heinichen's advice for the doubling of dissonances in the left hand. In 1733, Telemann[41] recommends the full-voiced style for the realization of opera and cantata thorough-basses; and in the exceptionally informative *Vorgemach*, Georg Andreas Sorge (1703–78) suggests a full-voiced accompaniment for the thorough-basses of symphonies and concertos:

> The accompaniment with 5, 6, 7, and more parts can be used only on the harpsichord in many-voiced symphonies and concertos. One does not need this [kind of accompaniment] on the organ and also it does not sound well on the latter. . . . One needs to see [with the full-voiced accompaniment] only that the right hand resolves its dissonances according to rule, because the higher tones strike the ear more sharply than the lower; the left hand, however, is not bound exactly to these rules and laws.[42]

Sorge approves essentially the same rules for doubling dissonances in the left hand that appeared first in Heinichen's treatise.

Descriptions of full-voiced accompaniments do not appear in every thorough-bass manual, partly because many of these books are too elementary. Also, some writers hesitated to give prominence to the special art of *Vollstimmigkeit*, lest their students neglect completely the four-part accompaniment and its valuable musical discipline. Sorge discloses his own apprehension when he cautions: "Spare the beginners this [the full-voiced accompaniment] and preferably restrain them so that as much as possible they double the bass in octaves and prepare the dissonances in the right hand alone, because otherwise they could easily fall upon the wrong way. Nobody should venture into this full-voiced manner of playing until first he is correctly trained and prepared in the four-part accompaniment."[43]

In treatises after 1750 the full-voiced style appears most frequently as a separate device reserved for accompanying recitatives, although Quantz (1752) leaves no uncertainty about his use of the style: "A full-voiced work accompanied by many instruments also necessitates a full-voiced, strong accompaniment. This [latter] part already requires some strengthening in a concerto with a few instruments, particularly during the concerted sections."[44] In 1756 the important post-Baroque theorist Johann Friedrich Daube (1733–79) recorded his preference for the full-voiced accompaniment in recitatives: "[This type of accompaniment] is used in accompanying a recitative, in the church as well as the theatrical style. It calls for such a fullness as both hands are able to grasp."[45] Although Daube[46] automatically repeats the familiar axiom restricting full-voiced accompaniments to stringed keyboard instruments only, he contradicts himself and surprises the reader by proposing that organists should consider this style for accompanying church recitatives with strong instrumental support, "as is the occasion on high feast days when numerous strophes are expressed by full choruses." He disallows the doubling of all dissonances in the left hand, except when the musical texture incorporates a large number of instrumental or vocal parts.

As late as 1781, in the midst of an era of full-grown Classicism, Kirnberger[47] (1721–83) devotes an entire section of his thorough-bass treatise to full-voiced accompaniments, although with few exceptions, he would not tolerate dissonances in the left hand. Undoubtedly the most intriguing allusion to a full-voiced style of accompanying comes from Johann Christian Kittel (1732–1809), a student of J. S. Bach: "When Sebastian Bach conducted church music, one of his most proficient pupils had to accompany on the harpsichord. It may be imagined that he could not venture on playing too meager an accompaniment from the thorough-bass. Notwithstanding, he had always to be prepared to find Bach's hands and fingers suddenly coming in under his own, and without troubling him any further, completing the accompaniment with masses of harmony, which amazed him more than the unexpected proximity of his strict master."[48]

Notes

1. Heinichen, *General-Bass*, 95–96.

2. François Couperin, *L'art de toucher le clavecin* (Paris, 1717). Tr. into German and English, A. Linde and M. Roberts (Wiesbaden, 1933), 24.

3. Mattheson, *Kleine General-Bass-Schule*, 48.

4. Bach-Mitchell, *Versuch*, 173.

5. Translation based on Couperin-Linde, *L'art*, 25.

6. Heinichen, *General-Bass*, 123–24.

7. Ibid., 127.

8. Ibid., 199.

9. Ibid., 548 (footnote h).

10. Werckmeister, *Nothwendigsten Anmerckungen*, 35.

11. Saint-Lambert, *Nouveau traité*, 65; Kellner, *Treulicher Unterricht*, 14; Telemann, *Generalbass-Übungen*, 11.

12. Bach-Mitchell, *Versuch*, 201.

13. Michael Prætorius, *Syntagma musicum* 3 (Wolfenbüttel, 1619); facs. ed. W. Gurlitt (Kassel, 1958), 145.

14. Lorenzo Penna, *Li primi albori musicali* (Bologna, 1672), 82–83: "A otto, a trè Chori, è à quattro Chori, etc. si empia, e radoppi pure le repliche, li ♯♯, e ciò si vuole, perchè fara bel sentire con tanta varietà di armonia."

15. Jean-Henri d'Anglebert, *Pièces de clavecin* (Paris, 1689); new ed. M. Roesgen-Champion (Paris, 1934), 136–40. Delair, *Traité*, [xi–xii].

16. Saint-Lambert, *Nouveau traité*, 129.

17. Ibid., 129.

18. Muffat-Federhofer, *Essay on Thoroughbass*, 109.

19. Gasparini, *L'armonico pratico*, 23.

20. Ibid., 87.

21. Ibid., 90–91.

22. Heinichen, *General-Bass*, 132 (footnote d).

23. Saint-Lambert, *Nouveau traité*, 126.

24. Heinichen, *General-Bass*, 156.

25. Ibid., 156.

26. Ibid., 202.

27. Ibid., 202.

28. Ibid., 204.

29. Ibid., 206.

30. Ibid., 207 (footnote a).

31. Ibid., 211.

32. Ibid., 212.

33. Ibid., 212–15.

34. Ibid., 218.

35. Ibid., 220.

36. Ibid., 222–23.

37. Ibid., 224–25.

38. Arnold, *Thorough-bass*, 344.

39. Reprinted in Ludwig Landshoff, "Über das vielstimmige Accompagnement und andere Fragen des Generalbassspiels," *Festschrift Adolph Sandberger* (Munich, 1918), 189–208. A facsimile of a portion of this Arietta, showing the full-voiced accompaniment, appears in *MGG* 6, col. 1125–26.

40. Kellner, *Treulicher Unterricht*, 15.

41. Telemann, *Generalbass-Übungen*, 40.

42. Sorge, *Vorgemach*, 417.

43. Ibid., 418–19.

44. J. J. Quantz, *Versuch einer Anweisung die Flöte traversiere zu spielen* (Berlin, 1752). (3rd ed. Breslau, 1789) facs. ed. H. -P. Schmitz (Kassel, 1953), 224.

45. J. K. Daube, *General-Bass in drey Accorden* (Leipzig, 1756), 202.

46. Ibid., 202–3 (footnote f).

47. J. P. Kirnberger, *Grundsätze des Generalbass* (Berlin, 1781), 83–86.

48. J. C. Kittel, *Der angehende praktische Organist* (Erfurt, 1808) III, 33.

5

The Accompaniment of Quick Bass Notes

Among the essential skills contributing to the art of accompanying is the ability to recognize nonharmonic tones in a thorough-bass. The performer must be trained to judge at sight which consecutive bass notes require no harmonic changes in the right hand, even when a lack of figures fails to make this clear. This problem hardly existed during the early Baroque because of the elementary character of thorough-basses, which usually demanded that each bass note support a new chord. Yet, as composers wrote more elaborate keyboard basses, heavily laden with passages of quick notes, accompanists were forced to seek means of eliminating chords from some of the bass notes.

Theorists of the seventeenth century offer little advice; in rare instances help can be derived indirectly from their rules for accompanying unfigured basses. The extent of these directions is confined generally to recommending that groups of four to eight notes sound under a single harmony. The first methodical study of quick bass notes and their accompaniment appeared in Heinichen's *Neu erfundene Anweisung*, later expanded to one hundred and twenty-two pages of rules and musical illustrations in chapter IV of the *General-Bass*, the only comprehensive source for the eighteenth century. The importance of Heinichen's explanations lies not solely in the sheer volume of words and musical illustrations but also in his logical organization of a difficult subject. The following examination of quick bass notes retains his orderly sequence of ideas, condensing only the natural volubility of Heinichen's speech into a more easily assimilated enumeration of rules and their explanations.

Before we can understand Heinichen's principles of accompanying quick bass notes, we must first establish the meaning of *transitus*, or passing tone, the contrapuntal device underlying most of the rules to follow.

Transitus means *insensu proprio* — or in its real sense — a free passing up or down to the third in which, namely, the middle note does not have its own harmony but passes through freely. To which it should be noted: that just as is well known with notes of the same value, the first, third, fifth, etc., are called *Notae virtualiter longae* or long notes (according to their inner value) while, in contrast, the second, fourth, sixth, etc., are called *Notae virtualiter breves* or short notes (according to their inner value), so too the same occurs with the *transitus*; and the first and third notes of like duration are always inherently [*virtualiter*] long, the middle one, however, inherently short.[1]

A *transitus* may be either *regularis* or *irregularis*; the former results "if the inherently long bass note sounds correct in the chord or *consoniret*, while the following inherently short bass note in passing through becomes a dissonance." The latter occurs "if the inherently long bass note sounds incorrect or *dissoniret* and becomes a consonance first on the immediately following inherently short bass note, or [in other words] coincides with the previously played chord."[2] The *transitus irregularis* appears in various guises in the following example:

Example 48. *General-Bass*, 259–60.

The definition of *transitus* could be broadened to encompass all varieties of passing tones, as Heinichen makes clear in the following passage: "*In sensu lato & improprio*, or in a broader sense, *transitus* also means a free passing to a fourth or fifth. Indeed, ultimately one can extend the *transitus* as far as the sixth, seventh, and octave, if all the notes in between, whether descending or ascending, have no harmony of their own but pass through freely, as often occurs in the invention of composers; all cases of which are illustrated in the following examples."[3]

Example 49. *General-Bass*, 260–61.

In this all-embracing definition the *transitus* could also be irregular; that is, the nonharmonic tones could fall on inherently long tones. An important clue suggesting a *transitus irregularis* (which Heinichen stresses repeatedly) is a figure over the last inherently short note or a leap following that note, for example:

Example 50. *General-Bass*, 262.

Common Time—Eighth Notes

Two factors are most important in determining the form of accompaniment for any group of quick notes: the meter and the tempo. Proceeding from this assumption, Heinichen divides his principles of accompaniment into four sections according to the basic meters: common, triple, *allabreve*, and overture; within these sections he separates the forms of accompaniment resulting from a slow or fast tempo. Beginning with common time, there are three rules for accompanying quick eighth notes in a thorough-bass.

1. Groups of two or four eighth notes, moving by step and not followed by a leap, have chords on inherently long notes; the inherently short notes pass through freely unless figured (note the last eighth note in bars 3 and 4 below):

Example 51. *General-Bass*, 263–64.

Although the preceding example sounds well on an organ, it requires modifications when played on the less resonant harpsichord. For this purpose Heinichen suggests the following version in which he strives to maintain a fuller sound by repeating each chord:

Example 52. *General-Bass*, 264–65.

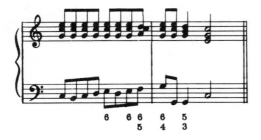

To improve this monotonous arrangement, the accompanist may add thirds in the right hand parallel to the bass line, simultaneously repeating the remaining tones first struck on the inherently long notes. As Heinichen's example illustrates, besides eliminating somewhat the excessive repetition of right hand chords, the parallel motion enriches the harmony by adding dissonances as passing tones.

Example 53. *General-Bass*, 266.

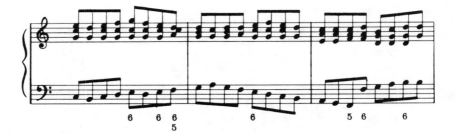

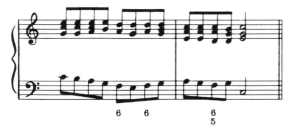

Heinichen[4] enumerates the sources of harmonic enrichment found in the right hand part of the preceding example:

(a) Passing Seventh (*7ma in transitu*[5]): bar 1, bass note 2 (hereafter 1/2); 4/4, 4/6; 5/2, 5/6; 6/6; 8/6.

(b) Chords of the Sixth: 2/4; 4/2; 5/4, 5/8; 7/4.

(c) Triads: 1/4; 2/8; 3/6; 7/8.

Like many to follow, this example reveals much about the art of accompanying as practiced by Heinichen. Note particularly the characteristic freedom with which he allows the right hand to reduce its parts from the standard three, permitting an easy escape from parallel fifths and octaves.

2. When a leap follows a group of two or four eighth notes moving by step, the inherently short notes have their own chords.

Example 54. *General-Bass*, 267.

3. Inherently short notes also have their own chords when they move by leaps only in a moderate tempo.

Example 55. *General-Bass*, 267.

Before turning to the rules for sixteenth notes in common time, let us consider first the following suggestion by Heinichen, a rule that should be inscribed in capital letters in any book treating basic principles of Baroque performance practices: "If, however, the tempo [*Mensur*] of this slow common time goes very quickly, e.g., in *semi-allabreve*, in overture meter or where, in addition to the indication of C or ₵, an *allegro* or *presto* is written, etc., the eighths, because of their quickness, are no longer viewed as eighths, but as sixteenths and so treated."[6]

Since in the context just described eighth notes borrow their treatment from the rules for accompanying sixteenth notes, the following examples for sixteenths, therefore, are equally applicable to eighth notes merely by making two bars out of one. The full meaning of this quotation will become clearer after we examine quick notes in *allabreve* and so-called *semi-allabreve* meters. It will suffice here to say that in Baroque music the signature C frequently denotes a spurious rather than a true *allabreve* (in which quarters and eighth notes are used like eighths and sixteenths in common time).

Common Time — Sixteenth Notes

1. When four sixteenths ascend or descend by step and are not followed by a leap, they have one chord only. If, however, the ascending or descending motion is interrupted and the fourth sixteenth moves in the reverse direction, then each group of two notes has a chord. If after four ascending or descending sixteenths a leap follows or the fourth sixteenth is figured, then in both cases this is a sign of the irregular passing

tone, and the chord on the third sixteenth will anticipate the harmony of the fourth sixteenth.

Although not actually stated by Heinichen, we can draw an additional qualification from the following example: When the third (and not the fourth) sixteenth reverses the direction of the notes, all four sixteenths belong to the same chord (see below bar 1, 4th beat; bar 4, 1st beat).

Example 56. *General-Bass*, 270.

To demonstrate the notational guise of the preceding example when written in eighth notes for a very fast tempo, Heinichen adds the following version (the same rules as those for sixteenths, of course, would apply):

Example 57. *General-Bass*, 269–70 (footnote*).

2. When a single leap occurs within a group of four sixteenths, the accompaniment is determined by the nature of the fundamental bass from which the sixteenths originated. If it was a single quarter, one chord is played; if two eighth notes, then two chords are played.

To aid the beginner in recognizing fundamental basses from which groups of sixteenths are formed, Heinichen gives examples of the most common bass figurations of (1) four sixteenths to one chord and (2) four sixteenths to two chords.

Example 58. *General-Bass*, 271–75.

Common Figurations of the Quarter Note,
with a Single Chord to Four Sixteenths

Common Figurations of the Eighth Note,
with Two Chords to Four Sixteenths

(a) Arnold, *Thorough-bass*, 739 (footnote) makes an important observation related to this measure: One notes that Heinichen was careful to avoid parallel octaves between the bass and lowest note of the right hand chord at this point. He observes an unwritten rule throughout the examples of avoiding parallel fifths or octaves between a quick bass note and the adjacent part. He does not, however, avoid the same parallel intervals between a quick bass note and a part not adjacent, for example the parallel octaves between the bass and middle note of the right hand chord at (b) and (c), and an abundance of similar progressions in the second half of this example given below.

Heinichen appends the following analytical comments regarding the preceding examples (for easier reference they have been divided into enumerated paragraphs rather than the one continuous footnote of the original text):

> Concerning these figurations we wish to make the following remarks:
>
> (i) In the first and second examples the fundamental notes are always contained in the first and third sixteenth notes.
>
> (ii) In the third example, however, the fundamental notes always remain in the first and fourth sixteenths, whether or not a leap follows. For in this bass figuration the second sixteenth is regarded as an anticipation of the following chord and the third sixteenth as an irregular passing tone.
>
> (iii) The fourth example shows that also in a figured thorough-bass the same bass patterns can sometimes have a completely different accompaniment. For previously [see pp. 112–13 above] we found this very bass pattern with a single chord amid [each of] the quarter note figurations. Here, however, the figures below [the bass] show that they already need to resolve on the third sixteenth and that, therefore, the two eighth notes in this case are the fundamental notes.
>
> (iv) In the fifth example the second sixteenth again passes as an anticipation of the following chord; and the first and fourth sixteenths furnish the two fundamental notes each time, whether a leap follows or not, excepting the single case when they [the group of four sixteenths] are treated as a figuration of a single quarter if a triad appears on the first sixteenth and the second sixteenth leaps up by a third only, as is demonstrated by the first half of the second measure and the last four sixteenths [as well as the first four sixteenths of the revised measure] of the example.
>
> (v) In the sixth and final example the two fundamental notes are contained in the first and fourth sixteenths. The distinction here, however, lies in the leap that follows, because we have seen this same pattern previously [see pp. 112–13 above] under the quarter note variations with one chord only.
>
> (vi) Therefore, instead of examining many more examples that could be added for eighth-note bass figurations of this kind, one can take special note of this rule: That, whenever sixteenths, between which a single leap occurs (NB., immediately after the first sixteenth) are in turn followed by a leap, then as a fundamental note the fourth sixteenth has its own chord.[7]

In the *Zusätze* to chapter IV, Heinichen[8] adds an important exception to the previous rule (vi): some groups of sixteenths in the bass, while meeting the conditions of this rule (i.e., a leap after both the first and fourth sixteenths), are a variation of the chord played to the first sixteenth and require no further chord as accompaniment. The next example exhibits various bass figurations of this type:

Example 59. *General-Bass*, 370–71.

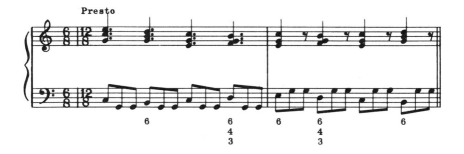

3. When two or three leaps exist within a group of four sixteenths and the third and fourth sixteenths do not belong to the chord on the first note of the group, then a new chord is played on the third note.

In the example below, four different bass figurations move variously by leaps while conforming to this general rule. In bar 1, two leaps always occur between the first three sixteenths; in bar 2, however, the leaps are between the first and second groups of two notes. In bar 3, three leaps are characteristic of each group (i.e., the sixteenths move entirely by leaps), but neither the third nor fourth sixteenth belongs to the chord on the first note of the group (however, Heinichen inadvertently breaks his own rule with the fourth sixteenth C that does agree with the first chord $\frac{g}{e}$). Three
c

leaps also separate the sixteenths in bar 4, and even though the third note of the group belongs to the chord of the first note, the fourth sixteenth does not. Consequently, each group of two notes requires a different chord.

Example 60. *General-Bass*, 276.

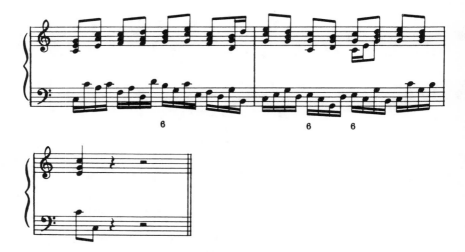

4. When all four sixteenths of a group derive from the first chord, making an arpeggio of the same, they have one chord only, which is played once on the organ but can be repeated on the harpsichord.

Example 61. *General-Bass*, 278–79.

(a) (b) (c) (d) In each appearance of a chromatically raised bass note Arnold, *Thorough-bass*, 742 adds a [6]. This misleads the student to the extent that he will regard the figure six as the normal indication, while Heinichen clearly considered the opposite true for this bass figuration. Particular attention should be given to the care with which Heinichen avoids doubling these raised bass notes serving as leading tones; and in (b) (c) and (d) one should not mistake the repetition of the right hand chord as the kind of repercussion that Heinichen suggests for harpsichord accompaniments. Rather these repetitions are essential in order to retain the leading tone after the bass leaves it for other chord tones.

5. When, with four or more consecutive sixteenths, the inherently long notes always proceed by step and the inherently short notes by leap; in this case also, four sixteenths are played to one chord. For such bass patterns, there is a special inclination to accompany the inherently long notes in thirds.

Example 62. *General-Bass*, 280.

The next two rules describe special bass figurations in which a rest is substituted for the first sixteenth in a group of four.

6. The chord belonging to the note following the rest may be played over the rest while the bass follows. All the previous rules for accompanying sixteenths are applied *mutatis mutandis*: When the three sixteenths proceed by step and no leap follows, a single chord is sufficient; if, however, a leap does occur, then a chord on the second sixteenth will anticipate the harmony belonging to the third sixteenth.

The special distinction between accompaniments as defined in the two parts of this rule is shown by the following example:

Example 63. *General-Bass*, 281.

7. Should a leap appear between the second and third sixteenths or between first and second and second and third, and should the last two not belong to the first chord (over the rest), then a new chord is played on the second sixteenth. If, however, all three notes are separated by leaps and they belong to the first chord, they require only a single chord.

Example 64. *General-Bass*, 282.

The last three rules for groups of sixteenths in common time concern combinations with other note values.

8. Two sixteenths that rise or fall by step after a quarter, eighth, or dotted eighth note usually pass through freely when no leap follows. If a leap occurs, this indicates an irregular passing tone and the chord on the

first sixteenth anticipates the harmony of the second (see ex. 65). In a rapid tempo such as *semi-allabreve*, two sixteenths proceeding in this way may also pass through freely in *ascendendo*, when a leap follows. But this is almost the only case; and should they move in *descendendo* while a triad is played to the preceding note, then a seventh is formed and requires resolution on the next bass note (see ex. 66, bars 4, 5).

Example 65. *General-Bass*, 284–85.

Example 66. *General-Bass*, 285.

Although a cursory glance at the immediately preceding bass part might suggest that each group of three notes (a dotted quarter and two sixteenths or an eighth and two sixteenths) requires two harmonies, actually a single chord suffices. The reason lies in the embellishment of the fundamental bass by three-note figurations. The true nature of this bass line is shown in the following example.

Example 67. *General-Bass*, 283 (footnote k).

Here then is a significant and not uncommon example in which a leap after a group of quick bass notes does not indicate an irregular passing tone.

9. When, in a moderate tempo, the first sixteenth following an eighth moves by step and the second one returns to the previous bass note,

then a new chord should be played on the first sixteenth. In rapid tempos (such as *semi-allabreve*), however, all three notes become simply a variation of one fundamental note and require one chord only. The distinction between the two accompaniments is clear in the following examples.

Example 68. *General-Bass*, 286.

Example 69. *General-Bass*, 286–87.

10. When a leap occurs between an eighth note and two sixteenths or after the first sixteenth, then a new chord is played on the first sixteenth, unless all three bass notes belong to the chord on the first note. In the latter case one chord only is needed. Both forms of accompaniment and their characteristic bass figurations are given in the next example.

Example 70. *General-Bass*, 287.

11. When an eighth note is followed by a dot and a sixteenth, both in progressions by step and leap, this sixteenth is treated exactly as if it were a true eighth note and with an accompaniment distinguished according to tempo. Thus, in example 71 below, the sixteenths follow the rules for eighth notes in a moderately paced common time; in example 72 they follow rules for quick eighth notes (i.e., sixteenths in common time).

Example 71. *General-Bass*, 288.

Example 72. *General-Bass*, 289.

Those wishing to practice additional dotted eighth and sixteenth figurations should follow Heinichen's suggestion: Place an imaginary dot after
the inherently long eighth notes and transform the inherently short notes
into sixteenths (instead of played consecutive eighth notes as ♪ ♪ ♪ ♪ substitute ♪. ♪ ♪. ♪).

Heinichen includes in the *Zusätze* to chapter IV a special bass figuration that was intended to follow example 66 above; rather than interrupt
the sequence of rules for sixteenths, we append it here (ex. 73) as the
concluding remark for this section on sixteenths in common time. Characteristic of the bass in question is a group of two sixteenths following a
syncopated quarter note. Heinichen[9] explains the bass part in the first
eight measures of example 73 as figurations built from fundamental half
notes proceeding by step. One chord for each measure suffices until the
pattern of the figuration is altered, that is, when the quarter note no longer
leaps a third or the remaining notes are changed in some way. When this
takes place, one should view the first half of the quarter note as an anticipation of the chord belonging to the second half of the note, and the
sixteenths may pass through freely to the next measure. Otherwise the
correct chord may be played with the syncopated quarter note, and this
chord may be repeated or a new one played with the sixteenths (see bars 9,
14, 16 below). This style of accompanying is particularly suited to moderate tempos.

Example 73. *General-Bass*, 374–75.

In a very rapid tempo the previous accompaniment would be altered so that the second eighth (e.g., the first half of the quarter note) passes through freely as an anticipation of the harmony on the second beat of the measure. The bass of this accompaniment would appear as follows when reduced to fundamental tones:

Example 74. *General-Bass*, 374.

Triple Meters

As a prerequisite to understanding the rules for accompanying quick notes in triple meters, we need to know Heinichen's definition of what constitutes a quick note in these meters: "All those notes from which each triple [meter] takes its name [i.e., the units of the meter: half notes in 3/2, quarter notes in 3/4, eighths in 6/8, etc.] are treated like the slow eighth note in common time with signature C; on the contrary, the notes half the value of those notes from which each triple [meter] derives its name are treated like the sixteenth in the same common time."[10]

Supplementing these definitions are two important exceptions:[11] the quarter note in 3/2 and the eighth note in 3/4 may be used as slow notes (each bearing its own chord when not moving as a passing tone) when (a) the tempo is very slow, and (b) in an *allegro* dominated by even quicker note values. Illustrations of both musical contexts occur in the following example:

Example 75. *General-Bass*, 376.

Prefacing his suggestions for accompanying quick bass notes in triple meters Heinichen offers a pertinent observation on strong and weak beats in triple meters: "The notes from which each triple meter takes its name, have this characteristic *ratione quantitatis intrinsecae*: that each time the first [note] is inherently long while the second and third are inherently short, so that sometimes the second, sometimes the third passes through freely and sometimes both together. . . ."[12]

Four rules[13] describe the accompaniments usually found with quick bass notes having a rhythmic value equal to one unit of a triple meter.

1. When three of these notes move up or down by step, then usually the middle, inherently short note passes through freely while, in a moderate tempo, the third note has a new chord, as no. 1 in the example below indicates.
2. But, if a leap follows the first note, then a new chord is played on the second note, and the third note passes through freely as a passing tone when no leap follows it, as no. 2 in the example below indicates.
3. Should a leap occur after the second or third note or should all three notes be separated by leaps, then each has its own chord, as no. 3 below indicates.
4. If the third note is preceded by a note of double its duration, then this third note may pass through freely as a passing tone when no leap follows. If, however, a leap does occur or if the note stands in the midst of leaps, then a new chord is played, as no. 4 below indicates.

Example 76. *General-Bass*, 294–97.

Another set of four rules[14] describes the principal characteristics of accompaniments for eighth notes in very rapid tempos, when the eighth note is the metrical unit (i.e., in 3/8, 6/8, 9/8, 12/8). Under these circumstances the eighth note is treated like a sixteenth in common time. Rapid tempos comparable to those used with meters based on the eighth note are seldom associated with 3/4 or 6/4 time, but when the exception arises quarter notes are accompanied as if they were eighth notes:

1. When three of these eighths move by step, then normally they have one chord only, as no. 1 in the example below illustrates.
2. If just the first and third eighths move continuously by step while the middle one leaps to an interval belonging to the chord played on the first, then all three are accompanied by one chord. In this case it is preferable to accompany the first and third notes in parallel thirds, as no. 2 below illustrates.
3. Apart from the preceding circumstance, when the second eighth leaps and the third note is not included in the chord or the first eighth, then one plays a new chord to the third note, as no. 3 below illustrates.
4. When all three notes proceed by leap in such a way that all are included in the chord played on the first eighth, then they have one chord only, as no. 4 below illustrates.

Example 77. *General-Bass*, 298–99.

Notes half the value of the metrical unit should be considered[15] the same as sixteenths in common time (except for the two special cases demonstrated previously in ex. 75). Four of the five rules to follow, therefore, approximate the instructions given previously for the accompaniment of sixteenths in common time.

1. When four of these notes (the first or last four) move up or down by step and no leap follows, then all four have one chord only. If the fourth note of a group returns to the note preceding it, then each

group of two notes has a chord.[16] If all four move up or down by step and a leap follows or a figure appears over the last inherently short note, this is a sign of an irregular passing tone and the penultimate note will have a chord that anticipates the harmony of the last note. Various examples of these accompaniments labeled no. 1 are given below.

2. When six of these notes move up or down by step and no leap follows, then a new chord will be played on the fifth note. If, however a leap follows or the inherently short sixth note bears a figure, then again this is a sign of an irregular passing tone, and the chord on the penultimate note will anticipate the harmony belonging to the sixth note, as the examples labeled no. 2 below show.

3. As long as each group of two of these notes is separated by a leap and the notes of the following group do not belong to the preceding chord, then a new chord is played for each group, as the examples in no. 3 below show.

4. But if four or six of these notes moving by leap belong to the chord of the first note, which simultaneously they divide into an arpeggio, then one chord is sufficient for all of them, played two or three times; see no. 4 below.

5. When, however, with four, six, twelve, or more similar notes, the inherently long notes move continuously by step and the intervening inherently short notes move by leap, then a group of four (the first or last four) is played to one chord, while the inherently long notes are effectively accompanied in parallel thirds; see no. 5 below.

Example 78. *General-Bass*, 301–8.

No. 3

No. 4

No. 5

No. 1

6. When a single leap occurs in a group of four (the first or last four) or six of these notes, then the accompaniment depends on whether the bass figuration originated in one or two fundamental notes. In the latter instance, the four or six notes have two chords; in the former, one chord only is required.

Doubting the beginner's ability to distinguish between these two types of bass figurations, Heinichen offers the following series of examples giving the most typical forms of each:

Example 79. *General-Bass*, 309–12.

Common Variations with a Single Chord to
Four or Six of the Same Notes

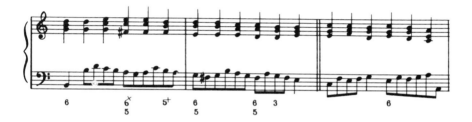

In the fifth example of the immediately preceding series (second half of bars 2 and 5), Heinichen has written a bass passage apparently contradicting his rule limiting a series of notes to one leap. Arnold[17] suggests these figurations are misprints and that the following may have been intended:

Example 80.

This is not entirely convincing, and one suspects that Heinichen intended the passage as printed. Heinichen's figurations are identical in both cases; and rather than having two chords as an accompaniment (or at least the same chord in different inversions), Heinichen merely repeats the same triad a second time. Thus, the context tends to suggest that he considered this particular figuration merely a variation of one fundamental note despite the two leaps.

Rather than wasting valuable space with examples of the preceding bass figurations as they would appear in other similar triple meters, Heinichen gives the opening bars only of example 79 as they would be notated with the eighth note or half note as metrical unit:

Example 81. *General-Bass*, 313.

7. When the first quick note is replaced by a rest of the same value, then the chord belonging to the next note can be played over the rest; in addition, all the previously given rules for sixteenths in common time apply here as well as the first five rules in this present section regarding half units in triple meter.

Example 82. *General-Bass*, 314–15.

(a) Heinichen frequently employs a triad on the inherently long note that is held while the bass falls a third and forms a seventh. See also bars 7, 9 of this example.

The next group of rules[18] concerns bass figurations in notes equal to a unit of a triple meter that are joined with notes equal to half units.

8. When, after a note with the value of a metrical unit, two notes half this value move by step up or down and no leap follows, then the two notes pass through freely. If, however, a leap follows or the second of the two notes is figured, then, as an indication of an irregular passing tone, the chord on the first of the two quicker notes will anticipate the harmony belonging to the second note; see examples below marked no. 1.

9. However, when the second note does not continue in the same direction, but reverses its motion and returns to the previous note, then a new chord will be played on the first of the two quicker notes; see no. 2 below.

10. When, with a group of three notes as described in rule 9, a leap occurs between either the first and second or the second and third notes, and the second and third are not related to the harmony of the first, a new chord is played on the second note. If, however, all three notes belong to the first chord, then they have one chord only; see no. 3 below.

Example 83. *General-Bass*, 317–21.

No. 2

No. 3

No. 1

No. 2

No. 3

11. In a very fast tempo, the three notes of the preceding rules, as long as they move by step, are usually played to one chord; and the last two notes of the group may ascend, descend, or reverse their direction, and a leap may follow, as the example illustrates:

Example 84. *General-Bass*, 321–22.

The preceding rule can be applied with equal validity to 3/2 meter for a quarter note followed by two eighths and also to 3/4 or 6/4 meter for an eighth note followed by two sixteenths.

Example 85. *General-Bass*, 324.

12. In triple meters, when the tempo is very fast, one finds figurations that follow a quarter or eighth note and consist of four notes of half the value, all four of which pass through freely.

Heinichen gives an example of each:

Example 86. *General-Bass*, 325–27.

13. In 3/2 meter, eighth notes are accompanied as if they were sixteenths in slow common time.

The following example serves to review all the previous rules for sixteenths in four-note figurations, but cast in the guise of eighths in 3/2 meter:

Example 87. *General-Bass*, 329–31.

Thirty-second notes rarely appear in thorough-basses, but when they do occur Heinichen recommends that the accompanist view them as having one flag less.[19] The following passage is notated both in thirty-seconds and sixteenths to illustrate this suggestion.

Example 88. *General-Bass,* 332.

Allabreve Meter

The final section on quick bass notes and their accompaniment concerns several "unusual" (*extraordinaire*) meters; the first of these, *allabreve*, comprises not just a metrical organization of notes but rather an entire style.

> This antique, affective style is certainly the most beautiful and convenient in which a composer can best show his fundamental understanding and exactness in composing. For the chords in this style must at all times be pure, their progression and resolution strict and removed from all liberties, the *cantabile* preserved without numerous leaps in all parts. The latter [should be] laden with syncopations and beautiful suspension of consonances and dissonances, and all the parts [should be] filled throughout with affective thoughts, themes, and imitations [but] without anything fanciful in character. Here one seeks the strict composer.[20]

For practical purposes, the only quick notes used in *allabreve* are quarter notes; and when, on rare occasions, eighth notes occur they must be joined together in groups of two. The signature of *allabreve* according to Heinichen[21] may be C or ₵, which testifies to the complete retreat of the Renaissance system of proportions and the total decline in the original meaning of these symbols.[22]

Heinichen[23] has organized the principles for accompanying quarter notes in *allabreve* into three rules and several important exceptions:

1. When quarter notes move by step or leap (though leaps should be used with discretion and in a limited number of figurations), they normally are grouped two to a chord. In two special contexts four quarters may be played to one chord: (a) when the first of the group has a triad and the remaining notes proceed by step up a fifth or the fourth note returns to the preceding note (see below, bars 8, 19, 20); (b) when the irregular passing tone is found on the third quarter (see bars 4, 12).

Example 89. *General-Bass*, 334–35.

2. If a leap occurs after a group of four quarter notes moving by step or if the last quarter note of the group is figured, this indicates an irregular passing tone, and the chord on the third quarter will anticipate the harmony belonging to the fourth quarter.

Example 90. *General-Bass*, 336.

3. When, after a half or whole measure, two unfigured quarter notes move up or down by step and no leap follows, then in *allabreve* style, this is an unexcelled indication of an irregular passing tone, and the chord on the first quarter will anticipate the harmony on the second quarter.

Example 91. *General-Bass*, 337–38.

Heinichen offers the following example as a rare exception to the two preceding rules. In example 92 the figure for each dissonance, which in *allabreve* must be prepared, signals the accompanist that an irregular passing tone has been used in the previous measure. Therefore, the second quarter note of the two-note group in the preceding measure must have its own chord in order to prepare the suspension.

Example 92. *General-Bass*, 338.

Another exception to these rules for quarter notes is found in the bass figuration of the next example, which receives special sanction as a *transitus in 4tam* in *allabreve*. Even though lacking one passing tone to complete the stepwise descent, a new chord is played for each group of its two notes.

Example 93. *General-Bass*, 339.

Heinichen[24] attributes the origin of the *transitus in 4tam* (*nota cambiata* in Fux's terminology) to composers in the past who wished to avoid frequent repetitions of interpolated eighth notes. The bass of the previous example would require the following form if this freedom were not permitted:

Example 94. *General-Bass*, 339 (footnote e).

In concluding this brief and incomplete investigation of the *allabreve* style, Heinichen gives an example that is arranged so that the student can compare the full-voiced and four-part realizations. As in earlier examples of this type, Heinichen appends a brief analysis of important dissonant structures occurring in the left hand.

Example 95. *General-Bass*, 340–42.

(NB. In this example the left hand proceeds (according to the rules of the previous chapter) together with some dissonances in the right hand as follows: In the second and fifth measures a fourth is prepared and resolved together with the right hand in octaves. In the third measure one observes that the right hand joins in forming the $\frac{4}{2}$ with the bass. In the eleventh measure the left hand appears to resolve the prepared seventh above itself. In the thirtieth measure an anticipated resolution of the seventh is used and, in the following measure, the fourth, instead of resolving, breaks off by leap.)[25]

Of much more importance to us than Heinichen's limited discussion of *allabreve* style are his comments on other so-called *allabreve* meters. These share in common a duple metrical arrangement with a new chord, generally, on each quarter note. Their relationship to the true *allabreve* is tenuous, which Heinichen implies in the following passages:

> Now there are other kinds of *Allabreve*. For, instead of the previous *allabreve*, in which the harmony of each measure is divided into only two parts and thus no fewer than two quarter notes can go to one chord, some [composers], on the contrary, divide each measure into four parts and give each quarter note its own chord. [They] also take the liberty of proceeding with various bass figurations and bizarre leaps with these quarter notes, contrary to the nature of the antique *allabreve*, although at the same time they try to imitate the latter by [employing] the usual syncopations [*Rückungen*] and suspension [*Syncopationes*] of consonances and dissonances.[26]

Other composers carry these modifications to even greater extremes: "and, although their *allabreve* does not make a profession out of syncopations, tied notes, and suspensions, [these composers] proceed beyond these in the bass with numerous fanciful figurations and leaps in eighth notes, just as occurs in slow common time with sixteenths. Justifiably, therefore, one usually calls this *allabreve* an *allabreve spurium* because it exhibits nothing of the true *allabreve* but the outer dress, I mean the notes, and the borrowed *allabreve* meter; in itself, however, it is nothing more than a translation of common, duple time."[27]

Examples of these meters occur in *ausländische*[*n*] *Concerte, ingleichen so viele Cantaten und Oper-Arien.*[28] The foreign country to which Heinichen alludes must be Italy, and the composers might be Alessandro Scarlatti, Vivaldi, or other of Heinichen's Italian contemporaries. Both spurious forms of the *allabreve*, Heinichen continues, employ an accompaniment typical of what previously has been called *semi-allabreve*[29] meter. In the latter metrical context the quarter note is accompanied as if it were an eighth in slow common time (i.e., a chord to every quarter note, except on a passing tone, and treating the eighth notes like sixteenths). The next example includes numerous illustrations of both quarter notes and eighths, as well as what Heinichen describes as *Inventiones* giving a "not unpleasant *Bizarrerie*" to the thorough-bass and permissible for that reason.

Example 96. *General-Bass*, 344–46.

Semi-Allabreve Meter

The differences between true *semi-allabreve* and true *allabreve* are purely a matter of notation and tempo, the tempo in the former being very fast. Otherwise, the accompaniment of *semi-allabreve* remains the same as for other rapid tempos that treat eighth notes like sixteenths in slow common time. Heinichen informs us that the next example represents the *antiquen semi-allabreve*; and he notes that bars 3, 4, and 5 contain the *transitus in 4tam*, a figuration that Heinichen interprets as a clue to the close relationship between this meter and the true *allabreve*.

Example 97. *General-Bass*, 347.

Additional exercises in true *semi-allabreve* can be created from previous examples of the true *allabreve* by making two measures of the latter meter into one, and by changing the half notes into quarters and quarter notes into eighths.

Overture Meter

"*Ouverteur-Tact* is distinguished by the signature 2 as well as its slow tempo and takes its name from the familiar *Ouverteur*, because it is used there for the most part, not only for the introduction but also in various pieces of same."[30] Heinichen uses the word "overture" in the meaning of an entire instrumental suite; some authors[31] limit its application to the introduction only. In this meter, quarter notes, as well as eighths following dotted quarters by leap, have their own chords; other eighth notes should be accompanied as if they were sixteenths in ordinary slow common time. In the following example (see bars 7–9) exceptional bass *Passagien* characteristic of this meter take a single chord only on the first note.

Example 98. *General-Bass*, 348–50.

Composers frequently employ the overture meter in pieces requiring quick tempos, and then the signature 2 should appear as either $\frac{2}{2}$ or $\mathbb{C}$. Heinichen reports that this distinction no longer is made, and 2, $\frac{2}{2}$, C, and $\mathbb{C}$ have become unreliable indicators of tempo. He urges[32] the beginner to remember, as a guide to accompanying these meters: "that whenever the tempo of an overture is fast, the quarter note will be used like an eighth in slow common time" (see pages 106–10 above). The following serves as an example of a quick tempo with overture meter:

Example 99. *General-Bass*, 351–52.

One characteristic of accompaniments in slow overture meter is the prevalence of passing dissonances originating in the parallel thirds between the bass and the right hand chords (ex. 98, bars 1, 3, 5, 11). In the immediately preceding example this stress on parallel thirds becomes even more prominent, for "in this lively style the right hand does not willingly rest for half measures and much less for whole [measures], particularly since overtures usually are accompanied on *Clavicins* [*sic*] and not with the sustained tone of an organ."[33] The accompaniment of a figuration with a quarter and two eighth notes should observe two rules:

1. If the three notes move up or down by step and no leap follows, then they have a single chord only (though frequently it will be repeated a second time). If, however, a leap follows, then the chord on the second bass note (the first eighth) will anticipate the harmony of the third note, as example 100 below illustrates.
2. If only the first two notes move up or down and the third reverses its motion, then all three notes customarily have one chord. The first section of example 100 shows, however, that in this meter and when a figure 6 appears on the first note of said figuration, a triad is particularly appropriate on the second note when it rises a step.

The only distinction between these rules for quick overture meter and those for slow common time is found in rule 2 directing "customarily" (*ordentlicher Weise*) one chord to the three notes, while in common slow meter a second chord would be played to the first eighth note in that figuration.

Example 100. *General-Bass*, 353–54.

To conclude, Heinichen[34] reviews the exceptional procedures permitting an accompanist to delay the resolution of a dissonance or bound consonance. Earlier in the *General-Bass* these suggestions had been applied to slow bass notes (see page 55 above); the restatement here will illustrate how they affect accompaniments of quick bass notes.

1. (a) A dissonance or bound consonance may delay its resolution by proceeding to other dissonances or bound consonances until, finally, the last note resolves for all the foregoing.

Example 101. *General-Bass*, 355–56.

(b) When a dissonance or bound consonance is played on a fundamental note that is divided up into many quicker bass notes, the dissonance or consonance must delay its resolution down a step until these bass figurations are completed.

Example 102. *General-Bass*, 357–61.

2. As with slow bass notes, with quick bass notes too, dissonances may resolve to dissonances in one of two ways:

(a) When a resolution of a dissonance falls to another dissonant note in the next chord:

Example 103. *General-Bass*, 361.

(b) When, with very quick bass notes, the dissonance resolves to a chord built on an irregular passing tone that has no harmony of its own; the chord of resolution, therefore, also is dissonant until the anticipated bass note is played.

Example 104. *General-Bass*, 362–63.

The full-voiced style has little application to the accompaniment of quick bass notes, because the left hand fingers are fully engaged in performing the bass part. Nevertheless, Heinichen[35] stresses that the accompanist need not limit his right hand to the usual three parts but may grasp as many chord tones as the fingers can reach. Of course, such freedom should be limited generally to accompaniments on stringed keyboard instruments.

The formidable bulk of the preceding materials constitutes the principles for accompanying quick bass notes that Heinichen gleaned *aus der gantzen Massa der weitläufftigen Composition.*[36] No writer before or after Heinichen proposed any other method to aid students in solving this particular riddle of thorough-bass realizations. C. P. E. Bach[37] ignores the whole problem and, though admitting certain rules (Heinichen's) existed for recognizing nonharmonic bass notes, he says they are not always dependable. In their place Bach proposes only that composers should mark each passing note in the bass with a horizontal line. This method of indicating that a right hand chord should be held for one or more additional bass notes had been used sporadically by composers, particularly in France, but never gained wide acceptance. Even if it had, Bach does not prepare the student for the "total mass of vastly numerous compositions" that leave nonharmonic notes unmarked. In addition, many subtle possibilities (such as ex. 92) must be neglected by the use of any oversimplified indication.

In general, theorists seem perplexed by their obligation to give students some explanation for accompanying quick bass notes. Gasparini[38] acknowledges the difficulty of accompanying quarter and eighth notes, particularly when they move by step, unless one has had a great deal of experience and has studied counterpoint. This facile evasion of the problem fails to satisfy Heinichen, who expresses a more forceful and practical educational philosophy:

> Gasparini makes short work of this material [quick bass notes] and states . . . that the accompaniment of quick notes is subject to many problems; and without considerable experience and an understanding of composition [Gasparini uses the word *Contrapunto*] one can succeed therein only with difficulty or not at all. Nevertheless, it is just as true that many hundreds, indeed thousands, of accompanists and organists wish to and must learn to accompany quick notes without being forced first to learn the entire [art of] composition, which would be all too long a path. How then can the matter be solved if one will not depend solely on the protracted [method of] experience? Answer: No other method can help the matter except to extract from the vast numbers of compositions most of the familiar cases of quick notes and to explain them carefully to the beginner, one by one. . . . Similarly, he who gives a little effort to the study and practice of this entire chapter [chap. IV, *General-Bass*] will, eventually, learn to form his own judgment from these many cases; and in the end he will find that the imagined difficulties (in the figured thorough-bass as well as here) are not insurmountable for long. For there is a mighty distinction between the difficult, and the impossible; and in music there are many difficult, toilsome things that, nevertheless, we must learn and with which we come to a happy ending.[39]

Notes

1. Heinichen, *General-Bass*, 257–58. The Baroque terminology *Notae virtualiter longae* and *Notae virtualiter breves* (inherently long and short note values) is another means of expressing strong and weak beats of a measure.

2. Ibid., 259.

3. Ibid., 260.

4. Ibid., 265.

5. Arnold, *Thorough-bass*, 734 (footnote 24) makes the following criticism of Heinichen's terminology: "The term *septima in transitu* . . . properly designates *a true passing Seventh*, i.e., a 7th which is *itself* a passing note, but it was also used indiscriminately to denote *a stationary Seventh*, which owes its existence to passing notes in *other parts*. Marpurg called attention to this misuse of the term." It would seem questionable to say that a term was misused when no other application of the word was common at the time. Baroque writers did not distinguish between two forms of passing note (*transitus*), nor did they specify how an interval *in transitu* should be formed. See J. G. Walther, *Praecepta der musicalischen Composition* (MS Weimar, 1708), ed. P. Benary (Leipzig, 1955), 150–51, who gives examples of both variants under one general heading of *Transitus*.

6. Heinichen, *General-Bass*, 268.

7. Ibid., 273–75 (footnote**).

8. Ibid., 369–70.

9. Ibid., 373–74.

10. Ibid., 292–93.

11. Ibid., 376.

12. Ibid., 293'(footnote q).

13. Ibid., 293–94.

14. Ibid., 297–98.

15. Ibid., 299.

16. Ibid., 299–300 (footnote t) makes the following important exception to this rule: In example 75, bar 6, the sixth in actual practice may not be indicated with a figure; nevertheless all four notes are accompanied by a triad on the first note. Concerning notes moving by step in a slow tempo, particularly *descendendo*, Heinichen suggests that a more harmonious effect can be obtained by playing a new chord on each group of two notes, for example:

17. Arnold, *Thorough-bass*, 756 (footnote).

18. Heinichen, *General-Bass*, 316.

19. Ibid., 331.

20. Ibid., 333 (footnote a).

21. Ibid., 332.

22. Curt Sachs, *Rhythm and Tempo* (New York, 1953), 269–71 discusses the "Decline of the Proportions in the Baroque," and gives several earlier instances of the rapid waning of the proportions in German music after 1600. It comes as a surprise, nevertheless, when Heinichen concludes that *alla-semibreve*, which also uses either C or ₵ as a signature, is faster than *allabreve*. According to the proportions, the former implied a slower tempo, although this distinction gradually lost force, until the two became almost synonymous; see Sachs, *Rhythm and Tempo*, 222–24. The present author is not aware, however, of any source before Heinichen that considers *alla-semibreve* as the faster of the two.

23. Heinichen, *General-Bass*, 333–39.

24. Ibid., 339.

25. Ibid., 343.

26. Ibid., 343. A difficult point in translating this passage involves the words *Rückung* and *Syncopationes*. No satisfactory word exists in English today for *Rückung*, which German treatises of the Baroque generally reserve for purely melodic suspension. In English practice, according to Morley these melodic syncopations were "drivings"; see Thomas Morley, *A Plaine and Easie Introduction to Practicall Musicke* (London, 1597); new ed. R. A. Harman (New York, [1952]), 257, which includes the following example:

The present author restricts the use of "syncopation" to this one meaning. *Syncopationes*, on the other hand, generally involved a dissonance structure (a suspension that is prepared and resolved). It is not unusual, unfortunately, to find the terms applied interchangeably. Also, *Bindung* (see footnote 28) has had a similarly chameleonic history. Some authors substitute it for *Syncopationes*; others use it to refer specifically to the suspended note, i.e., the "bound" note. See also Arnold, *Thorough-bass*, 127–28 (footnote 2).

27. Heinichen, *General-Bass*, 343–44.

28. Ibid., 343 (footnote f).

29. Ibid., 945, in the *Supplementa*, explains that *semi-allabreve* is a prevalent German corruption of *alla-semibreve*.

30. Ibid., 348.

31. For example, Walther, *Lexicon*, 456, defines the *Ouverture* as the "doorway to the suite," as well as an introduction to operas.

32. Heinichen, *General-Bass*, 350.

33. Ibid., 352 (footnote i).

34. Ibid., 354–63.

35. Ibid., 365.

36. Ibid., 366.

37. Bach-Mitchell, *Versuch*, 412.

38. Gasparini, *L'armonico pratico*, 32.

39. Heinichen, *General-Bass*, 947–48.

6

The "Art" of Accompaniment:
Specific Aspects of Style

In reconstructing the complex art of accompaniment we might well retain Heinichen's emphatic counsel as one of our golden rules:

> Until a beginner has thoroughly practiced the first principles of the thorough-bass, he should be left undisturbed by the considerable equipment of embellishments and the too confusingly ornamented thorough-bass. To play an embellished thorough-bass requires much experience, discretion, and judgment. How can one preach these things to a beginner when he is still not trained in the fundamentals? Besides, the thorough-bass was not conceived to enable one to perform with it as in preludes, but only so that the concerted parts would be accompanied. Consequently, all that one can expect of a beginner is that he knows how to accompany with chords; that means (not in the old style of three parts, but) in 4, 6, 8, and more parts. Also, the full-voiced accompaniment gives the fingers so much to do that in addition few embellishments can take place. When, however, one is trained previously in the fundamentals, only then is it time to think of secondary things, *flosculos* and decorations of the thorough-bass, in order that they can be applied discreetly to music of a few parts, and where a full-voiced accompaniment is not always necessary (particularly on the organ).[1]

Most important is his statement that "the thorough-bass was not conceived to enable one to perform with it as in preludes. . . ." Although an accompanist must improvise harmonies to a thorough-bass, the character of this improvisation differs vastly from the solo style required for *präludieren* or *fantasiren*.[2] Indeed, beginning with the first printed rules for playing from a thorough-bass, by Viadana,[3] every significant Baroque source stresses the functional role and essential simplicity of keyboard accompaniments, and each admonishes the performer against obscuring the solo part or parts with overly elaborate realizations.

The Embellishments

Accompanists who turn eagerly to Heinichen expecting guidance in forming highly ornamented accompaniments will close his treatise unrewarded.
Quite the contrary, Heinichen regards melodic ornamentation as a rela-
tively unimportant skill for accompanists. He freely admits the incompleteness of his explanations for ornaments, and he describes adequately
only those embellishments applicable to chords as distinct from melodic
ornamentation. "The art of the embellished thorough-bass, however, really
consists of not always simply playing chords but [rather] of using an
ornament here and there in all parts (particularly in the outermost part of
the right hand, which usually stands out), and thereby giving more elegance to the accompaniment, which can be applied with ease in four parts
and, upon occasion, in five- and six-part accompaniments."[4]

"The ornaments are numberless," Heinichen confesses, and they
change according to each performer's experience and good taste. Because
embellishments depend less on rules than on practice and judgment, he
offers only a short introduction to their interpretation. "The rest we must
leave to the visual demonstration of a teacher or to the individual industry
and experience of the student."[5] He divides the embellishments into two
groups, the first consisting of those with a single, unchanging execution:
(1) trill, (2) *transitus*, (3) appoggiatura (*Vorschlag*), (4) slide (*Schleiffung*), (5)
mordent, and (6) acciaccatura.

(1) A trill can be applied to any part of the accompaniment, in the left
hand as well as the right.

> In a three-part chord of the right hand, it [a trill] is not readily adaptable except
> on the middle note; therefore the thumb and little finger (for we always require
> the application of all five fingers) take the remaining parts, as the following
> example illustrates on the third quarter of the second measure. If one wishes a trill
> on the top or lowest part of the right hand, then the thumb or little finger plays the
> second part and the remaining chord tones are given to the left hand, because in
> such cases the right hand cannot satisfactorily manage more than two parts, as the
> following example illustrates on the second and fourth quarters of the first mea-
> sure. Should the left hand find opportunity to apply a trill to the bass, then for
> convenience it can give up all remaining parts, and the right hand can take a
> greater number of chord tones. Also, the little finger of the left hand can play the
> bass while the remaining fingers apply a trill in a middle part, a distinction made
> clear by the following example between the third quarter note of the second
> [measure] and the second quarter [not third quarter according to text] of the third
> measure.[6]

Example 105. *General-Bass*, 523.

(NB. This example does not mean to imply that in so few measures no embellishments other than pure trills should be used, but it shows in brief the many ways
the trill can be applied. Which is also to be understood in the examples of all the
following embellishments.)[7]

(2) A passing tone (*transitus*) between notes a third apart adds very
little harmonic or melodic interest to keyboard music. This ornament
gains considerable elegance, however, when combined with a trill; and in
the following example,

Example 106. *General-Bass*, 524.

each melodic leap by a third invites the accompanist to employ a *transitus* and a trill. The practical value of the *transitus* arises only in music of rather slow tempo, as the following version of example 106 illustrates:

Example 107. *General-Bass*, 524–25.

(3) Similarly, the appoggiatura is an ornament familiar to beginners; and, actually, it can be applied by experienced players to all intervals. Most commonly and easiest, however, it is used with ascending and descending seconds and thirds in both the right and left hands. The art of doubling it in parallel thirds in either hand, and particularly in the right, may be observed in the following example, where the appoggiatura is always indicated by the familiar *custos* w .[8]

Example 108. *General-Bass*, 525–26.

This unique application of the *custos*[9] was forced on Heinichen because his printer[10] lacked the smaller notes generally used to indicate appoggiaturas. There is, however, a striking similarity between the *custos* and the various signs for mordents and trills found in eighteenth-century music.[11] Perhaps this external resemblance has some bearing on the origin of these signs.

(4) A two-note appoggiatura beginning a third below the ornamented note is appropriately named a slide (*Scheiffung*). Heinichen[12] suggests the character of this ornament is particularly suited to *cantabile* (i.e., vocal) music, in which it fills in melodic skips of ascending thirds and embellishes passages ascending by step. He places an *x* on the staff to mark the first note of the ornament. The slide is best applied to the right hand part, which must be limited to two parts in these instances while the left hand fills in the harmony. The accompanist should exercise particular care to avoid forming parallel fifths and octaves between the slide and another part; the first three examples below illustrate common errors of this type:

Example 109. *General-Bass*, 528–29.

Heinichen[13] makes a surprising distinction in the interpretation of the appoggiatura and slide separating vocal from instrumental practice. He asserts that the passage given below at (a) would generally be sung as in (b); however, instrumentalists would anticipate each ornament with a short note as illustrated in (c):

Example 110. *General-Bass*, 527–28 (footnote a).

One looks in vain for a similar interpretation of the appoggiatura and slide in later German sources or in modern studies. Most of the latter predicate their interpretations of embellishments either on French sources from the turn of the eighteenth century or on German treatises written after 1750 (i.e., Quantz, L. Mozart, C. P. E. Bach, Marpurg). Even though there can be no doubt that German composers drew from the galaxy of French *agréments*, the anachronistic application of instructions from late eighteenth-century sources to music written a generation earlier is an uncertain historical procedure.[14] In addition, we know very little about the all too elusive Italian art of embellishment, which apparently was never crystallized into neat tables of signs and explanations. Heinichen's seemingly unique interpretation of the appoggiatura and slide may well represent a clue to contemporary Italian performance practice in the first half of the eighteenth century.

(5) "The *mordent* . . . is indeed another familiar ornament; we shall see, however, . . . that there is more connected with it [than with the previously explained ornaments], and therefore it must be examined more carefully. Generally a *mordent* is properly formed if one plays a note almost simultaneously with its adjacent lower whole or half tone, yet releases the latter [note] immediately while continuing to sustain the main note. This striking [of the ornament], however, can occur in [one of] three different ways."[15] Taking the note C as an illustration, the three forms of a mordent consist of:

1. Striking the adjacent semitone B at almost the same time as the C and immediately releasing it again while sustaining the C.
2. Striking the C first and immediately following it with the B and a repetition of the C, playing the three notes so rapidly that the C has only one accent.
3. Forming a trill with the lower auxiliary by repeating the two notes (as in the previous method) one or more times, which Heinichen says is used by some performers for slow notes.

The first type of mordent initially appears in Gasparini's treatise, where he describes it picturesquely as resembling the bite of a little animal which can hardly bite and lets go immediately without leaving a wound.[16] Mattheson good-naturedly finds Gasparini's description inadequate; and "if the little animal could be kept out I should rather derive the word from an amorous kiss."[17]

In Heinichen's opinion the method used to play a mordent in unimportant, since it can be altered to conform with the musical context; for an accompanist, however, it is indispensable to know whether a mordent requires a whole tone or semitone for the lower auxiliary. This decision calls for a precise understanding of the *ambitus modi* for each key, that is, the pattern of whole and half steps forming each major and minor scale.

In addition, we must mention that in three- and four-part chords of the right hand the mordent can successfully occur in a middle part only. . . . If, however, one wishes to play this ornament comfortably in the outermost part of the right hand, then as with previous ornaments this hand cannot easily perform more than two parts. The mordent can also be used in the bass, in which case the right hand carries the full accompaniment. The distinction [between a mordent in the right and one in the left hand] is illustrated in the following example; the lower whole tone or semitone for each mordent is indicated with two little lines.[18]

Example 111. *General-Bass*, 533.

(6) Heinichen also endorses a very different type of mordent, the acciaccatura, praising its "grand effect" on the harpsichord and its particular usefulness for expressing the affective meaning of words in recitatives as well as other vocal music. His explanation relies almost entirely on Gasparini:

Above all, he [Gasparini] distinguishes between a mordent and the so-called acciaccatura. He considers [as] a mordent only a semitone struck below [the main note]. . . . However, he would have one play the entire chord including the mordent with a slightly spread arpeggio (concerning which more shortly), holding all the notes except the dissonant semitone that is released immediately. . . . In addition, he observes that this mordent has a good effect particularly in three circumstances, namely: with the octave, [with the] sixth, and [with the] minor third.[19]

Example 112. *General-Bass*, 534.

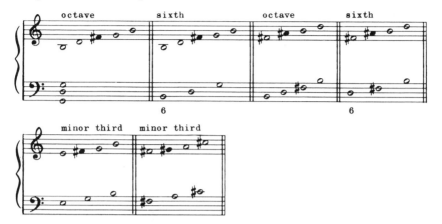

On the other hand, he [Gasparini] speaks of an acciaccatura if, because of the *ambitus modi*, one plays not a semitone but a whole tone below [the main note] or also, according to the opportunity, [one plays] almost simultaneously even three or four adjacent notes in a slightly spread arpeggio while releasing the false, or nonchordal notes, as was said of the mordent in the previous paragraph.[20]

For instructional purposes Heinichen divides the acciaccatura into four types, according to the four harmonies with which the ornament most frequently appears. First, with chords of the sixth.[21]

1a. By playing a fourth to a chord with major sixth and minor third. The following example includes the fourth both as an acciaccatura and as a mordent.

Example 113. *General-Bass*, 536.

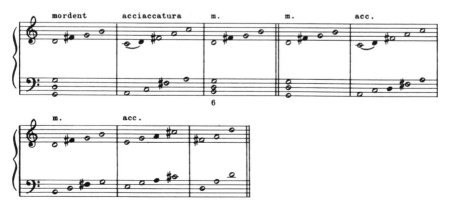

1b. By playing a seventh between the sixth and the octave, either as a
single acciaccatura or mordent or in combination with the fourth of
the previous example.

Example 114. *General-Bass*, 536–37.

1c. By playing the two tones between the major third and sixth or minor
third and sixth (though the latter does not appear in Gasparini's treatise).

Example 115. *General-Bass*, 537.

2. In the second harmonic context, chords of a diminished fifth, a ninth
between the octave and tenth is played alone or in combination with the
fourth between the third and fifth. In the latter case the acciaccaturas
form a sixth between themselves.

Example 116. *General-Bass*, 538.

3. When a chord includes a major third and a minor seventh, the acciaccatura is formed from the fourth between the third and fifth.

Example 117. *General-Bass*, 538–39.

4. In the last harmonic context, chords including an augmented fourth together with a second and sixth, the acciaccatura is formed from the fifth between the augmented fourth and sixth.

Example 118. *General-Bass,* 539.

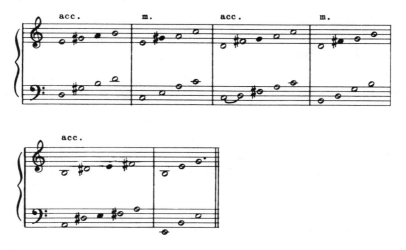

Finally, this author [Gasparini] says that one must try to discover other acciaccaturas, and [he] gives still another [example] that (as he says) fell into his hands as soon as he searched further, in which one strikes 13 keys at once and the thumb and little finger each play two keys. And this acciaccatura follows, which should be used with the familiar $\frac{7}{4}$ [*sic*] chord in the recitative.[22]

Example 119. *General-Bass,* 540.

When looking for new acciaccaturas one needs only a free finger in either hand of an arpeggiated chord to play the note between any interval of a third. Heinichen cautions (1) that these dissonances should not be played too frequently; (2) that not more than three of four adjacent notes be played at one time; and (3) that these "false notes" of the arpeggiated chord be released immediately while the chord tones are sustained with the fingers.

The abundant enthusiasm Heinichen evinces for the acciaccatura stands out in bold relief when compared to his treatment of other ornaments. This disproportionate emphasis is easily understood: the acciaccatura had real value as a means of introducing dissonances at dramatically strategic moments in recitative accompaniments. It had not been explained in any other German thorough-bass manual and, in fact, must have been something of a novelty to German accompanists. The acciaccatura quickly became just another ornament in the *Manieren-Equippage*, and a decade later Mattheson thought that "Heinichen makes more of it than the thing is really worth."[23] Mattheson also blames the acciaccatura for the frequent occurrence of harmonic impurities in full-voiced accompaniments.

The almost universal appeal of Italian operatic music undoubtedly implemented the rapid spread of the acciaccatura throughout Europe. The reputable reporter Walther[24] carefully describes it in his *Lexicon*; and across the English Channel the British composer and writer on music Charles Avison cites the acciaccatura as one "of the peculiar Beauties of this Instrument [harpsichord]. But these graceful Touches are only reserved for a masterly Application in the Accompanyment of a fine Voice, or single Instrument; and therefore, besides the Difficulty of acquiring a complete Skill in them, they are not required in the Performance of full Music."[25] Although C. P. E. Bach vigilantly avoids impure harmonies, he too recommends acciaccaturas as an addition to arpeggios in solo keyboard music.[26]

The latter's illustrious father demonstrated the wonderful eloquence of the acciaccatura in the opening measures of the Sarabande from his *Partita in E minor* (*Clavier-Übung, Teil II*):

Example 120.

Neither Gasparini nor Heinichen uses the oblique line found in Bach's works,[27] nor does either suggest any particular symbol for the acciaccatura.

The second main class of embellishments in Heinichen's account "depends on each [performer's] inventiveness";[28] and they include: melody, *passaggi*, arpeggios, and imitation, each of which must be improvised without the aid of interpretive signs or instructions from the composer.

> . . . a weak-[sounding] four- or five-part accompaniment becomes more elegant if the upper part of the right hand has a melody, i.e., a singing line, and does not always remain on the same note. Thus the following example would be very simple to accompany in the latter form:[29]

Example 121. *General-Bass*, 543–44.

Now to improve this [example] and especially to give a better turn to the upper part, one can proceed in [one of] two ways. Namely, one either (1) divides the accompaniment between both hands so that the right hand generally has two parts only and the left hand [has] the remaining two- or three-part accompaniment; or (2) the left hand takes the entire full-voiced accompaniment and by this means gives the right hand more convenience to invent a particular song or melody on the bass, [which will be] as good as our imagination, taste, and talent will allow. If one wishes to try an embellished performance of the previous example according to the first method with the accompaniment divided between both hands, then it [the previous example] becomes more elegant in the following form. . . .[30]

Example 122. *General-Bass*, 545–47.

If, however, one wishes to accompany this same bass according to the second method and, as far as the concerted parts are not impaired, to sound a particular melody in the right hand for several measures, or perhaps as a test throughout (the best opportunities for which are found in a *cantabile* solo and in the empty ritornello of an aria without instruments), then the following accompaniment will serve as an illustration. In this connection should be noted: with this method the deeper bass notes are better taken full-voiced an octave higher in order that the grumble of numerous low notes (particularly on an organ) does not pain the ear and [so that] both hands will be brought more closely together.[31]

Example 123. *General-Bass*, 548–51.

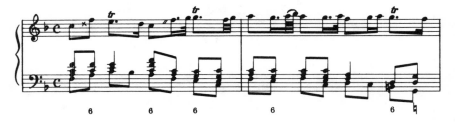

Just as melody is suited primarily to *cantabile*, affective, and slow pieces, in contrast *passaggi* . . . are more applicable to lively and quick pieces. We know that the term *passaggi* includes all kinds of running and leaping quick notes. Their number, however, is limitless, and their invention over a thorough-bass depends similarly as does melody on our imagination and skill. When an active or quick bass part has *passaggi* one can, by omitting most or all of the other parts, proceed simply with thirds and sixths, particularly when the *passaggi* have a wide range in themselves, for here such an accompaniment tends generally to have a great effect.[32]

Example 124. *General-Bass*, 551–52.

However, should the bass not include *passaggi*, then the right hand can endeavor to apply such *passaggi* where they do not detract from the concerted parts; and here again the left hand proceeds by itself with as full-voiced an accompaniment as is possible. Examine the following bass and the several variations of *passaggi* over it; countless other forms with various note values could be found over this very same bass. Moreover, one must take pains to play all *passaggi* cleanly, distinctly, and without a slipshod manner of striking, because in this lies a great brilliance of performing, which in itself is easier to hear than to describe.[33]

Example 125. *General-Bass*, 553–56.

The *arpeggio* overshadows in importance all other embellishments of this second group. In the most common form of the arpeggio, a full-voiced chord is broken from the lowest note of the left hand to the highest of the right. These arpeggios can also be played doubly (from the lowest to the highest tone and back to the lowest in reverse order) or repeatedly (by repeating the double arpeggio one or more times). This last variety may conclude by striking a solid chord in the right hand "as is frequently applied to the harpsichord in the recitative and with other motionless bass notes. Moreover, with somewhat active or moderately quick notes the left hand frequently plays a full-voiced chord with a simple arpeggio while the right hand concludes with a solid chord on the same beat. One must seek to learn from fine performers the many other similar ways of breaking [chords]."[34]

Heinichen speaks at length about another category of arpeggios that in effect are nothing more than various special kinds of broken chords. For example, one need not play two-part chords solidly but instead can alternate the parts in manner of Heinichen's example:

Example 126. *General-Bass*, 558.

Thus:

Now should the right hand find an opportunity to apply such arpeggios, then, in addition, whenever possible pick two parts [in the left hand] forming a triad with the bass or the three fundamental parts of the chord. Additional skill is unnecessary for this type [of arpeggio], since one plays the arpeggio according to his pleasure, first striking one of the two parts, then the other afterward, and the left hand manages the remaining accompaniment. The following example will sufficiently illustrate the point.[35]

Example 127. *General-Bass*, 559–60.

Exactly the same procedure applies to three-part chords, and Heinichen's examples demonstrate the variety of arpeggios that may be substituted for unbroken chords:

Example 128. *General-Bass*, 561–62.

Unlike the three-note figurations, those based on four-part chords lack variety, and Heinichen illustrates only three forms:

Example 129. *General-Bass*, 564–65.

These same chordal figurations may replace the single notes of a thorough-bass if they do not interfere with the concerted parts or distort the composer's music. Heinichen observes wisely that "not all composers are content with these bass variations. Nevertheless if, for example, in a solo, a cantata *a voce sola*, or in the empty ritornello of an aria without instruments, such things are introduced *à propos* and with discernment, they embellish the accompaniment and are certainly admissible. Only one must not irritate the singer with these things and [must] not make a prelude out of the accompaniment."[36] The target of this pointed rebuttal was Gasparini, who had flatly rejected substituting figurations for the actual thorough-bass part because "it is very easy to miss or depart from the intention of the writer, from the good taste of the composition, and to offend the singer."[37]

In the last six sections of example 130 Heinichen demonstrates the doubling of two-, three-, and four-part figurations in the right hand, either in full-voiced form or in two parts moving in parallel thirds and sixths. In certain *pompös und lebendig gesetzten Sachen*[38] this mode of accompanying adds substantially to the brilliance of harpsichord performances.

Example 130. *General-Bass*, 566–73.

2-Part Figurations [Harpeggiaturen]

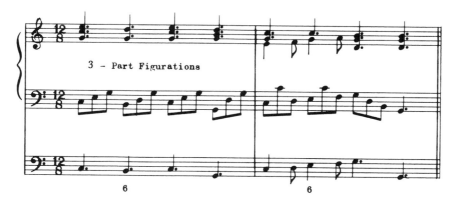

3 - Part Figurations

¼-Part Figurations

Doubled 2-Part Figurations between Hands

Doubled 3-Part Figurations between Hands

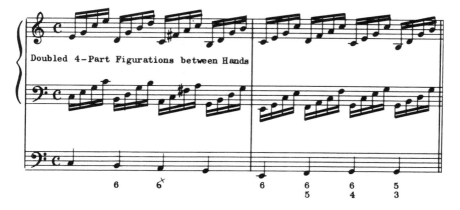

Doubled 4-Part Figurations between Hands

(NB. From these variations one sees in every case that the fundamental bass note is played first and is followed by the variation. Therefore, those thorough-bass variations are not of the best sort in which one of the unsuitable middle parts substitutes for the bass, and the correct bass note is not played until afterwards.)[39]

Arpeggios have an important role in the special problem of performing repeated tones of a thorough-bass. Earlier (as a supplementary comment to his study of quick bass notes) Heinichen had anticipated the question, advising that

one must not allow himself to be misled by many quick repetitions of a note, for one repeats the previous chord in slower note values, one or more times (according to the opportunity [offered by] the meter), as long as no other figure occurs over such notes. And the performance of the quick bass notes is left to the other accompanying bass [instruments]. For example, these three measures:

Example 131.

could be accompanied somewhat in the following way . . . :[40]

Example 132.

Such accompanying, however, would quickly become oppressively dull, especially with lengthy passages of rapidly repeated bass notes. For this reason, Heinichen[41] suggests modifications such as melodic improvisation, *passaggi*, and particularly the two types of arpeggios. Once again, however, he cautions us to avoid assiduously any element in an accompaniment that will detract from the solo part.

The first four sections of example 133·show how to improvise variants over reiterated bass notes; the final three sections given various embellishments of the bass part (which is printed in its original form below the left hand part). Heinichen's simplifications of rapidly repeated bass notes are exceptionally instructive and exemplify the frequent disparity between a thorough-bass notation and the sound of its realization.

Example 133. *General-Bass*, 574–77.

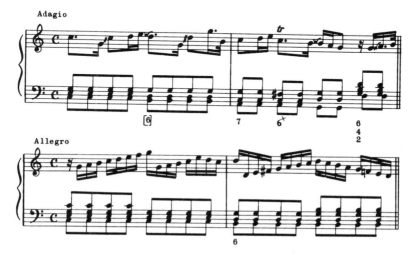

Baroque sources offer few concrete suggestions for using imitation as a decorative device with the thorough-bass, and consequently Heinichen's characteristically specific observations have great significance:

Finally, the second class of embellishments concludes with imitation, which differs from said embellishments in that it does not depend like the former on our own ideas but must be taken from the notated composition itself. Therefore, imitation in this context results if an accompanist seeks to imitate a composer's melodic motive or invention in places where the composer himself HAS NOT USED IT. The accompanist has few opportunities left for imitation, because (1) one must never hinder a singer or instrumentalist with these melodic motives, and, on the other hand, (2) one can expect that a composer will himself fill out those places where the imitation he has initiated will fit. Thus, clearly on a keyboard instrument this embellishment is the very poorest in use. Because, however, rare cases can occur in a composition (particularly in cantatas and arias without instruments) where a little place remains in which the skilled accompanist can repeat a melodic motive begun in the thorough-bass or a concerted part several times more than the composer has done, the following example, therefore may serve as an illustration. Regarding which is still to be noted: that the right hand seeks willingly to accompany the concerted part in thirds and sixths and at the same time to form a concerted duet with that part. This form of imitation is particularly suited to vocal pieces and is also easier to accomplish, because in chamber and theatrical music one can observe the singer exactly from the voice-part usually written above [the thorough-bass], varying from him and again following him.[42]

Example 134. *General-Bass*, 579–81.

Now certainly it would be profitable and necessary to show the application of all these ornaments to entire thorough-basses as well as to include the concerted part so that one could point out to the beginner where this or that ornament would be applicable or inapplicable. But every informed musician realizes that such numbers of examples would belong not to a single chapter as here, but to an entire book. Now we would willingly make up this deficiency at least by recommending other authors who have pursued the same material *ex professo*; however, at this time I do not know a single writer who has given much effort to this [material] except for the just recently cited *Organisten-Probe* of Capellmeister Mattheson. The great merit of this book for the beginner already well-acquainted with thorough-bass fundamentals is that it makes him fast to the saddle in various ways and gives him (1) the difficulties of all the modes, (2) a well-practiced technique, and (3) the diverse *Galanterie* belonging to the thorough-bass. And I believe (without vanity on my part) that those who place the *Organisten-Probe* next to this treatise need a third author neither in theory nor in practice.[43]

Heinichen's warm-hearted and exceedingly generous compliment was returned by Mattheson in the *Grosse General-Bass-Schule*, in which the latter ranks the *General-Bass* first among works on the thorough-bass. Furthermore, "it would be a disgrace, both to a musician and to every proper connoisseur and amateur, not to possess it or to value it as it deserves.[44]

The *Bassetti*

A thorough-bass becomes a *bassetto* (also *Basset* or *Bassetgen* in German sources) when a C or G clef replaces the usual bass clef. This device serves essentially to warn an accompanist to stop the normal style of realization for the moment. Heinichen effectively explains the details of performing *bassetti* in connection with a specially valuable illustration in fugal form.

> (1) One finds the inscription *tasto solo* twice in this example [ex. 135]. In Italian the wooden keys of the harpsichord, organ, etc., are called *tasti*, from *tastare* [meaning] to touch [or] to feel; therefore, the words *tasto solo* fully signify that one should play these same notes as single keys or [with] single fingers, without additional accompaniment, until another part or another clef appears.
> (2) One sees at various places just two parts written one over the other, which means that in such circumstances one should never play more than is notated.
> (3) Always bear in mind with the occurrence of soprano, alto, and tenor clefs in the thorough-bass that one never doubles such *bassetti* at the lower octave (as is permitted with the ordinary bass clef). However, one certainly can
> (4) Realize the harmony over the *bassetto* with both hands as full-voiced as the circumstances and the available space in the upper octave of the keyboard permit (but with a discreet regard for the many or few concerted parts for voice or instruments).[45]

Example 135. *General-Bass*, 516–20.

Tasto solo

Heinichen's concluding remarks about example 135 reëmphasize the important distinction existing between thorough-bass accompaniments and solo improvisations:

> . . . the countersubject [which was first introduced in bars 11–17] occurring in the last four measures of the right hand has been allowed in order to shorten the fugue. An accompanist, however, is not usually expected to find the place for such elaborated *themata, inventiones,* or *variationes* of a composer and, by imitating the same, to encroach upon the other [instrumental] parts dedicated to this task. Such

arts the amateur can better utilize in [extemporizing] preludes; this is where they really belong.[46]

Numerous Baroque works (including fugal sections in overtures and cantatas) require such an accompaniment; and the length of the previous example helps us to penetrate the means of continuing a realization, a problem left unsolved by the brief examples found in most treatises.

The measures of example 135 that double the left hand part in octaves would appear as single notes in actual practice; and Heinichen uses this notation to stress the need for playing the basses of *bassetti* in single notes. The most remarkable and significant feature of example 135 is the freedom with which Heinichen moves from four to five parts and his unconcern for parallel octaves and fifths between inner parts: Bars 8–9, for example with parallel octaves; bar 16, with parallel fifths and octaves (second and third beats); bars 21–22, with parallel octaves. Even more unusual, however, is bar 9, which Arnold[47] points out as an example of a doubled leading tone. Heinichen undoubtedly would have had a colorful retort for this objection to a doubled leading tone arising from the convergence of a five-part chord into a four-part harmony. Clearly, keyboard harmony in this period continues to display a remarkable freedom from the strict principles of voice leading. Arnold also criticizes the bass of bar 9

stripping it of passing tones to form

and emphasizing the additional doubling of the leading tone as well as the parallel octaves. Although the E functions harmonically, perhaps we might consider other factors tending to mask from the ear the effect of the doubling and the parallelism: the approach of the bass through a dissonance, the position of the E on the rhythmically weak portion of the beat, and its very short duration.

Arnold perceived the unique lesson to be drawn from Heinichen's fugue: "The object [of Arnold's detailed analysis of the parallels in Heinichen's examples] was merely to call attention to the kind of liberties (liberties which in a harmony exercise would rightly provoke the severest censure) which, at this period, were taken in the treatment of a figured bass, not by the ignorant or unskilled, but by one of the soundest musicians of his day. . . ."[48]

Relationship of the Accompaniment to the Whole

Heinichen's discussion of the *manierlichen General-Bass* confirms unequivocally the limited applicability of embellishments to accompaniments. He reiterates frequently that accompanists must avoid an overly florid or melodically independent style detracting attention from the soloist. Clearly he regards a ritornello or other rest in the solo or concerting parts as the only suitable places for an ornamented or imitative thorough-bass realization.

Basically then, the art of accompanying consists of a refined style of improvising harmonies; and Heinichen's examples show that the most important features of this style are a full-voiced realization and an avoidance of large melodic skips in all parts. Although Baroque sources fully confirm the accuracy of Heinichen's information, we continue to be plagued with the widest disagreement among writers over the character of thorough-bass accompaniments and their relationship to the solo or ensemble being accompanied. Apel,[49] for example, says "within the course of time from 1600 to 1750 the style of improvised accompaniment changed from simple homophony to real counterpoint." Where, however, is the evidence for contrapuntal realizations? Even Bukofzer treats the sources lightly by generalizing that "Gasparini and, especially, Heinichen called for the addition of improvised melodies against the figured bass, a practice that Bach carried in his realizations to the highest level."[50] Quite to the contrary, according to Heinichen or Gasparini, the only circumstances warranting the improvisation of melodies were occasions when the keyboard performer must play alone. The very fact that Heinichen treats melody as a special embellishment underlines its limited role in accompanying.

Those who oppose the kind of accompanying Heinichen recommends invariably evoke the spirit of J. S. Bach.[51] These skeptics refuse to believe that the great master of contrapuntal techniques would have permitted purely harmonic realizations for his thorough-basses. To prove their contention they quote statements of two younger contemporaries of Bach, the first by Lorenz Mizler: "Whoever wishes to hear truly the delicate in thorough-bass [realizations] and what is called really good accompanying, need only trouble himself to hear our Capellmeister Bach, [for he] accompanies each thorough-bass to a solo so that one would think it was a concerto, and that the melody he makes with the right hand had been composed beforehand."[52] Less specific is the report by Heinrich Nicolaus Gerber's son that his father had learned the art of realizing thorough-basses from J. S. Bach, whose accompaniments were characterized by an equality of the parts and were so beautiful that the solo part could be omitted without being missed.[53]

As long ago as 1880 Philipp Spitta correctly interpreted these testimonies of Mizler and Gerber in a brilliant and pioneering essay on Bach's thorough-bass accompaniments.[54] Spitta acquired a thorough-bass realization by H. N. Gerber to an Albinoni sonata that contained corrections by J. S. Bach.[55] The accompaniment is obviously the work of a student, but its general style apparently satisfied Bach since he made only minor changes. It has

> no imitative use of motives, whether taken from the solo parts or freely invented. It is simple — a flowing movement in several parts, in which we never for a moment lose the feeling that the motive power is external to itself. It is only in so far as an unconstrained progression of harmonies, which never encounters any obstacle, must of itself have a certain melodic effect that we can speak of melody at all in this accompaniment, and this exactly suits the definition of a good accompaniment given by the younger Telemann: 'a good flowing song (*ein guter Gesang*), i.e., a well-proportioned and pleasing succession of sounds.'[56]

Gerber's manuscript tends to indicate that the "beauty" characterizing Bach's method of accompanying did not depend on an independent melodic improvisation. Similarly, Spitta believes the melody in Bach's realizations, which Mizler found so perfect, entailed "such a variety in the succession of notes that they could be sung with ease and would be pleasant to listen to. But since in the best melodies we notice the fewest leaps, it follows that the figured bass player must make no unusual leaps if he wishes to preserve intact the melodic element. Apparently his description of Bach's method of accompanying tends the same way as what we already know from Heinrich Nicolaus Gerber's manuscript, namely, to a smooth combination of harmonies, the result of which is the production of a kind of melody in the upper part."[57]

Despite Spitta's clear interpretation, many musicians still refused to accept merely harmonic accompaniments for Bach's music. They rejected the few examples by Bach's students[58] as the work of amateurs and explained the numerous examples in treatises as simplified exercises for beginners. Fritz Oberdoerffer,[59] however, has attacked this Philistine incredulity, and in his reëxamination of Bach's thorough-bass practice he fully supports Spitta's conclusions. Also, Oberdoerffer's article casts fresh light on the proper relationship between accompaniment and the total composition, including the following observations:

1) A distinction must be made between accompaniments in general and thorough-bass realizations. We cannot take as models for the latter the keyboard parts Bach wrote to a number of chamber music compositions. In these instances Bach employs the harpsichord as a concerted instrument by freely exploiting contrapuntal devices, and these accompaniments are in no sense analogous to thorough-bass accompaniments.

2) Writers who postulate melodic independence for the upper part forget the important melodic character of the bass itself. It is not merely a harmonic outline to be brought to life by introducing motives and themes in the right hand, but has a thematic character of its own that freely interacts with the composed melodic line.

3) When Baroque treatises refer to melodic interest in the right hand of an accompaniment it is in the sense that all unnecessary leaps are to be avoided. The right hand was responsible for supplying a "neutral" harmonic background to the composed parts (*für die komponierten Stimmen einen neutralen harmonischen Hintergrund zu liefern*). The chords must not belong to the thematic structure of the composition and must not enter into a contest of motives or free melodies with the composed parts. In the case of a bass theme, every hint of melodic emphasis of the upper part must be avoided.[60]

Actually the character of thorough-bass accompaniments should never have been in doubt, for the sources are abundantly clear in this regard. Therefore, it is only fitting to close this chapter with the advice of a few eighteenth-century authors, the first from Andreas Werckmeister:

Since the thorough-bass must be nothing more than a gentle murmur and the foundation of a musical composition on which its entire structure rests, it must, therefore, be employed without many *passaggi* and complexities. For if singers and instrumentalists use the *passaggi* and ornaments the composer has written and the organist wishes to mix in his own ornaments, then the harmony would be ruined. Still, one must not always make the simple chords too full, particularly if a weak singer or instrumentalist is at hand. An experienced [player] can, now and then, play a thorough-bass with arpeggios. In short: it [the thorough-bass] requires musical talent and judgment also. For if one has no musical aptitude 1,000 rules could be illustrated with 10,000 examples and still the purpose would not be achieved. Whoever has a natural aptitude, diligence, and ambition can learn a great deal from these few rules.[61]

Undoubtedly a common fault of accompanists was a tendency to perform with virtuosity; and this led many writers to express concern that the accompanist might divert attention unduly from the soloist. Saint-Lambert's description of musicians who prize their "clever vanity" has the authentic ring of one who had known many such performers.

For the purpose of the accompaniment is to second the voice and not to stifle or disfigure it by an unpleasant racket [*mauvais carillon*]. There are those accompanists who have such a good opinion of themselves that, believing themselves alone to be worth more than the other [players] in the concert, they try to shine above all the other players. They burden the thorough-basses with *passaggi*; they embellish their accompaniments; and [they] make a hundred things that are, perhaps, quite pretty in themselves, but that at the time are extremely injurious to the performance and that serve only to show the clever vanity of the musician who performs them. Whoever plays in a concert must play for the honor and perfection of the performance and not for his own particular honor. It is no longer a concert when each plays only for himself.[62]

Mattheson also confirms Heinichen's frequent insistence that elaborate keyboard realizations were out of place in thorough-bass accompaniments. Mattheson's *Grosse General-Bass-Schule* (a misleading title since the work has nothing to say about thorough-bass realizations) contains forty-eight test pieces planned to teach organists the art of improvisation. Mattheson suggests various means for making these figured basses (*Probe-Stücke*) into organ solos, including melodic invention in the right hand and the addition of imitative passages and embellishments. He stresses, however, "that the ornamental and variegated playing of [the] thorough-bass has little place in pieces where the fundamental part itself has been purposely written in an ornamental and variegated style. On the other hand, if the bass is written without any special ornamentation, and if one plays alone, be it in the beginning of an aria, in the middle, or wherever else an interlude appears, then and there do these ornaments, these figures, these ideas, these niceties . . . find their proper setting — yes, almost their necessary place."[63]

Even after 1750 composers and theorists admonish accompanists to avoid unnecessary embellishments and superfluous melodies.[64] Of all these authors, C. P. E. Bach offers the most colorfully phrased advice, words that span the centuries without losing their force:

Gratuitous passage work and bustling noise do not constitute the beauties of accompaniment. In fact, they can easily do harm to the principal part by robbing it of its freedom to introduce variations into repetitions and elsewhere. The accompanist will achieve eminence and attract the attention of intelligent listeners by letting them hear an unadorned steadiness and noble simplicity in a flowing accompaniment which does not interfere with the brilliance of the principal part. He need feel no anxiety over his being forgotten if he is not constantly joining in the tumult. No! An understanding listener does not easily miss anything. In his soul's perception melody and harmony are inseparable. Yet, should the opportunity arise and the nature of a piece permit it, when the principal part pauses or performs plain notes the accompanist may open the draft on his dampened fire. But this demands great ability and an understanding of the true content of a piece.[65]

Notes

1. Heinichen, *General-Bass*, 521.

2. Jacob Adlung, *Anleitung zu der musikalischen Gelahrtheit* (Erfurt, 1758), facs. ed. H. J. Moser (Kassel, 1953), 752, suggests that *fantasiren* better describes this art than *präludieren*, since the latter refers only to *vorspielen* on a chorale and not to music improvised while the congregation leaves a church or for other occasions.

3. Lodovico Grossi da Viadana, *Cento concerti ecclesiatici* (Venice, 1602). The title-page to Viadana's *Concerti* and the extended prefatory remarks (including his rules for the thorough-bass) are quoted in Claudio Sartori, *Bibliografia della musica strumentale italiana stampata in Italia fino al 1700* (Florence, 1952), 111-15. For an English translation see Oliver Strunk, *Source Readings in Music History* (New York, 1950, 419-23.

4. Heinichen, *General-Bass*, 521-22.

5. Ibid., 522.

6. Ibid., 522-23.

7. Ibid., 524.

8. Ibid., 525.

9. *GroveD* VI, 445, in a table of ornaments and their signs, overlooks Heinichen's use of the *custos*.

10. *General-Bass*, 527 (footnote a) alludes to the inadequacy of his printer's typography for indicating both the appoggiatura and the slide.

11. *GroveD* VI, 444-445 shows at a glance the wide variety of signs for embellishments that seem to be derived from the form of the *custos*.

12. Heinichen, *General-Bass*, 527.

13. Ibid., 527-28 (footnote a).

14. Since the publication of the first edition of the present study, Frederick Neumann's magesterial study, *Ornamentation in Baroque and Post-Baroque Music, with Special Emphasis on J. S. Bach* (Princeton, 1978), has appeared, which examines in great detail the complexities of ornamentation from various viewpoints, including national characteristics.

15. Heinichen, *General-Bass*, 529.

16. Gasparini, *L'armonico pratico*, 91.

17. Mattheson, *Capellmeister*, 119 (footnote **).

18. Heinichen, *General-Bass*, 532–33.

19. Ibid., 534.

20. Ibid., 535.

21. Heinichen indicates arpeggios in example 113 and succeeding examples by printing chord tones successively rather than in vertical alignment. The slur beneath the lowest tones of the right hand chord means that both notes should be struck by the thumb.

22. Heinichen, *General-Bass*, 540.

23. Mattheson, *Capellmeister*, 120.

24. Walther, *Lexicon*, 6.

25. Charles Avison, *An Essay on Musical Expression* (London, 1752), 119–20.

26. Bach-Mitchell, *Versuch*, 159.

27. The short, unaccented appoggiatura or grace note erroneously became known as an acciaccatura in the nineteenth century, an unfortunate confusion in terminology that continues to plague many popular music dictionaries.

28. Heinichen, *General-Bass*, 552.

29. Ibid., 543.

30. Ibid., 544–45.

31. Ibid., 547–48.

32. Ibid., 551.

33. Ibid., 552.

34. Ibid., 557.

35. Ibid., 558.

36. Ibid., 565 (footnote k).

37. Gasparini, *L'armonico pratico*, 104.

38. Heinichen, *General-Bass*, 565.

39. Ibid., 573.

40. Ibid., 377–78.

41. Ibid., 573.

42. Ibid., 578–79.

43. Ibid., 582–83.

44. Mattheson, *Grosse General-Bass-Schule*, 10.

45. Heinichen, *General-Bass*, 515–16.

46. Ibid., 516.

47. Arnold, *Thorough-bass*, 377.

48. Ibid., 379.

49. Willi Apel, *Harvard Dictionary of Music* (Cambridge, Mass., 1944), 746.

50. Bukofzer, *Music in the Baroque Era*, 384.

51. For example see Rudolf Steglich, "Nochmals: Über die Generalbassbegleitung," *Mf* 10 (1957), 422–33.

52. Lorenz Mizler [von Kolof], *Neu eröffnete musikalische Bibliothek* . . . 1 (pt. 4 Leipzig, 1738), 48.

53. E. L. Gerber, *Historisch-biographisches Lexicon der Tonkünstler* . . . (Leipzig, 1790–92), col. 492: "Den Beschluss machte der Generalbass, wozu Bach die Albinonischen Violin-solos wählete; und ich muss gestehen, dass ich in der Art, wie mein Vater diese Bässe nach Bachs Manier ausführete, und besonders in dem Gesange der Stimmen untereinander, nie etwas vortrefflichers gehöret habe. Dies akkompagnement war schon an sich so schön, dass keine Hauptstimme etwas zu dem Vergnügen, welches ich dabey empfand, hätte hinzuthun können."

54. Spitta–Fuller-Maitland, *J. S. Bach* II, 292–300.

55. Ibid. III, 388–98.

56. Ibid. II, 294. "The younger Telemann" refers to Georg Michael Telemann (the son of Georg Philipp) who wrote *Unterricht im General-Bass-Spielen* (Hamburg, 1773).

57. Spitta–Fuller-Maitland, *J. S. Bach* II, 295.

58. Another student of Bach, J. P. Kirnberger, published (in his *Grundsätze des Generalbasses*) a realization of the thorough-bass to Bach's Andante from the Trio Sonata (No. 7) in the *Musicalisches Opfer*. This has been reprinted in Arnold, *Thorough-bass*, 790–92.

59. Fritz Oberdoerffer, "Generalbassbegleitung," *Mf* 10 (1957), 61–74. See his concluding remarks in *Mf* 11 (1958), 79–82 in which he effectively dismisses the objections raised by Rudolf Steglich in *Mf* 10 (1957), 422–33. See also Oberdoerffer's excellent general survey of the entire thorough-bass practice in *MGG* 4, col. 1708–37.

60. Oberdoerffer, "Generalbassbegleitung," *Mf* 10 (1957), 73.

61. Werckmeister, *Nothwendigsten Anmerckungen*, 40–41.

62. Saint-Lambert, *Nouveau traité*, 121.

63. H. P. Reddick, *Johann Mattheson's 48 Thorough-Bass Test Pieces: Translation and Commentary* (Diss. Univ. of Michigan, 1956) II, 40.

64. For examples see: Quantz, *Versuch*, 225, 235; Daube, *General-Bass*, 198; Adlung, *Anleitung*, 653–54.

65. Bach-Mitchell, *Versuch*, 367–68.

7

Unfigured Basses

Divergent opinions concerning the practicality of unfigured basses split theorists and composers into two opposing groups during the very first decade of the seventeenth century. As early as 1607 Agazzari warned composers of the ambiguities inherent in unfigured basses; and in 1619 Praetorius vigorously rejected all thorough-basses lacking figures,[1] a characteristically German conviction: throughout the Baroque, German writers opposed the omission of figures from thorough-basses more vigorously than either the French or Italians.

In the same year that Agazzari cautioned against the practice, Bianciardi wrote a set of rules for unfigured basses,[2] *Breve regola per imparar'a sonare sopra il basso con ogni sorte d'istrumento.* Many Italian theorists, including Sabbatini and Penna,[3] attempted to codify bass progressions into specific formulas to which they could assign appropriate harmonies; and similar directions soon appeared in French sources.[4] As late as 1708 Gasparini relied on this long-established Italian practice[5] for the lengthy section of his treatise instructing the accompanist in the mysteries of the unfigured bass.[6]

How different German sentiments were in approximately the same period; Werckmeister effectively summarizes the attitude of his compatriots: "Those . . . who say that the figures over the notes in a thorough-bass are quite useless and unnecessary, display no slight ignorance and folly; for it is clearly impossible for even an adept accompanist, who understands the natural course of harmony and composition, to play everything correctly in accordance with the ideas of another, since the progressions and resolutions may take place in many different ways."[7]

Mattheson expresses even greater contempt for unfigured basses, particularly for the belief of some that accompanists could realize basses even without the aid of a score or solo part.[8] No one, however, opposed unfigured basses so eloquently as C. P. E. Bach; and though no mention is made of Heinichen by name, Bach clearly has the former's instructions[9] in mind when he says:

> We learned in the Introduction to Part II that even when a bass is figured as it should be, a good accompaniment comprises many additional factors. This alone exposes the ridiculousness of the demand that accompaniments be realized from unfigured basses, and makes evident the impossibility of fashioning even a passable accompaniment. . . . Some have gone to great trouble to systematize the realization of unfigured basses, and I cannot deny that I have undertaken similar experiments. But the more I have thought about it, the richer I have found harmonic usages. And these are increasing to such an extent, what with the fineness of our tastes, that it is impossible to formulate hard and fast rules. . . . Even granting that some formulating is possible, are we to rack our memories in learning rules which by their nature must be numerous and not always valid? And having finally learned the given rules, are we then to squander endless time and energy on mastering of exceptions? Even if we did all of this, the results would be of only small value, for the ablest musician can err when presented with only one alternative, let alone several.[10]

Bach's words are weighted with good sense; undeniably the lack of figures diminishes the utility of thorough-basses and makes the art of accompanying less certain. In addition, the whole problem of Baroque performance practice would be immeasurably simpler if composers had only reached Bach's conclusion. Unfortunately for us, they did not. A significant portion of Baroque music lacks figures in the thorough-bass parts; the cantata literature alone teems with examples. Therefore, Heinichen's assistance in this difficult area of performance practice has irreplaceable significance. His general suggestions and rules are not a compilation of sterile theories but rather the sound basis for developing a skill possessed by the best accompanists of his day.

It is self-evident that before a student attempts to realize unfigured basses he must have practiced the figured bass in Heinichen's words, *en perfection*. Also, he requires a thorough acquaintance with the various chords and progressions and needs to have memorized the *ambitus modi* for each scale. After this material is firmly in hand and once the student learns three important methods of deriving figures from unfigured basses (see below), then Heinichen assures us there can be no reason to make such a *Hahnen-Geschrey* about the impossibility of the task.[11]

I. Deriving Figures from a Solo Part Given above the Bass

This technique presents the fewest problems and contains the best approach to the unfigured bass, especially to find dissonances and their appropriate resolutions. If, for example, the accompanist finds a D in the thorough-bass against a C in the solo vocal line, he will recognize immediately the dissonant seventh and add the usual third and fifth to the chord. Heinichen illustrates this important skill with a somewhat extended example;[12] the example and a translation of Heinichen's commentary are given on the following pages.

Example 136. *General-Bass*, 727–30.

No. (1) indicates the major 3d in connection with the triad.
   (2) gives a 6th to which we know belong 3d and 8ve.
   (3) shows the minor 3d in connection with the triad.
   (4) shows a ♭7 to which we know belong 3d, 5th, and 8ve.
   (5) signifies a diminished 5th to which belong the 3d and 6th.
   (6) specifies the 7th to which in this case belong the major 3d with the 5th and 8ve, according to the guidance of the preceding bass note.
   (7) gives the diminished 7th to which we know belong the 3d and diminished 5th.
   (8) since no ordinary resolution of the preceding diminished 7th occurs with this chord, one recalls,[13] therefore, . . . that this is an inversion of the

harmony to which one may play either $\frac{6}{4}_{\flat 3}$ or $\frac{6}{4+}_{2}$. This very chord demonstrates how important it is for an accomplished accompanist to understand what was taught previously about the theatrical inversions of harmony, if he does not wish to grope in the dark and wants to be completely in command of his art.

(9) gives the 6th and (10), the diminished 5th. The remaining parts are well known.

(11) shows the 7th to which in this case belong the major 3d, 5th, and 8ve.

(12) presents the 7 6 to which we know belong the 3d as well as the diminished 5th until the 6th enters. Here, however, one can also consider the two sixteenths in the voice part as a mere variation and, therefore, hold the chord of the 7th for the duration of the entire bass note, looking for the resolution of the 7th first on the following bass note. . . .

(13) shows the major 3d, (14) the 6th, and (15) the common cadence 4 ♯, to which we know belong the 5th and 8ve.

(16) gives the 6th, (17) the major 3d, and (18) the augmented 4th, and to the latter we know belong the 2d and 6th.

(19) and (20) both give the 6th.

(21) gives the diminished 7th. Because, however, the notes in the vocal part repeat the same tone through the next bass note while, on the other hand, the bass represents a simple variation of the first chord $\frac{\flat 7}{F\sharp}$ until (22), therefore, one recognizes here the . . . form of an inverted harmony and retains the first-mentioned full-voiced chord in the right hand until

(23) the former dissonance becomes a 9th, which in this instance may use the major 3d and 5th as well as the 7th for auxiliary parts; and finally on

(24) resolves to the 6th with which the previously held diminished 5th C can also be retained and finally resolved over the next bass note.

(25) and (26) give the major 3d, but (27), the 6th; at

(28) the $\overset{b}{5}$ and 6^+ both are given successively in the vocal part, forming the well-known chord $\overset{6^+}{\underset{}{\overset{}{5}}}$.

(29) gives a 6^+ , together with its natural minor 3d. The immediately following F♯, however, does not fit into this chord [and], therefore, is only an anticipation of the next chord that normally would be omitted from the accompaniment. (NB. Then one would want to anticipate the entire next chord $\overset{a}{\underset{d}{f♯}}$ with the right hand, a form of accompaniment one might note specially since it can be used for many similar anticipations. . . .)

(30) gives the major 3d; the 4th that follows is another anticipation of the next chord and can be omitted from the accompaniment, or the entire chord of the next bass note can be anticipated in the right hand as was discussed previously.

(31) gives the 3d and immediately following the augmented 6th, both of which stand together and can be played simultaneously.

(32) concludes with the familiar cadence $\overset{6}{\underset{4}{}}\,\overset{5}{\underset{♯}{}}$ in which the [solo] part is led through the 6th and 5th to the final note.

An obvious inadequacy of the preceding method is its disregard of dissonances in the harmonic texture when they fall in a part other than between melody and bass. Even more important, however, it fails completely when there is no solo part to draw upon. Heinichen sees no problem in these instances, and his answer to such criticism reaches a rather startling conclusion that can be summarized into three major points:[14]

1. For the accompanist's "daily bread" (cantatas and arias unaccompanied by instruments other than the *continuo parts*), one should not be concerned that the solo part fails to indicate all of the important dissonances; in this music the accompanist has the right to form harmonies freely based on the *ambitus modi* of the scale (see below pp. 227–30).

2. In accompanying from a complete score, the accompanist can always draw assistance from other parts, for when the solo part stops the instrumentalists continue and the harmony is always fully represented. The inexperienced performer, of course, must first learn to grasp the contents of a score at sight, in order to recognize modulations and important dissonances.

3. The greatest problems for an accompanist arise when the thorough-bass includes only the solo part, even though the piece includes a substantial orchestral accompaniment. In these circumstances the accompanist seems to have no means for determining the harmonies of the composition during short pauses in the vocal line and particularly in a ritornello. Nevertheless, Heinichen believes confidently that since the vocal line carries most of the musical substance and is the source of the ideas (*die Vocal-Stimme gleichwohl das meiste, und die Force eines solchen musicalischen Stückes ausmachet*), the accompanist, therefore, should have

no difficulty selecting appropriate consonances and dissonances for those sections in which the solo part is silent. If, however, he should permit a dissonance to escape his attention now and then, this is not serious, since

> the accompanist need not always express fully on the keyboard all the dissonances found in the remaining parts. If this sounds strange to someone, then I ask each educated musician if he would not agree with me that even the most perfect composer and thorough-bass player cannot hear all the dissonances and other *minutiae* found in the inner parts or, in concert music, other [instrumental] parts far removed from him. However, this makes little difference as long as he does not play conflicting chords that cannot stand together with the chords of the work in question.[15]

This remarkable statement stresses the indispensable ingredient of improvisation in accompanying as well as underscores the exceedingly free outlook of keyboard performers who felt no responsibility for matching each note in the over-all harmonic texture. For

> an accompanist would need to have a Siberian ear not to be able to perceive the full concentration [of sound] of a $\frac{6}{4}$ chord formed in the instrumental parts, even though his unfigured bass offers him no opportunity for [this chord]. In the same way, an augmented fifth and augmented sixth, a diminished seventh, or similar sharp dissonances will be easily heard no matter where they are hidden. Never mind if now and then a seventh or ninth is not observed because it does not occur in a solo part. It does not matter if in place of these one takes a simple triad, because this [chord] as well as the seventh and ninth have the third and fifth for auxiliary parts; thus one does not form [incorrect] dissonances with the remaining musicians. Likewise, nothing is lost in the expression of the diminished fifth if the sixth appearing over such bass notes is not omitted, for the third, sixth, and octave belong as much to the diminished fifth as to the sixth alone. . . . Nevertheless, it is true that one must not make an asylum of ignorance from such liberties. For the more fully and accurately the accompanist expresses the consonances and dissonances of the harmony down to the smallest detail, the more his dexterity is praised, even where [this attention to detail] is not required.[16]

II. Deriving Figures from Some Easy General Rules or from Notable Intervals of the Scale

The conventional means for teaching accompanists to play from unfigured basses consisted of a long list of typical bass progressions and their harmonies. To memorize the prodigious number of bass formulas would tax the most retentive minds. Heinichen, however, is more practical: he retains only eight of these rules and restricts his choice to those pertaining to triads and chords of the sixth.[17]

General Rule 1

When the bass of a triad descends a semitone, ascends a third (or descends a sixth), the next bass note has a sixth.

Example 137. *General-Bass*, 734.

General Rule 2

When the bass of a major triad ascends a semitone, descends a major third (or ascends a minor sixth), the next bass note has a sixth. If the major triad descends a whole tone, the next bass has the $\begin{smallmatrix}6\\4+\\2\end{smallmatrix}$ chord.

Example 138. *General-Bass*, 734.

General Rule 3

When the bass of a minor triad descends either a whole tone or a major third (ascends a minor sixth) the next bass note has a sixth.

Example 139. *General-Bass*, 735.

General Rule 4

When the bass of a minor sixth chord (usually including a minor third) ascends a semitone, descends a major third (or ascends a minor sixth), the next bass note has a triad. If this sixth chord ascends a whole tone then the next bass has a sixth.

Example 140. *General-Bass*, 735.

General Rule 5

When the bass of a major sixth chord (usually including a major third) ascends or descends a whole tone, then the next bass note has a sixth. If this chord descends a minor third (ascends a major sixth) the next bass has a triad.

Example 141. *General-Bass*, 735.

General Rule 6

When the bass of a major sixth chord, including a minor third, descends a whole tone, then the next bass note has the triad as its natural harmony. If it descends a minor third or ascends a semitone, a whole tone, or a minor third, then in all four cases the next bass has a sixth.

Example 142. *General-Bass*, 736.

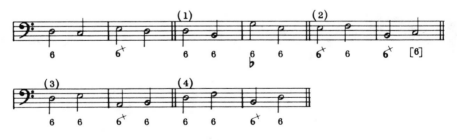

General Rule 7

If two bass notes ascend or descend a third and one includes an accidental before the note, then the accidental is usually retained for the preceding or following chord.

Example 143. *General-Bass, 737.*

General Rule 8

A bass note chromatically raised by a sharp or natural sign foreign to the key has a sixth chord, whether it moves by step or leap.

Example 144. *General-Bass, 738.*

III. Deriving Figures by Special Rules, or from the Natural Structure (*Ambitus*) of the Scale

In Heinichen's opinion,[18] the major source from which to draw thorough-bass figures was the *Schemata modorum*, giving the natural harmony for each of the seven tones in the major and minor scales. The fundamental chord for each scale degree is determined by six natural laws of tonal harmony that Heinichen lists as Special Rules:

Special Rule 1

The fifth degree of major and minor scales has a major third over it, whether or not this third appears major in the key signature. (Reason: The leading tone of major and minor scales must be a semitone below the first scale degree.)

Special Rule 2

The fourth degree of minor scales has as its natural harmony a minor third over it. (Reason: The sixth degree in minor scales must be minor.) The triad is the most natural chord on the fourth degree in both major and minor, while the sixth or $\frac{6}{5}$ chords are exceptions. In one instance, when the bass moves as a passing tone from the fifth degree to the third, the $\frac{6}{4+}{2}$ chord is natural to the fourth degree (see final two sections of ex. 145).

Example 145. *General-Bass*, 740–41.

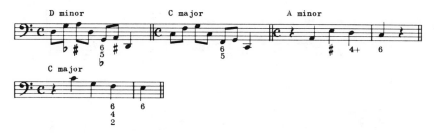

Special Rule 3

The leading tone of major and minor scales uses a sixth chord. (Reason: The scale structure does not include a perfect fifth over the leading tone.)

Special Rule 4

The third degree of major and minor scales uses a sixth chord. (Reason: The third and fourth degrees in major are only a semitone apart, and one does not usually place triads on adjacent semitones. The third in minor requires a sixth chord because no perfect fifth exists in the scale structure.)

Special Rule 5

The second degree of minor scales uses a sixth chord. (Reason: Because no perfect fifth exists above the second degree in the minor scale.) In major scales one may employ either a triad or sixth chord on the second degree. It is natural to use a sixth when the bass moves to the third degree (see ex. 146, nos. 1 and 2); if the bass leaps from the second degree then the triad is preferable (see ex. 146, nos. 3 and 4):

Example 146. *General-Bass*, 743.

Special Rule 6

The sixth degree of minor scales uses as its natural harmony a sixth chord. (Reason: Because the fifth degree is only a semitone apart and requires the triad.) In major, however, one may use either a triad or sixth chord. The sixth is more natural when one leaps to or from the fourth degree (see last section of ex. 147); otherwise, the triad is the more natural accompaniment:

Example 147. *General-Bass*, 744.

Keeping these six rules in mind, the following *Schemata modorum* for A minor and C major require no additional explanation. For the former, Heinichen gives both ascending and descending forms of the scale; the double figures over the second and sixth degrees in major suggest alternate chords for these bass notes and do not mean that the triad and sixth chord are played successively.

Example 148. *General-Bass*, 745.

Heinichen[19] also lists the remaining twenty-two scales with their *schemata* even though the figures are identical with those in example 148.

An accompanist will gain almost no help from these *schemata*, however, if he does not recognize modulations as soon as they occur in a composition. To aid in detecting them, Heinichen offers another rule:

Special Rule 7

When a bass note is raised chromatically by a sharp or natural sign, the composition modulates to the key beginning a half tone above the chromatically altered note. If, however, the altered bass note is accompanied by a chromatically altered major third or sixth in an upper part, then the piece modulates to the key beginning a half tone above either the third or the sixth.

In concluding his chapter on the unfigured bass, Heinichen presents a comprehensive example[20] combining the various special rules. The music is given here with a translation of his detailed analysis.

Example 149. *General-Bass*, 755–60.

This example begins in B♭ major. Now as long as the *ambitus modi* remains in this key, figures of the *schema* for B♭ major apply. Therefore, the bass note

(1) normally has the 6th above it, because it is the third degree of the scale. Special Rule 4.

(2) normally has the triad above it, because it is the second degree in major standing within a progression by leap. Special Rule 5.

(3) has the 6th, because it is the leading tone. Special Rule 3.

Note (4) in the upper part introduces a foreign sharp indicating the scale has changed to another a half tone higher, i.e., G minor; therefore, one now applies the figures from the *schema* of G minor, and on the following

(4) the bass note will be considered the second degree, requiring the major 6th given in the upper part. Special Rule 5.

(5) and (6) have a major 3d above, because they are the fifth degree of a minor scale.

(7) has a major 6th above it, because it is the second degree of minor. Special Rule 5.

(8) has the 6th, because it is the third degree of the scale. Special Rule 4.

(9) has the major 3d, because again it is the fifth degree of the scale. Special Rule 1.

(10) has the 6th, because it is the leading tone. Special Rule 3.

The chromatically lowered note (11) indicates that the previous leading tone has been relinquished and that in its place there is a new leading tone at (12); i.e., the chromatically raised bass shows the scale is changed to another a half step above this bass, which is F major. Therefore one begins now to use the *schema* of F major, which requires that the following notes

(13) and (15) have a 6th above, because they are the third degree. Special Rule 4.

(14) and (16) have the major 3d above, because they are the fifth degree. Special Rule 1.

(17) as the second degree in major would normally have the major 6th over it, even if it were not already given in the upper part. Special Rule 5.

Note (18) indicates a new leading tone in the upper part that alters the scale to D minor. We apply, therefore, the figures belonging to the *schema* of D minor, which requires the following notes

(19) and (20) have a 6th, because they are the third degree of the scale. Special Rule 4.

(21) has the major 6th above it, because it is the second degree in minor. Special Rule 5.

(22) and (24) have the major 3d, because they are the fifth degree of the scale. Special Rule 1.

(23) has the 6th, because it is the leading tone. Special Rule 3. At the sign (*) we should remember in passing that this same bass note must normally have the minor 3d, even if it does not occur in the key signature, because it is the fourth degree of D minor. Special Rule 2.

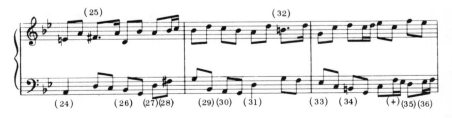

(37)(38)(39)   (40)

Note (25) in the upper part again indicates a new leading tone that changes the scale to the one a half tone higher, which in this case is G minor again. If we apply the figures of this *schema*, then

(25) this bass note is considered the fifth degree of the scale and together with (27) and (31) has the major 3d above it. Special Rule 1.
(26) and (29) have a 6th above, because they are the third degree of the scale. Special Rule 4.
(28) has the 6th, because it is the leading tone. (30), however, has the major 6th, because it is the second degree in minor, according to the frequently cited rule.

Note (32) in the upper part shows a new leading tone, i.e., a chromatically raised [B natural] that alters the scale to C minor. Therefore, we apply the natural figures from the *schema* of C minor according to which bass note

(32) is considered the fifth degree and, therefore, has [together] with (37) and (40) the major 3d above. Special Rule 1.
(33) and (36) have a 6th above, because they are the third degree. Special Rule 4.
(34) has the 6th above it, because it is the leading tone.
(+) naturally has the minor 3d above it, because it is the fourth degree in minor. Special Rule 2.
(35) has a major 6th above it, because it is the second degree in minor. Special Rule 5.
(38) has the unusual dissonance of a diminished 7th above it, which one . . . would never find except through [the indication of] the upper part. The sharp before this bass note seems to alter the scale to G minor, but the leading tone of C minor in voice part over (39) contradicts the former [key] and shows that the previous $^{7}_{F\sharp}$ should have been viewed only as a bizarre chord, of which the sharp was to be abandoned immediately afterwards.

Note (40) indicates by means of the chromatically raising natural sign that the minor sixth of the previous C minor scale no longer is valid and, therefore, the scale is altered by this natural sign to B♭ major. Consequently, we again apply the *schema* of B♭ major, upon the strength of which

(41)   (42)   (43)(44)   (+ +)   (45)(46)   (47)

(40) and also (42) have the 6th above, because they are the leading tone.
(41) has the 6th, because it is the third of the scale, according to the frequently
     cited rule.

Note (43) shows another foreign natural sign that should alter the scale to
another a half tone higher, i.e., C minor. However, the new natural sign appearing immediately afterwards in the upper part at (44) contradicts this [key] and
indicates that the scale changes to F major. Thus this very note

(43) is treated simply as a bizarre chord, of which the natural sign does not
     continue [in effect]. The diminished 5th in the voice part (which one can
     never find except from the given part) is played together with its well-known
     harmony.
(44) and (+ +) have the major 3d above, because they are the fifth degree.

Note (45) lowers the previous leading tone, and since no new leading tone
follows in the notes [of the bass or voice part], we are back again to the key of the
signature, i.e., Bb major. According to this

(46) has the 6th above it, because it is the third degree.
(47) again has the 6th, because it is the leading tone.

(48)   (49)

(48) naturally has the triad above it, because it is the sixth degree, which here
     does not leap from the fourth degree of the scale. Special Rule 6.
(49) similarly has the triad, because it is the second degree in major standing in
     the midst of a progression by leap. Special Rule 5.

Since it is important for the accompanist to find modulations quickly, he will be aided in this skill if he knows the regular modulations to be expected for each key. As Heinichen explains, if the performer realizes beforehand that the key of G major generally modulates to D major, B minor, or E minor, he can look for these tonalities during the course of the music. He suggests, therefore, one more special rule:

Special Rule 8

All major scales usually modulate to the third, fifth, and sixth degrees, exceptionally to the second and fourth. Minor scales, however, modulate usually to the third, fifth, and seventh degrees, exceptionally to the fourth and sixth.[21]

Several additional observations regarding refinements in accompanying unfigured basses will be examined in the course of the example in chapter 9. First, however, we must consider some special problems encountered in the accompaniment of recitatives.

Notes

1. Agostino Agazzari, *Del sonare sopra'l basso con tutti li strumenti* (Siena, 1607); facs. ed. *Bollettino bibliografico musicale* (Milan, 1933). Praetorius, *Syntagma* III, 147.

2. Reprinted in Robert Haas, "Das Generalbassflugblatt Francesco Bianciardis," *Festschrift für Johannes Wolf* . . . (Berlin, 1929), 48–56.

3. Penna, *Li prima albori*, chaps. 2–5; Galeazzo Sabbatini, *Regola facile e breve per sonare sopra il basso continuo* (Venice, 1628), chaps. 6–13.

4. Delair, *Traité*, 32–43 and Saint-Lambert, *Nouveau traité*, 90–117; both devote considerable space to unfigured basses.

5. In the foreword to *Symphoniae sacrae* III (1650) Heinrich Schütz states: "Die Italianer/zum guten Theil/pflegen heutiges Tages keine *Numern* sich dabey zu gebrauchen. . . ."

6. Gasparini, *L'armonico pratico*, chaps. 4–5.

7. Werckmeister, *Harmonologica musica*, 65.

8. Mattheson, *Kleine General-Bass-Schule*, 42. This opinion, however, contradicts an earlier viewpoint given in his *Neu-eröffnete Orchestre* (Hamburg, 1713), 72: "Ein wohlerfahrner Musicus tractiret auch wol einen solchen General-Bass . . . ohne überstehenden Ziffern."

9. Heinichen, *General-Bass*, 725–68.

10. Bach-Mitchell, *Versuch*, 410–11.

11. Heinichen, *General-Bass*, 725–26.

12. Ibid., 727–30.

13. See Appendix C, 000.

14. Heinichen, *General-Bass*, 730–32.

15. Ibid., 731–732.

16. Ibid., 732–33.

17. Ibid., 734–38.

18. Ibid., 738.

19. Ibid., 746–50.

20. Ibid., 755–60.

21. Ibid., 761. The second half of this rule reads in the original: "alle *modi minores* weichen aus, ordentlich: in die 3e and 5te, ausserordentlich: in die 4te, 6te *min.* and 7me." This does not agree with Heinichen's table of modulations in minor scales nor with general practice, since the minor seventh degree (the dominant of the relative major) is not an exceptional modulation. We have, therefore, revised the original in presenting Heinichen's rule.

8

Accompanying the Recitative

To accompany recitatives the student of the thorough-bass cannot rely on Heinichen's general and special rules for unfigured basses examined in the preceding chapter, because they require the presence of clearly defined tonalities, an element conspicuously absent in most Baroque recitatives. Italian secular recitatives in particular explore uncharted areas of harmony; frequent modulations that result from the expression of specific affections of the words cause the music to shift back and forth between remote tonal centers. To further complicate the accompanist's role, he is often cast adrift without even a key signature to guide his thorough-bass realizations.

The best source of information for determining the harmonies of a recitative accompaniment is the solo part. Frequently the composer writes out the complete harmony of a measure in the solo part, broken up into a melismatic figuration. For example:

Example 150. *General-Bass*, 770–71.

The solo part in this example gives us the following harmonies: a $\overset{6+}{5\flat}$ chord on (1); a $\overset{6}{4+}_{\natural3}$ chord on (2); first a triad and then a $\overset{+7}{4}_{2}$ chord on (3); a triad on (4); a complete diminished seventh chord on (5); an inversion of the preceding harmony showing all the notes of the $\overset{6}{4+}_{2}$ chord on (6); a diminished seventh chord with diminished fifth and minor third on (7); a "very foreign chord" with third and sixth on (8); and finally a triad on (9).

This means of discovering the proper figures for a recitative thorough-bass is delightfully uncomplicated; the problem, however, grows considerably more difficult when the solo part fails to give more than one or two tones of an appropriate chord. Heinichen suggests three avenues by which the accompanist can arrive at the remaining chord tones:

I. From the Rules for Inverted Harmonies

Dissonances may occur in one part and be resolved in a different part.[1] Consequently, when the solo part contains a dissonance that lacks a resolution, the accompanist is obligated to make the proper resolution in his realization. He must exercise care that the resolution occurs before a new harmony arises in which the resolving tone is unsuitable. For example:

Example 151. *General-Bass*, 772.

In the first section of example 151 no resolution occurs in the solo part for the seventh (the second note, E). the accompanist must play a 7 6 progression on successive beats over the F, since the seventh cannot resolve on the next bass note. Similarly, in the second section the sixth (B) must be played in the accompaniment in the second half of the measure to resolve the seventh in the vocal part. In the third part of the example the accompanist plays a sixth (A) with the C as the resolution for the seventh in the solo part over the preceding bass note C♯.

When inverting chords with diminished fifths, tritones, minor or diminished sevenths new forms of these dissonances result;[2] the accompanist should play them even though they are omitted from the vocal part:

Example 152. *General-Bass*, 773.

The C over the bass note E♭ in the first section of example 152 might mislead the accompanist into adding only the G of a sixth chord. Actually this E♭ bass is part of the inverted harmony for the previous 5♭̸ chord; therefore, the correct harmony should be a $\overset{6}{\underset{2}{4+}}$ chord. In each of the following sections of this example a sixth occurs with the bass of the inverted harmony (i.e., the G♯, E, and F♯), but the accompanist should also include the diminished fifth belonging to the original chord. In these instances, however, the omission of a diminished fifth is less serious, since in these cases the sixth chord is part of the original dissonant chord.

Another type of inversion substitutes a sixth chord for a triad in the resolution of a diminished fifth and minor or diminished seventh. The accompanist must not omit this sixth even though it does not appear in the solo part.

Example 153. *General-Bass*, 774.

In all three sections of this example the accompanist would err if he played a fifth on the second bass note rather than the sixth.

II. The Different Resolutions and Different Uses of Three Related Chords

Three closely related harmonies ($\overset{+7}{\underset{2}{4}}$, $\overset{6}{4}$, $\overset{6}{\underset{2}{4}}$) pose difficulties for the accompanist who is unable to distinguish between them from only the bass and solo parts. Therefore, he must rely on certain characteristics of each chord to aid him in this choice.

First, one can decide between a $\overset{+7}{\underset{2}{4}}$ and a $\overset{6}{\underset{2}{4}}$ from their resolutions. The former retains the same bass note in resolving, while the latter resolves one degree lower:

Example 154. *General-Bass*, 755.

In contrast, however, a $\overset{+7}{4}_{2}$ and a $^6_4$ both resolve over the same bass note. There is doubt in choosing between these chords only when the upper part gives only the fourth: "One uses the $\overset{+7}{4}_{2}$ in the recitative, while in contrast the $^6_4$ is used in the *arioso* style, when the voice part gives the fourth only (without the indication of a 7, 2, 6, or 8, which clearly distinguishes between the two)."[3]

Heinichen examines the three chords separately and suggests the following principles to help the accompanist determine which chord is appropriate to a given musical context:

1. Following a triad on the same bass, a $\overset{+7}{4}_{2}$ chord is indicated if the solo part has only a seventh or joins the latter with the second or fourth and subsequently returns to the previous triad.

Example 155. *General-Bass*, 776–77.

2. A $\overset{+7}{4}\underset{2}{}$ is suitable when the solo part over a sustained bass has only the fourth, second, or $\frac{4}{2}$ alone and then returns to the triad again.

Example 156. *General-Bass*, 777.

3a. The $\frac{6}{4}$ is used with its octave if over a sustained bass the solo part proceeds from a triad to a sixth or a $\frac{6}{4}$ and then moves on to $\overset{+7}{4}\underset{2}{}$.

Example 157. *General-Bass*, 778.

3b. A $\frac{6}{4}$ is also used when the solo part progresses from a triad through $\frac{6}{4}$ and back again to a triad.

Example 158. *General-Bass*, 779.

This particular use of a $\frac{6}{4}$ chord is the one mentioned earlier as suited to the *arioso* style (in distinction to the $\overset{+7}{4}\overset{}{2}$ used in the recitative for the same musical context). To make this ambiguous case somewhat clearer Heinichen adds the following comments: "Actually this type [ex. 159] is seldom used in the recitative. On the other hand, vocal parts in the *arioso* style [written] over a constant repetition of the same bass note frequently proceed from a triad or minor seventh chord to the sixth or fourth alone or to the $\frac{4}{8}$ and then return again to the former chord. In each of these cases the $\overset{6}{\underset{8}{4}}$, and not the $\frac{6}{3}$ or $\overset{+7}{4}\overset{}{2}$, must be played as the natural chord, which should be carefully noted, because many accompanists make various errors in this regard. For example":[4]

Example 159.

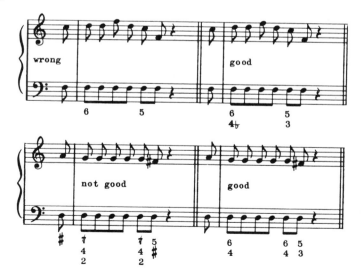

Still dissatisfied with his explanation for this $^6_4$ chord, Heinichen adds to the Supplement of his treatise the following observation, which expands on the phrase "seldom used in recitative": "I would almost say NEVER (for my taste) if the $^{+7}_4$ did not follow the $^6_4$, as occurred . . . in the previous example [ex. 157]. And though the second example on p. 779 [i.e., the second half to ex. 158] is used frequently in recitatives, I would prefer to play the $^7_{4\flat}$ instead of the $^6_{4\flat}$ and to consider the apparently contradictory D in the voice part as a mere melodic turn, which does not determine its own harmony in the recitative."[5]

4a. A $^6_4$ chord is played when the solo part proceeds from either a triad or dissonant chord to the second or fourth alone or to a $^4_2$, and the bass resolves down a step:

Example 160. *General-Bass*, 781.

4b. A $\overset{6}{\underset{2}{4}}$ chord is also played when the solo part begins as in 4a, proceeds to a $\overset{6}{4}$, and the bass again descends by step:

Example 161. *General-Bass*, 782.

5. Finally concerning the $\overset{6}{\underset{2}{4}}$ chord, it is always the correct choice when the solo part has a tritone, augmented second, or a $\overset{6}{2}$, whether or not the other intervals are also given. It is preferable to accompany an augmented second with an augmented fourth, not a perfect fourth.

Example 162. *General-Bass*, 782–83.

One exception concerns the augmented fourth: When the bass of a $\overset{6}{\underset{2}{4+}}$ chord resolves down a semitone and the augmented fourth is retained as the fifth or ascends to the octave, then this fourth prefers the augmented second as accompaniment, and the resolving chord requires a major third:

Example 163. *General-Bass*, 784.

III. From the Notes of the Octave for Each Scale (*Specie octavae*)

The last of the three methods amounts to little more than the memorizing of twenty-four major and minor scales, knowledge that can help the accompanist determine sizes of intervals over an unfigured bass. Heinichen speaks extensively about the *Specie octavae* (the notes within the octave of each scale), and he prints each of the scales to assist the accompanist in learning them.[6] Though such an expansive treatment was necessary at a time when the well-tempered system of tuning had only recently made all the scales practical on keyboard instruments, there is no need to repeat this elementary material here. Instead we choose one example from several in order to illustrate how Heinichen applies the *Specie octavae* to the unfigured bass.

Example 164. *General-Bass*, 791.

At (1) the diminished fifth should be accompanied by a minor third and sixth. The resolution of this bass note indicates that the *Species octavae* of A♭ is required to determine the correct notes of the third and sixth, that is, the third on B♭ and the sixth on E♭. Without consulting the notes of the scale the third and sixth arrived at by counting lines and spaces of the staff would be the incorrect B♮ and E♮. At (2) the same scale remains in effect, giving E♭ as the fifth for the triad. The minor sixth at (3) requires the E♭ as the minor third. At (4) the vocal part and bass form a diminished fifth, and the latter resolves to G♭. The correct accompaniment for this diminished fifth is found in the notes of the octave for G♭ major, that is, A♭ and D♭. At (5) the same scale is used to locate the fifth of the chord. At (6) the vocal part in the second half of this measure forms a tritone; the correct accompaniment found in the scale of G♭ would be A♭ as the second and E♭ as the sixth. At (7) the vocal part forms a major 6th requiring a minor third in the accompaniment to agree with the scale of G♭. On the second half of this measure the vocal part forms a tritone, and a chromatic alteration (which

Heinichen calls a "metamorphosis") changes the scale from G♭ to the natural scale of A minor.

Notes

1. According to Heinichen's invaluable account of dissonance in the operatic style; see Appendix C, 000.

2. Ibid., 237–242.

3. Heinichen, *General-Bass*, 776.

4. Ibid., 779 (footnote c).

5. Ibid., 957.

6. Ibid., 785–87.

9

A Practical Demonstration

In concluding his study of unfigured basses, Heinichen demonstrates how one might add figures to Alessandro Scarlatti's solo cantata *Lascia deh lascia al fine di tormentarmi più.*[1] Heinichen considers this type of music the accompanist's "daily bread," and his meticulous analysis of its problems proves the utility of his principles for realizing unfigured thorough-basses. This lengthy example also accentuates the value of his procedures in accompanying compositions based on the theatrical style, embodying the bold chromaticism and frequently shifting tonalities displayed in Scarlatti's cantatas. In the course of Heinichen's explanation he proposes a number of important "practical observations"; and his entire presentation forms a uniquely complete lesson in thorough-bass accompanying that has no equal in any other Baroque source.

For these reasons, the Scarlatti-Heinichen example, together with a translation of Heinichen's commentary, affords an appropriate conclusion to this study of the art of accompanying, especially as this art is applied to music written in the operatic style.

Example 165. *General-Bass,* 798–836.

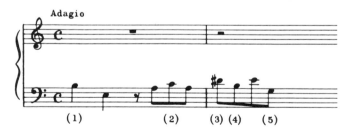

With the first bass note of this cantata it would appear as if we had the key of B minor before us, but the first cadence shows that here we have the incorrectly indicated scale of E minor without a F♯; and from this immediately arises *Observa-*

tio practica 1. That one must never judge the key of an unaccompanied aria [i.e., unaccompanied by instrumental ensemble] from the first bass note but rather from the first cadence of the ritornello. Reason: The ritornello of the bass usually gives in advance the initial modulation of the voice part. Since the latter need not always begin on the first note of the scale and frequently starts on the third or fifth degree as well, thus the same thing must occur in the first ritornello. Accordingly, at the beginning of our cantata the bass notes

(1) and (4) have a major 3d above, because they are the fifth degree of the scale and according to the familiar Special Rule 2. . . . However, one finds the correct form of the 5th for both bass notes not in the key signature but in the *Specie 8vae* for E minor, where the F♯ appears on the fifth degree above the bass note.

(2) has a 6th above it, because it is the sixth degree in minor. Special Rule 6.

(3) also has a 6th, because it is the leading tone. Special Rule 4.

(5) again has a 6th, because it is the third degree. Special Rule 3.

(6) could have a major 6th above it, because it is the second degree (according to Special Rule 5); here, however, we make the following

Observat. pract. 2. That whenever the second degree in minor immediately precedes a cadence, it is more beautiful to retain the prepared seventh over it. Reason: Because in this way the following cadence will be better prepared. One can bring this cadence to a conclusion on the two bass notes

(7) with $\frac{5}{4\sharp}$, or with $\frac{6}{4}\frac{5}{\sharp}$, or also with the simple major 3d, which have considerable value in pieces without instrumental [accompaniment]. In general, one can take particular note of the *clausul* [formed by] the last four notes A F♯ B B, because it occurs daily in all scales.

(8) has a 6th above it, because it is the sixth degree in minor.

(NB. For the sake of brevity, we shall omit such simple figures as 2, ♯, ♭, 4, $\overset{+}{5}$, 6, 7, etc., which are expressly given by the voice part and whose accompanying parts are correct according to the key signature, because they are particularly well known from the preceding chapters. We shall, however, mark each one of them with a (+) as an indication to the accompanist that for such bass notes he need only observe the voice part.)

(9) actually indicates the familiar $^{6}_{4+}_{2}$ chord, but one must again seek the correct 6th in the *Speciae 8vae* for E minor, where one finds F♯ rather than the F that appears on the sixth step above the bass according to the incorrect key signature. On bass note

(10) the voice part gives a 4th. Again one finds the correct 5th only in the preceding *Specie 8vae*. For bass note

(11) one finds only a diminished 3d in the key signature [i.e., $^{G}_{E♯}$] for the $^{7}_{5}$ chord given in the voice part. For this incomplete 3d either we can add an accidental . . . and without further hesitation form the correct G♯, or we can regard the ♯ before note (11) as the leading tone in F♯ minor and can look for the correct third in its *Specie 8vae*; here again we find the G♯. This double method of seeking the correct third for this case, frequently occurring in our cantata, is repeated here for the first and last time.

(12) For this chord indicated by the voice part one knows how to find the correct 2d in the *Specie 8vae* for B minor as well as the progression for the leading tone A♯ found in the voice part.

(13) has a 6th, because it is the natural resolution of the augmented 4th or $^{6}_{4+}_{2}$ chord (as long as the voice part does not expressly give the opposite . . .).

(14) and (16) do not have the correct 3d in the key signature; therefore, one must seek it in the previously discussed method.

(15) has the 6th, because it is the natural resolution of the augmented 4th.

(17) has a major 3d above it. It is the fifth degree of the scale, because the voice part modulates to A minor, which is indicated not only by the preceding and succeeding G♯ but also by the immediately following sixth degree in the bass, i.e., F. The D♯, however, coming between (14) and (16) is treated only as a bizarre chord whose accidental does not continue in effect. . . .

(18) has a 6th above it, because it is the sixth degree in minor. Special Rule 6. On bass note

(19) the voice part forms a diminished 5th to which we know a 3d and 6th belong. One finds them both correctly not in the key signature but in the *Specie 8vae* for B minor, whose leading tone is given by the bass. For on the third step above the bass one finds the correct 3d C♯ and on the sixth step the correct 6th F♯. If one plays the 7th in place of the 6th the effect will be richer harmonically.

(20) has the usual recitative cadence for which one easily finds the correct 5th from the *Specie 8vae* for E minor.

(21) has a major 3d and (22) a 6th above, because the former is the fifth degree and the latter, the third degree of the scale. The next two bars of this *arioso* repeat literally the first ritornello and, therefore, the same figures are also repeated. The recitative begins a new section in C major, and thus the following bass note

(23) normally has the 6th above it, because it is the leading tone.

(24) as the sixth degree in major can readily carry the 5th above it (Special Rule 6); an experienced accompanist, however, would prefer to give this note a major 6th, since the two bass notes C and B have preceded: according to

Observat. pract. 3. In a major scale, if a bass descends stepwise a fourth, the second bass note normally has the [minor] 6th and the third [note] the major 6th: C $^{6}_{B}$ $^{6+}_{A}$ G. Reason: This progression forms a half cadence with the fifth degree of the scale and requires the major 6th as leading tone over the third note. Even though the half cadence in our example is broken off after the $^{6+}_{A}$ and in place of the final G an unrelated $^{\flat 7}_{F\sharp}$ chord is taken, this [latter chord] is only an inversion of the preceding $^{6+}_{A}$ whose resolution to G follows. Besides, the progression of the first three bass notes would be sufficient to give the last [bass note] a major 6th, as long as the voice part does not contradict it.

(25) has an E♭ as its 3d, not the E found in the key signature, because the minor 6th always has the minor 3d in its natural harmony. We must, however, resolve an uncertainty here, the answer to which can be applied to many similar cases. Namely: the question arises in which *Specie 8vae* would the inexperienced [accompanist] find the natural third E♭ for note (25) if he did not know how to derive it from the minor 6th in the method described above? Actually in this case the scale seems to be so obscure that one really cannot name or distinguish it. This bass note with its minor 6th cannot belong to G minor, because the *Specie 8vae* of G minor does not include A♭ but A. Also one cannot consider it part of C minor, because otherwise the leading tone B instead of B♭ would follow [on the next bass]. It cannot belong to A♭ major, because the *Specie 8vae* for this scale does not contain a D. On the other hand, this D appears over the B♭, and from this it becomes clear that in this case the $\frac{6♭}{C}$ chord cannot be reduced to any scale. Consequently, one asks with justification in which *Specie 8vae* can one seek the correct 3d? As an answer serves:

Observat. pract. 4. That in such closely related and comparable scales it does not matter which *Specie 8vae* one uses to find the correct figures, [for] they will always be the same. Reason: Because otherwise the distinctions between such doubtful scales would necessarily be seen more clearly from both parts.

Accordingly, one can look for the natural 3d to bass note (25) in the *Specie 8vae* for C minor, A♭ major, or G minor, and in each case one will find the required natural 3d E♭.

(26) can be made more beautiful by retaining the preceding 7th with the triad. [For]

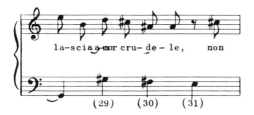

(27) one knows how to play the natural 5th F♯, which on

(28) forms the natural 6th in the $^{4+}_{2}$ chord.

(29) can actually retain the preceding minor 6th E together with its diminished 5th. But in this case the major 6th would be more effective harmonically, since both parts appear to form a half cadence in F♯ major, and the major 6th is the leading tone of this scale. [For]

(30) one knows how to find the natural 5th without looking for it in the *Specia 8vae* of the previously mentioned scale.

(31) again relinquishes the leading tone of this scale. Here one could play the major 3d with the major 6th found in the voice part, i.e., the G♯ belonging to the previous scale; however, at this point we formulate

Observat. pract. 5. That if the bass of a $^{5}_{\sharp}$ chord descends two whole tones (in this case F♯, E, D), then the middle bass note has a $^{6}_{\substack{4+ \\ 2}}$ chord for greater harmonic effectiveness. Should we wish to play this chord to note (31) we can find the correct figures (according to the example of the 4th *Observat. pract.*) in the *Specie 8vae* for the preceding scale of F♯ major or the succeeding scale of B minor; in both we will find F♯ as the correct 2d, A♯ as the correct augmented 4th, and C♯ as the correct 6th.

(32) has a 6th, not only as the natural resolution of the augmented 4th but also because it is the third degree of B minor, whose leading tone is given in the previous chord. [For]

(33) one knows how to find the correct 3d F♯, and on

(34) the usual recitative cadence follows.

Now we come to the first aria of this cantata, which also begins on the fifth degree of the scale as is apparent from the first cadence of the ritornello. Therefore, bass notes

(1) and (2) have a major 3d above, because they give this very fifth degree [and] according to Special Rule 1.

(3) (3) and (7) have a 6th above, because they are the third degree. The several bass notes

(3) (4) (4) (4) (4)

(4) all have a major 6th above, because they are the second degree in minor. Special Rule 5. One could be satisfied with this natural accompaniment for the first two measures. If, however, one wishes to make them more elegant and richer in harmony, then [to this end] serves

Observat. pract. 6. That if in a slow tempo an inherently long note repeats the previous tone and descends a step, then for greater beauty one forms a suspension with the repeated bass note using either a $\frac{6}{4}$ or $\frac{7}{4}$ chord. The first two bars just cited, therefore, would be accompanied in a grander style as:

One takes the final $\frac{7}{4}$ chord in place of the $\frac{6}{4}$ only if the major 6th has preceded and the *ambitus modi* would give rise to $\frac{6^+}{4}$, in which a harsh dissonance results between the major 6th and minor 2d. To avoid this one uses a $\frac{7}{4}$ chord. . . . We continue with our aria and note that both bass notes

Ti bas-ti   ti bas-ti a-mor cru-de – le cru-

(5)   (6)   (7)   (8)   (9)   (10)   (†)

(5)   and (6) must be satisfied with the usual sixth chord including a minor 3d. Yet, here again an experienced accompanist would proceed more artistically if he gave bass note (5) the previously prepared $\frac{7}{5}$ and bass note (6) the $\frac{6}{4+}$ chord in the form of an anticipated passing note . . . in which the rapidly approaching *ambitus modi* of the cadence would be more clearly expressed.

(8)   has the usual cadence: 4 ♯ or $\frac{6}{4}\frac{5}{♯}$.

(9)   has a major 3d above it, because it is the fifth degree.

(10) according to one's choice can have either the 6th or the 5th because it is the sixth degree in minor standing within a progression by leap. Special Rule 6.

de   -   le più non mi   tor-men - tar ch'io vuò   mo - ri -

(†) (11)   (†) (†) (12)   (13)(14)(†)(15)(†)   (16)

(11) does not have a perfect 5th in the *ambitus modi*. It seems doubtful, however, that one should use the minor 6th G from the previously established C major scale or the major 6th G♯ of the immediately following A minor scale. If one examines both the modulation to A minor in the bass ($_{A F B}^{\quad 7}$) as well as the G♯ in the voice part immediately following the bass note B, then no doubt remains that we are concerned here with A minor. Thus, bass note (11) has a major 6th, because it is the second in minor. Special Rule 5. It would be more effective, however, if we used a $\frac{7}{5}$ over note (11) and the next bass, and resolved it first on the third bass [third B] to the major 6th.

(12) retains a major 3d with the 7th, because it is the fifth degree and also because the leading tone C♯ on the preceding bass note indicates the scale of D minor. According to this

(13) also has a major 6th, because it is the second degree in minor, if one does not choose to use this bass as a passing tone with the well-known $\frac{7}{3}$ chord.

(14) has a 6th, because it is the third degree.

(15) gives a new leading tone, for G minor, and consequently has a 6th.

(16) cadences in G minor with the 6th ($\frac{6^\flat}{4}\frac{5}{♯}$).

(17) continues to have a minor 3d of G minor, and

(18) has the major 3d, because it is the fifth degree.

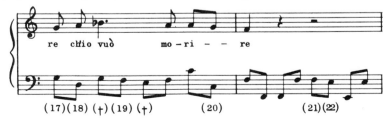

re   ch'io vuò   mo - ri - - - re

(17)(18) (†) (19) (†)   (20)   (21)(22)

(19) omits the leading tone of the preceding G minor and moves freely as a passing tone.

(20) cadences in F major with the 6th ($\begin{smallmatrix} 6 & 5 \\ 4 & \sharp \end{smallmatrix}$).

After this cadence the [bass] theme of the first ritornello is repeated, which one uses in the same way, giving to bass note

(21) the $\begin{smallmatrix} 6 \\ 4 \\ 2 \end{smallmatrix}$ chord, whose correct fourth from the scale of F major, i.e., Bb, one knows how to play. On the next bass note

(22) one must excuse the inexperienced [accompanist] if he remains in F major, playing the natural 6th to the three-fold repetition of note (22). However, because this accompaniment does not agree satisfactorily with the succeeding D minor, we make at this point the supreme and indispensable

Observat. pract. 7. That in such arias, recitatives, and two-part compositions one can more frequently see the structure of a scale from the succeeding modulation of both parts; one must learn, therefore, to look quickly in advance at the following bass notes. This foresight is obviously a rule founded on considerable experience and practice, [and] to train the inexperienced in it one must employ many examples. We shall meet such examples in this cantata. Thus, if we glance ahead at the notes of both parts following note (22), we not only see that the bass moves into D minor, but that the voice part also begins to establish this modulation. For this reason the entering D minor would be much better prepared if one figured the entire theme as:

Here it should be specially noted that one could actually keep the natural fourth Bb in the $\begin{smallmatrix} 6 \\ 4\natural \\ 2 \end{smallmatrix}$ chord, because this note is common to both F major and D minor. But this is a special type of progression based on what has been explained . . . concerning the unusual [melodic] motion in all minor scales (in which one usually ascends from the fifth of the scale through the major 6th and major 7th to the octave). One presupposes, therefore, that in this example the upper part moves from A (the fifth degree of the new scale) through the major 6th and major 7th to the octave of D minor, as actually occurs. Therefore, the passing note B requires the 4♮ even though it is contrary to both the preceding and succeeding scales. If these basic reasons seem all too difficult and obscure, then one can give the entire matter more succinctly by saying that this 4♮ is contrary to the *ambitus modi* only as the result of the motion of a passing tone in the upper part from A to C♯, necessitating the correct form of the 2d B; otherwise, the unnatural motion of an augmented 2d A, Bb, C♯ would result.

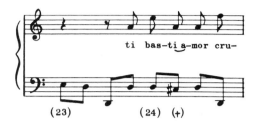

(23) receives the $\frac{7}{4}\frac{}{2}$ chord in place of the $\frac{6^+}{4}\frac{}{2}_\natural$ for the reason given at the end of *Observat. pract. 6.*

(24) The chord of a second formed by the voice part must have a minor 6th, which one finds in the *Specie 8vae* for D minor according to the reason included in Special Rule 2.

(25) has a 6th, because it is the third degree. For the A minor scale was indicated shortly before by the leading tone G♯. [To]

(26) one plays the correct 3d. [At]

(27) the voice part gives to both bass notes in succession an 8ve, 3d, and augmented 4th. Here one plays these parts together on the first bass note together with the proper 6th: $\frac{6}{4+}_{\flat3}$.

(28) Here one must be satisfied with the natural 6th G; however, an experienced accompanist would prefer the major 6th, because in this way the two successive sixths, i.e., 6♮ and 6^+ , ascend by semitones together with their bass and make the last chord more effective harmonically.

(29) must repeat the sharp of the preceding bass note together with its 7th.

(30) To the diminished 5th [one] can play either the natural 6th C or even better the major 6th C♯, since this leading tone follows immediately. [To]

(31) one takes the correct 3d.

(32) proceeds in the familiar manner through the 6th to the cadence ($^{6\ 5}_{4\ ♯}$). [To]

(33) the 4th will be given. Because the bass is prepared and resolves down, the $^{6}_{4\atop 2}$ chord is [the one to be used here]. . . .

(34) To the diminished 5th [one] plays in place of the natural 6th G the major 6th G♯, for we are now in A minor and this leading tone follows immediately. Over the next two notes the $^{6+}_{5♮}$ chord remains until on bass note

(35) [one] plays the $^{7}_{4\atop 2}$ chord in place of the $^{6+}_{4\atop 2♮}$ to avoid the frequently cited harshness of the previous major 6th. [To]

(36) one takes the correct 3d.

(37) has the 6th, because it is the third degree.

(38) proceeds through the 6th to the cadence ($^{6\ 5}_{4\ ♯}$).

(39) has the major 3d, because it is the fifth degree, and

(40) has the 6th, because it is the third degree.

(41) repeats the previous cadence in A minor.

(42) can have either the 5th or 6th; the latter usually follows naturally after the $\overset{6}{\underset{2}{4}}$ chord.

(43) expressly gives the 6th, which because it is major and because a minor 2d appears over the next bass note, requires the latter note

(44) to have the $\overset{7}{\underset{2\flat}{4}}$ chord instead of the $\overset{6\natural}{\underset{2\flat}{2}}$, according to the frequently cited rule.

(45) shows a diminished 5th in the voice part for which one must be satisfied with the related 6th. For a more harmonic effect one retains the previously prepared minor 7th, which one

(46) properly resolves [and] to which one can play either the previously prepared diminished 5th C or even better the $\overset{6}{\underset{2}{4\natural}}$ chord. This *passus compositionis* should be used just as in the 3d measure of the first ritornello.

cer–ba mor–te mi – a,   sol

(47) (†) (48) (†) (49)(50)(51)

(47) The 4th belongs with the $\frac{6}{2}$ given in the voice part. Here one must be satisfied with the perfect 4th A♭, because it belongs to the *Specie 8vae* of both the preceding C minor and the succeeding F minor established by the sixth degree in the bass. But an experienced accompanist would prefer the augmented 4th, since in such a form the harmony of this and the following bass note gives a correct imitation and transposition of the two immediately preceding notes marked with + + . Therefore, we formulate here

Observat. pract. 8. That when a bass part transposes its theme of a few or many notes, then at the same time one also transposes preferably the preceding accompaniment. One finds such examples in this aria whenever the second and third measures of the ritornello are repeated and transposed in the succeeding measures.

(48) will be regarded as the fifth degree in the previously cited scale of F minor and should have a major 3d. Since, however, this forms an unnatural chord with the minor 6th in the voice part, we must employ the previously recommended foresight as an aid in seeing how this minor 6th is resolved over the next bass notes, in which case

(49) and (50) indicate that it resolves to a 5th over a sustained or repeated bass. For this reason, it [the minor 6th] is accompanied by a 4th and not a 3d. . . . If we give a 4th to both basses (48) and (49) together with a minor 6th, then in place of this [previous procedure]

Observat. pract. 9. results, [giving] the following special progression that one must observe carefully, since it frequently occurs in two-part pieces in the [same] form as it is found in the cantata, and yet in itself is obscure without figures standing below it:

(51) contains a major 3d as the fifth degree.

(52) has a minor 2d; one looks for the correct 4th and 6th in the *Specie 8vae* for F minor, where one finds F on the fourth step above this bass and A♭ on the sixth step.

(53) normally has a 6th, since the previous $\overset{6}{4}$ chord regularly resolves to a 6th. The minor 3d, however, must be taken $\overset{2}{\text{here}}$, since this bass note is on the fourth degree of the scale. Special Rule 2. The next two notes can use either this 6th chord or the latter bass can have a 5th, which is all the same since the voice part is not contradictory. On bass note

(54) the 2d is given again. Because we are still in F minor, the augmented 4th as the leading tone must be used in place of the perfect 4th $\overset{6}{4\natural}$.

(55) has a 6th, because it is the natural resolution of the previous chord of the second. The next two bass notes can also use a 6th chord, or a 5th can be taken on the second bass, which is a note of short duration and at the same time omits the leading tone of the previous scale.

(56) Here again we have need of foresight. For though it appears because of the following F♯ that we are in G minor, this is contradicted by the immediately occurring cadence in C minor. According to this, we should use a major 3d over note (56) as the leading tone of C minor. But the minor 6th in the voice part together with the succeeding harmony shows that we have another case such as took place on notes (48), (49), and (50). Therefore, bass note (56) has the $\frac{6^\flat}{4}$ chord over it, and the repeated basses (57) after the F♯ have $\begin{smallmatrix}6\\4\end{smallmatrix}\begin{smallmatrix}5\\\natural\end{smallmatrix}$.

According to this, the following half bar marked (*) normally has the preceding minor 3d. On the next connected or prepared bass note

(58) a doubt arises as the result of the chord of the second. Here an inexperienced [accompanist] would easily stay within C minor and play the $\frac{6^\flat}{4}{}_2$ chord, which actually would not be too incorrect. Yet, whoever understands foresight and casts just a glance at the F♯ following in the voice part would prefer to give this bass note (58) the $\frac{6}{4}{+}{}_2$ chord, because through it the following scale of G minor is better prepared.

(59) has a 6th together with the next two bass notes, because it is the natural resolution of the augmented 4th.

(60) has a minor 3d together with its 6th above it, because it is the fourth degree. However, for a more harmonic effect one can give this bass the $\frac{6}{4}{+}{}_{\flat 3}$ chord.

(61) has a major 3d, because it is the fifth degree. [To]

(62) we must play the minor 3d together with the 5th, because the sharp before the preceding bass note has changed the scale to D minor. Special Rule 7. [On]

(63) one can play the major 6th, because it is the second degree in minor, if one does not wish to use this bass as a passing tone with the 7th in the well-known $\frac{7}{3}$ chord.

(64) has the 6th, because it is the third degree, and

(65) also has the 6th, because it is the sixth degree in minor. Special Rule 6.

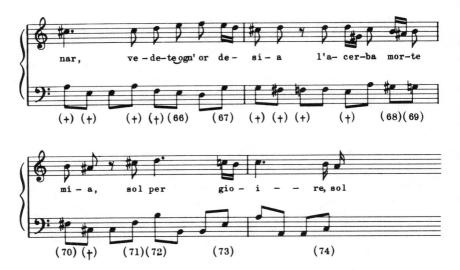

(66) again has the 6th, because it is the second degree.

(67) has the minor 3d above it, because it is the fourth degree.

(68) has a 6th, because it is the leading tone of the preceding A minor; on

(69) this scale changes again but, nevertheless, retains the 6th, because of

Observat. pract. 10. With such descending minor semitones, the perfect 5th over the last bass note sounds absurd and contrary to the natural harmony.

(70) gives a 4th for which one can find the correct 5th in the *Specie 8vae* of B minor, [the scale] established by the preceding and succeeding A♯ in the voice part.

(71) has a major 3d, because it is the fifth degree. Again the correct 5th is found in the *Specie 8vae* for this scale, which also gives

(72) the correct 5th F♯.

(73) can be satisfied with a triad; however, an experienced accompanist would prefer to use a $\frac{7}{♯}$ chord, since at the same time it seems to form a cadence in the following key of A minor.

(74) has a 6th; one can consider [this bass] either the third degree of the previous A minor scale or the sixth degree of E minor that follows. [For]

(75) one knows the correct 5th.

(76) could actually have a triad. But here we make the following

Observat. pract. 11. That if this bass note (which is the fourth degree) precedes the fifth degree and the usual cadence immediately follows, it is preferable for this fourth degree to have the $\frac{7}{5}$ chord. Reason: This bass note will then be considered a simple embellishment and variation of the succeeding firmly held cadence:

According to this then

(77) has the usual cadence 4 ♯ or $\begin{smallmatrix}6&5\\4&♯\end{smallmatrix}$, both of which are identical.

(78) has a 6th, because it is the sixth degree in minor. The accompaniment would be more effective harmonically if the previously prepared 7th were retained over this bass note and not resolved to the 6th until the next bass. [For]

(79) one knows how to play the correct 3d, and on

(80) the voice part proceeds in the familiar way through the 6th to the cadence $\begin{smallmatrix}6&5\\4&♯\end{smallmatrix}$·

After this extravagant aria we come to a recitative where over bass note

(1) a 4th belongs to the figure $\frac{6}{2}$ given by the voice part.

(2) can have either a triad or preferably the chord of the immediately following minor 7th.

(3) can actually retain the preceding minor 3d. The major 3d, however, better suits the transformation to the exceedingly unrelated scale that follows.

(4) has a major 6th above it, because the voice part already gave this accidental in a note of short duration. From this the composer's intention is found to be a progression to B minor and, therefore, this bass note (4) is regarded as the second degree of the scale.

(6) gives the leading tone of the following C♯ minor scale. In this *Specie 8vae*, however, one finds the correct 5th for this bass note (6) as well as the correct 5th to the next bass note (7) and, further on, the correct 3d to bass note (8).

(9) actually could have the natural 3d joined to a minor 6th. An experienced accompanist, however would prefer to give this bass the $\frac{6♮}{4}$ chord, which becomes the $\frac{7}{5}$ chord on the next bass (10) and then resolves formally to bass (11). These four basses F♯, E, D♯, and E represent the very *passus compositionis* previously investigated in the example of numbers (49) and (50).

(12) must actually be satisfied with a natural 6th with the diminished 5th and a triad with bass note (13). However, foresight again shows one how to improve on this, for an experienced accompanist needs only to glance at the following cadence to be able to prepare it more satisfactorily by giving bass (12) a major 6th and bass (13) the natural 3d, viewing the former bass as the second degree in B minor and the latter as the third degree in the same scale. In this way, the cadence 4 ♯ on bass

(14) is prepared, which, after the voice part ends will usually be repeated briefly. The correct 5th for the cadence is found in the *Specie 8vae* for B minor.

Finally we come to the last aria of this cantata, [and it] proceeds for the most part in a natural [style]; therefore, we will not find such difficulties of accompanying as in the first aria above. Considering the first cadence of the ritornello according to *Observat. pract. 1*, we find that bass note

(1) again begins on the fifth degree of the scale and has a major 3d above it. Special Rule 1.
(2) has a 6th above it, because it is the sixth degree in minor. Special Rule 6.
(3) (9) and (12) have a major 6th above, because they are the second degree in minor. Special Rule 5.
(5) and (6) have a 6th above, because they are the third degree. Special Rule 6.
(10) and (11) have a major 3d above, because again they are the fifth degree.
(13) forms the usual cadence with 4 ♯ or $\begin{smallmatrix} 6 & 5 \\ 4 & ♯ \end{smallmatrix}$·

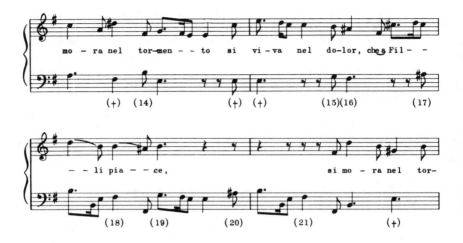

(14) has a major 3d because it is the fifth degree.

(15) has a 6th, because it is the third degree.

(16) Here the voice part gives the leading tone of B minor; thus, one will look to the *Specie 8vae* of this scale for the correct 5th.

(17) and (20) have a 6th, because they give the leading tone of the scale; one finds the correct 3d in the same *Specie 8vae*.

(18) and (21) form the familiar cadence 4 ♯ or $\begin{smallmatrix}6\\4\end{smallmatrix}\begin{smallmatrix}5\\♯\end{smallmatrix}$ in B minor to which one plays the correct 5th C♯. [On]

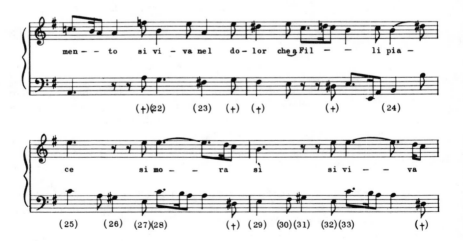

(22) the voice part gives a 6th only with the second note [over this bass]. Actually this 6th can be played on the first [of the] bass notes; however, for greater

beauty one plays a 7th to the first [part of the] bass and resolves it to the 6th on the second [part].

(23) To this note an inexperienced [accompanist] undoubtedly would want to give the natural 6th D. An experienced accompanist, however, judges from fore-sight of the immediately following ♯ in the voice part that this bass note (23) requires a major 6th; because in this form the following E minor scale will be better prepared, and this very bass will be regarded as the second degree.

(24) has the usual cadence 4 ♯ or $\begin{smallmatrix} 6 & 5 \\ 4 & ♯ \end{smallmatrix}$.

(25) has a 6th; one may consider [this bass] either the sixth degree of the preceding A minor scale or the third degree of the immediately following A minor scale.

(26), (31), (35), and (38) have 6ths, because they give the leading tone of A minor to which [the passage] firmly modulates, while the few appearances in between of a D♯ are viewed only as a bizarre chord whose accidental does not continue [in effect].

(27), (29), (32), (34), (36), and (39) all have major 3ds, because they are the fifth degree.

(28) and (33) have a 6th, because they are the sixth degree in minor.

(37) and (40) would actually be correct with a 5th. But since the voice part has previously given the minor 6th, it can also be retained for these bass notes. On the other hand, on bass note

(41) one must repeat immediately the F♯, so that this bass note has the correct 3d. Since we are in E minor again, therefore

(42) has the major 3d, because it is the fifth degree.

(43) has a 6th, because it is the third degree.

(44) has the usual cadence 4 ♯ or $\begin{smallmatrix} 6 & 5 \\ 4 & ♯ \end{smallmatrix}$.

ra _____ si vi — — — va   nel tor-men - to ne l do -

(†)   (45)   (†)(46)   (47) (†) (†)(48)   (49)   (50)

lor, che a Fil — — li pia —

(†)   (†)   (51)

(45) has the previously given minor 3d, which on

(46) can be retained, because the transposition of the bass notes in this measure can have a full repetition of the harmony and accompaniment belonging to the preceding measure according to the principle of *Observ. pract. 8.*

(47) passes freely through the preceding chord because the voice part expressly retains the 4th. [To]

(48) one knows how to find the correct 3d without difficulty. On bass note

(49) a new leading tone is given, indicating B minor. From the *Specie 8vae* of this scale, one will know how to find the correct 6th for the $\frac{4+}{2}$ chord formed in the voice part.

(50) has a 6th, because it is the natural resolution of the preceding augmented 4th.

(51) and (52) proceed through the 6th to the cadence $\frac{6\ 5}{4\ \sharp}$.

ce _____ che a Fil - li pia — — — ce

(†)   (†)   (52)   (53)(54) (55)(56) (57)

Co-sì   mor-rò   con -

(58)   (59) (†)(†) (60)

(53) Here foresight must again do its duty. For the bass note immediately following and shortly thereafter the G♯ shows that the previous scale suddenly
changes to A minor; therefore, this bass (53) has a major 3d, because it is the
fifth degree.

(54) has a 6th, because it is the sixth degree in minor.

(55) has a minor 3d, because it is the fourth degree in minor.

(56) has a 6th, because it is the leading tone.

(57) has a major 6th, because it is the second degree in minor.

(58) has a 6th, because it is the third degree. All these [chords] are according to
the often cited special rules.

(59) Here the inexperienced [accompanist] might easily play the major 6th,
because [this bass] is the second degree of the previous A minor. Yet, foresight shows again in this case that the voice part changes to the C major
scale, because the next bass note has a G rather than the former G♯. Therefore, the preceding chord (59) must prepare for this and has the natural 6th
G, because the bass note now forms the leading tone of C major.

(60) has a 6th, as much for the reason just given as because it is the natural
resolution of the previous chord of a second.

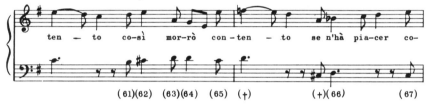

(61) again has a 6th, because it is the leading tone of the previous scale.

(62) gives the leading tone of D, [and] whether it is D minor or D major can most
quickly be determined from foresight. For a glance at the immediately following F in the voice part indicates we are in D minor. According to this,
bass notes (62), (65), and (67) have 6ths, because they are the leading tone of
the scale.

(63) has a minor 3d instead of the major 3d found in the key signature because, as
we know, the scale is D minor. [On]

(64) one must play the correct 6th B♭ and not the incorrect B to the $\frac{4}{2}$ chord
because, according to the principle of Special Rule 2, every minor scale uses
a minor 6th, which also agrees with the *Specie 8vae* for D minor.

(66) requires a minor 3d together with a minor 6th, because not only are we in D
minor but the minor 6th always has a minor 3d as part of its natural harmony, as explained previously.

(68) has a 6th, because here it is the leading tone of A minor.

(69) has the familiar cadence 4 ♯ or $\begin{smallmatrix}6\\4\end{smallmatrix}\begin{smallmatrix}5\\♯\end{smallmatrix}$.

(70) has a 6th, because it is the sixth degree in minor, since we are in E minor here.

(71) Here we are in B minor; thus one will know how to find the correct 5th in the *Specie 8vae* of this scale.

(72) For this chord one plays the correct 3d.

(73) has the useful cadence to which one again plays the correct 5th C♯. [For]

(74) one can play immediately on the [first part of the] bass note the 6th given in the voice part on the second [part of the] bass. More effective harmonically, however, is the retention of the previously prepared 7th that resolves together with the voice part to the 6th. On the next bass note

(75) one again proceeds in the same way and uses a 7th followed by a 6th instead of just the 6th.

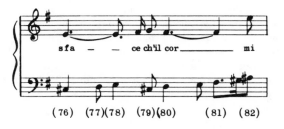

(76) Here an inexperienced [accompanist] would easily play the natural 6th A, believing that we are in D minor. Actually this seems to be true, and only the last bass notes of the measure contradict [this assumption].

One must be satisfied in this case if the accompaniment is built on D major from (76) to (80). An experienced accompanist, however, would not permit himself to err with the minor 6th on note (74) but would remain in the previous scale of B minor and prefer to give bass (76) a major 6th, because it is the second degree in minor. Then the bass note

(77) should actually pass through freely according to the rules for quick notes. However, instead we can make the following

Observat. pract. 12, observing this special *passus compositionis*, that if a minor 3d joined to a major 6th ascends a minor 3d or moves back from there, then for a richer harmony one gives the middle note a special chord of the sixth; and the note ascending a third can have a 5th or even better a major 6th. All cases are given in the following example:

According to this principle, note (77) is given a sixth chord, because it is the third degree of the scale; and the sustained note in the voice part does not affect this adversely.

(78) however, receives more naturally a major 6th in place of the more commonly used 5th.
(79) has another major 6th together with the diminished 5th in the upper part, because it is the second degree; and
(80) has the natural 6th, because it is the third degree. This harmony will be joined more smoothly to the following bass note, if over
(81) as the fifth degree of the previous scale, a major 3d is played, and over
(82) as the leading tone of the previous scale, a 6th is played. One finds the correct 5th to note (81) and the correct 3d to note (82) in the *Specie 8vae* for B minor.

(83) In looking ahead [we see] the scale changes to A major. Therefore this bass note has naturally a 6th, because it is the leading tone. The effect will be richer harmonically if one will anticipate in this chord the diminished 5th D appearing immediately afterwards in the voice part.

(84) has a 3d together with the minor 7th, because it is the fifth degree.

(85) has naturally the 6th, and one can consider [this bass] either the third degree of D major or the leading tone of the following G major scale. In addition, one can also retain as an anticipation the diminished 5th appearing in the voice part.

(86) can actually have a natural 6th, because it is the leading tone of the previous G major scale. But if an experienced accompanist casts a glance at the following *ambitus modi* of the B minor scale, he can better prepare this scale by giving bass (86) a major 6th, bass (87) a triad, and bass (88) the natural 6th, in which case

(89) with a major 6th again forms the *passus compositionis* that was explained above in the measure with note (76). Thus, one repeats those figures here, until

(90) where [the aria] closes with the familiar cadence 4 ♯ or $^{6\ 5}_{4\ \sharp}$.

Here Heinichen concludes his explanation of the cantata.

Note

1. MS copies of this cantata exist in the Santini collection, Univ. Bibl. Münster (Westfalen) MS 3898, and the Royal College of Music Library (presently in the British Library) MS 578. I am indebted to Edwin C. Hanley (Univ. of Calif., Los Angeles) for this information. Scarlatti's cantata is printed in Arnold Schering (ed.), *Geschichte der Musik in Beispielen* (Leipzig, 1931), 378–83 with a realization of the accompaniment based on Heinichen's demonstration. Schering uses a number of harmonies that deviate slightly from Heinichen's advice, largely in the form of added sevenths, and he very cautiously adds a few ornaments. He rebars Heinichen's original, halving the measures and shifting the bar lines in the two recitatives. For a different realization of this cantata, see appendix A of this book.

10

Heinichen Rediscovered:
Perspectives of Late Baroque
Musical Thought and Practice

Since the mid-eighteenth century, Heinichen as theorist and composer has been largely forgotten. Obviously, from the wealth of invaluable information found in preceding chapters, this obscurity has for too long deprived musicians concerned with Baroque performance practices of a comprehensive source of instruction and practical demonstrations. *Der General-Bass in der Composition* is a monumental work earning its author a place in music history among the great writers on musical theory and practices. Heinichen's book not only records a vast amount of practical information about the art of thorough-bass accompanying, but contributes an intensely vivid perspective of theoretical and philosophical considerations of the late Baroque composer. With typically Baroque logic, Heinichen viewed thorough-bass study not simply as a means of acquiring a technique but also as an effective method for learning the entire knowledge of a composer. In the very opening paragraph Heinichen announces: "No music connoisseur will deny that the *Basso Continuo* or so-called thorough-bass is, next to [the art of] composition, one of the most important and most fundamental of the musical sciences. For from what source other than composition itself does it spring forth? And what actually is the playing of a thorough-bass other than to improvise upon a given bass the remaining parts of a full harmony or to compose to [the bass]?"[1]

Clearly, the complex skill of thorough-bass realization, with its profusion of rules and often equally numerous exceptions, was an integral part of a composer's craft. That the device should assume such importance resulted naturally in a musical era dominated by stress on the bass-melody framework in many forms of music. But even the most clairvoyant monodist or early Italian opera composer, who had abandoned Renaissance polyphonic conventions, could not have foreseen the extent to which the thorough-bass would infiltrate every form of Baroque musical expression. What the monodists thought to be a simple technique connected with their attempts to revive a Greek style of dramatic music, spawned an art so intricate in its final stages that Heinichen, in describing it, filled more than a thousand pages with rules and examples.

Der General-Bass was Heinichen's second endeavor at writing a complete thorough-bass treatise. An earlier version, less than half the size and published in 1711, is usually dismissed as nothing more than a model for the second version. Without detracting from the all-inclusiveness of the second version, one can adequately judge the latter only after specific acquaintance with Heinichen's youthful accomplishment. Also, a comparison of the two works yields fascinating evidence of the growth of Heinichen's musical outlook and provides a number of valuable clues to the most meaningful influences experienced by Heinichen as he matured as an artist.

Der neu erfundene und gründliche Anweisung . . . zu vollkommener Erlernung des General-Bass (Hamburg, 1711) is the first German work to give instructions for accompanying from figured as well as unfigured basses and to establish numerous and carefully drawn distinctions between the *stylus gravis* and the *stylus theatralis*, so important to the tasteful usage of dissonances in operatic music. Heinichen also prescribes the elements of a stylistically correct realization of recitative accompaniments, and these valuable suggestions embody our earliest German guide for this area of eighteenth-century performance practice. This first treatise contains the essence of Heinichen's theories related to composing, including the formulation of a type of musical oratory to aid composers in the invention of musical ideas. The originality and historical impact of these concept in 1711 might elude us if we knew them from the 1728 treatise only. If Heinichen had written nothing but the *Neu erfundene Anweisung*, his work would still remain one of our best sources of information for the thorough-bass, the theatrical style, and as evidence of the important bonds between music and rhetoric existing in Germany at the end of the Baroque.

In the years separating the two publications, Heinichen left the periphery of the European musical stage, the provincialism of Leipzig, and sought the brilliance of the Venetian world of music. His exposure to the vitality and abundance of Italian music explains many of the alterations and additions to his revised treatise: the detailed explanations for dissonances in the theatrical style; the boldness of harmonic realizations; the numerous attacks on contrapuntal complexity; and particularly the appearance of the concept of *goût*. Heinichen defines *goût* (*gusto* or *guter Geschmack*) as, among other things, "an all-pervading *cantabile* as well as suitable and touching accompaniments."[2] This "all-pervading *cantabile*" — a superior description for what we often call *bel canto* in Baroque music — was an essential aspect of Italian opera, receiving Heinichen's enthusiastic acceptance.

A major difference becomes apparent when the title-pages of each edition are juxtaposed. The lengthy title of the *Neu erfundene Anweisung* (see fig. 1) outlines the author's three-fold goal: (1) to give a new and funda-mental method by which amateurs can learn the art of thorough-bass accompanying; (2) to apply this knowledge to recitative accompaniments; and (3) to augment the explanation with numerous musical examples and selected rules of composition.

Although the title of *Der General-Bass in der Composition* (see fig. 2) outlines a purpose generally similar to that of the first version, a new element strikes the eye with the suggestion *auch zu gleicher Zeit in der Compo-sition selbst, wichtige Profectus machen könne*. Heinichen was the first of numer-ous eighteenth-century writers to teach composition with principles derived from the thorough-bass. His definition of the thorough-bass (quoted above), identical in both editions, makes clear that he had always thought of it as part of the craft of composing; yet the broader emphasis on its instructive value for composition students stands out in each chapter of the second edition. Even the titles of the two versions testify to Heinichen's altered purpose: in 1711 he published a "newly discovered and basic method by which the amateur can fully learn the use of the thorough-bass," while in 1728 Heinichen chose the all-embracing "Thorough-bass in Com-position."

The *General-Bass* begins with a preface added to this revised version. Here Heinichen recommends that readers concerned more with com-posing than accompanying should study certain chapters only or portions of them. He urges a careful reading of the lengthy *Einleitung*, in itself a manual for composers that emphasizes musical rhetoric and the expression of affections.[3] Following the reading of this chapter Heinichen suggests the student turn to sections on intervals and the rules for consonances and dissonances; the *triade harmonica* and parallel and contrary motion; rules of harmony and the principle for anticipating resolutions of dissonances; regular and irregular passing tones; characteristics of the *stylus theatralis*; a musical circle aiding modulation; and finally a second reading of the *Einleitung*.

The preface offers us the only tangible clue to Heinichen's reasons for revising his treatise. With typical immodesty he expresses the hope that his new treatise might share the successful reception among amateurs that his first work enjoyed. Having been persuaded to take up his pen again he would rather "fully differentiate this work from the old treatise, making it four times as strong a work so that experienced as well as inexperienced, learned as well as unlearned, accompanist as well as composer could gain special usefulness from it. . . . [The new work includes] not only the necessary fundamentals of composing, but also such important and still partly unknown material about which, to date, we have been given nothing to read by old or new, German, Italian, or French authors."[4] Actually Heinichen wrought much more than just a second edition from the earlier model. The addition of new chapters, extensive footnotes, and a vastly increased number of musical examples makes the second version approximately three and one-half times larger in total number of pages.[5]

Immediately apparent when comparing the two versions is the absence of footnotes in the first and the really astonishing number and prolixity of them in the second. Many of Heinichen's most instructive thoughts often await the reader at the bottom of a page; and many of these notes contain personal observations on musical practices and malpractices invaluable to those curious about the later German Baroque. These digressions at times resemble a teacher's enthusiastic ramblings — tangential comments that result from a provocative word or idea in the text. They mirror the mature artistic credo of Heinichen, the theorist and aesthetician, which he had developed in the years following the publication of the first version of his treatise.

The very first footnote in the *General-Bass* focuses a sharp image of Heinichen's philosophical conception of music. Although both versions open with identical paragraphs, a simple expression of the thought that music is both a theoretical and practical art, this idea provokes a lengthy footnote in the revision, a whole summary of Heinichen's musical aesthetics. Why, he asks, do so many unnecessary controversies, contradictions and, particularly, disputes arise between young and old composers? The answer lies, according to Heinichen, in the inability of the protagonists to agree upon the first principle of music: is it based on reason or the ear?

> The old [musicians] side more with Reason, but the new with the Ear; and since both parties do not agree on the first fundamental, it is evident that the conclusions and consequences made from two contrary fundamental principles should breed just as many controversies of inferior rank and thousands of diametrically opposed hypotheses. Musicians of the past, we know, chose two judges in music: Reason and the Ear. The choice would be correct since both are indispensable to music; yet, because of the use of these two concomitants, the present cannot reconcile itself with the past, and in this the past is blamed for two errors. First, it wrongly classed the two judges and placed the Ear, the sovereign of music, below the rank of Reason or would divide its commanding authority with the latter.

Whereupon the blameless Ear must immediately cede half of its monarchical domain. In addition, unfortunately, the composers of the past poorly explained the word *ratio*. In those innocent times (in which one knew nothing of present-day good taste and brilliance in music, and every simple harmony seemed beautiful), they thought Reason could be put to no better use than the creation of supposedly learned and speculative artificialities of note writing. Therefore, they began on the one hand to measure out theoretically innocent notes according to mathematical scales and with the help of the proportioned yardstick, and on the other hand, to place these notes in musical practice on the staves (almost as if they were on a rack) and to pull and stretch them (or in the language of counterpoint, to augment them), to turn them upside down, to repeat and to change their positions, until finally from the latter resulted a practice with an overwhelming number of unnecessary instances of contrapuntal eye-music and from the former resulted a theory with amassed metaphysical contemplations of emotion and reason. Thus, one no longer had cause to ask if music sounded well or pleased the listener, but rather if it looked good on paper. In this way, the Visual imperceptibly gained the most in music and used the authority of the imprudent Reason only to cover its own lust for power. Consequently, the suppressed Ear was tyrannized so long that finally it hid behind table and chairs to await from the distance the condescending, merciful glance of its *usurpatores regni (ratio & visus)*. This grave injustice to the musical sovereign, the Ear, has been reprehended more by present-day musicians than by those of the past. They have begun vigorously to understand the many absurd and preposterous principles of the past and to form completely new ideas about the noble art of music unlike those of the learned ignoramuses. Above all, they return to the oppressed Ear the sovereignty of its realm; they displace Reason from its judicial duties and give it [Reason] to the Ear, not as *Domino* or co-regent, but as an intelligent minister and counselor with the absolute mandate to warn its master (the occasionally deceived Ear, if indeed "deceived" can be spoken of) of every false step; but otherwise, Reason differs in opinion, it must serve [the Ear] with complete obedience and employ all of its skill, not for the visual appearance on paper, but to give the Ear the satisfaction of an absolute ruler. Really! What has the visual to do with music? Could anything more absurd be stated? The [art of] painting is for the eye, music, however, for the ear. Similarly, food is for the [sense of] taste and flowers for the [sense of] smell. Would it not be ridiculous to say the dinner was especially good because it smelled good, even though it was disagreeable to the taste and stomach? It is just as absurd if one should say along with pedants: this is outstanding music because it looks so fine (I mean pedantic) on paper, even though it does not please the ear, for which music is solely made. . . . As we must now admit unanimously that our *Finis musices* is to stir the affections and to delight the ear, the true *Objectum musices*, it follows that we must establish all our musical rules according to the Ear. And in this *Frau Vernunfft* (that super-intelligent *ratio*) will have her hands full, even more than we can imagine in our times. . . .[6]

Heinichen's insistence that the only true aim of music is to stir the affections reminds one of the similar goal adopted by Johann Mattheson as his battle cry: *Alles, was ohne löbliche Affecten geschiehet, heisst nichts, thut nichts, gilt nichts.*[7]

Contrapuntal music, intricate compositions inspired by textbook rules, became one of Heinichen's favorite targets for barbs of criticism. One might think it strange, that Heinichen should bristle with such contempt for contrapuntists, when one sees the large number of church compositions in his catalogue of music.[8] His criticism seems aimed particularly at stereotyped contrapuntal devices, which were part of every second-rate church musician's composing techniques, composers he preferred to call arch-contrapuntists "who seek the *Summum bonum* or the entire art of music in the study of counterpoint only." He continues, assuring his reader that he is

> very fond of counterpoint, and in my youth I was an ardent champion of it; as in the past, in the future too I shall continue to demonstrate my willingness to deal with fugues, double fugues, and other artifices of themes on paper in the devout church style. I cannot deny, however, that after many years of experience I have lost my previous enthusiasm for it and absolutely cannot bear our excessive misuse of forced counterpoints, in which for the most part (and I do not say completely) nothing has validity unless it is a pedantic counterpoint, and in which generally the artificial play with notes on paper is given out as the most noble and most artful form of music.[9]

For Heinichen counterpoint has only two good purposes:

> First, [counterpoint] serves students and beginners in composition. With counterpoint they learn to climb or to spell, and with these given and restricted themes and toilsome exercises they are forced to master skilful progressions or *Passus compositionis*. . . . Second, counterpoint serves church music if it is mixed, according to the style of good church composers, with other techniques of good taste. Here is really its place and here the contrapuntist can best show his learned schooling. Because our usual devout church music (more in Germany than in other countries) tolerates neither too much fire, inspiration, nor gay ideas, thus sometimes even a contrapuntist with little taste and invention can slip through at the very first. For after he has a bit of a theme or something of a musical idea captured at the twelfth, then he whips it through all the usual transpositions and common inversions; this then is called erudition, and the man has accomplished Herculean feats.[10]

In *Seven Articles of Faith* Heinichen charges the following abuses to an excess of counterpoint:

> 1. Most of the [contrapuntal] *inventa* (with few exceptions) are based on the visual and lifeless manipulations of notes but not on the actual sound.

2. That the more one sinks into the excesses of such stereotyped artifices, the more one necessarily must depart from the Ear and the true *Finis musices*.

3. That, therefore, those lines of a composition (not the entire piece, for there one can alternate) must be considered *inter casus raros & accidentales* or rare masterpieces in which considerable sterile art is combined with equal amounts of good taste.

4. That the excessive abuse of too much counterpoint is the shortest path to musical pedantry, ruining many fine talents that otherwise could have been developed into something worthy.

5. That, for the most part, counterpoint in itself is something laborious (like the farmers' work when they load manure into wheelbarrows) but not artistic once one has learned the routines.

6. That one can make a dull contrapuntist *par force* out of any dumb boy but [one cannot make] a composer with good taste.

7. Finally, to promote the *Finis musices* rather than the forced rules of counterpoint, there are many more beautiful and artistic things in music.[11]

How far removed these statements place Heinichen from the stream of North German musical style — Kuhnau, Buxtehude, Böhm, and, of course, J. S. Bach — and also from the instrumental music of most Italian composers of the early eighteenth century. Contrapuntal techniques were indispensable to the principle of continuous expansion[12] or motivic development that was the seminal force of late Baroque music. Heinichen's bitter attack, on counterpoint and all those artificialities of composing he felt characterized German music, represents a symptom of the gradual disintegration of Baroque style.

Perhaps even more revealing of the change in musical outlook present at least in Dresden at the end of the second decade of the eighteenth century is the following remarkable passage by Heinichen, in which he contrasts German, French, and Italian music, and suggests the advantages inherent in a new style mixing the best elements of French and Italian music:

Experience teaches that . . . paper music receives more credit in one nation than in another. One nation [Germany] is industrious in all endeavors; another laughs over useless school work and tends to believe skeptically that the "Northerners" [*Tramontani*] (to use their manner of speaking) work like a team of draft horses. One nation [Germany] believes art is only that which is difficult to compose; another nation, however, seeks a lighter style and correctly states that it is difficult to compose light music. . . . One nation [Germany] seeks its greatest art in nothing but intricate musical "tiff-taff" and elaborate artificialities of note writing. The other nation applies itself more to good taste, and in this way it takes away the former's universal applause; the paper artists [Germans], on the contrary, with all their witchcraft remain in obscurity and, in addition, are proclaimed barbarians, even though they could imitate the other nations blindfolded if they applied themselves more to good taste and brilliance of music than to fruitless artificialities. An eminent foreign composer once gave his frank opinion . . . regarding the differences in music of two nations. "Our nation," he said, . . . "is more inclined to *dolcezza* (gracefulness, *tendresse*) in music, so much so that it must take care not to fall into a kind of indolence. Most "Northerners" [*Tramontani*], on the other hand, are almost too inclined to liveliness in music, so that they fall too easily into barbarisms. If they would take pains over adapting our *tendresse* and would mix it together with their usual *vivacité*, then a third [style] would result that could not fail to please the whole world." I will not repeat the comments I made at that time, but will say only that this discourse first brought to my mind [the thought] that a felicitous mélange of Italian and French taste would affect the ear most forcefully and must succeed over all other tastes of the world. . . . Nevertheless, the Germans have the reputation abroad that if they would apply themselves industriously they could usually surpass other nations in learning. From this principle I [derive my] hope that some day our composers will try in general (since there is no scarcity of special instances) to surpass other nations in matters of musical taste as well as they have succeeded long ago in artful counterpoint and theoretical accuracies.[13]

The extent to which the influence of the *style galant* had pervaded musical circles in Dresden is indicated by Heinichen's following advice:

I would never suggest to anyone to fill up the theatrical style with too many serious inventions. . . . For pathetic, melancholic, and phlegmatic music (in so far as it is based on tenderness and good taste) is effective in the church and chamber styles; but it is not well suited to the theatrical style, and one uses serious pieces simply for judicious changes. And if their lordships, the poets, overload us with pathetic and sorrowful arias, we must try to sweeten these either with mixed inventions or effective accompaniments; or in those arias containing a double affection, one turns the invention more generally to the lively element rather than the serious one. Thus, e.g., with the melancholy of love, one should rather express the pleasantness of love and not the blackness of melancholy. With the petition of a lover for a reciprocation of love, one should rather express more the tenderness of his affection than the seriousness of his plea or sad sighs. . . . In summary, the theatrical style for the most part requires something moving or adroit, though I should not call it simply merry. For merry music in itself can easily degenerate into barbarism and is unpleasant to sensitive ears. But if its noble vivaciousness is combined with good taste, tenderness, and an effective or brilliant style, this will always please the ear. . . .[14]

Most unexpected, however, of Heinichen's many random observations is his criticism of assigning an affection to each key. In commenting upon a music example he had included in the *Einleitung*, Heinichen interjects the following surprising opinion:

[The aria] begins in E♭; for this reason, however, the invention need not be sad, serious, or plaintive, for brilliant concertos as well as joyous arias in certain cases can be composed with the greatest effect in this beautiful key. Furthermore, the previous examples . . . clearly show that one can express the same words and affections in various and, according to the old theory, opposing keys. For that reason, what previous theorists have written and re-written about the properties of the modes are nothing but trifles, as if one mode could be merry, another sad, a third pious, heroic, war-like, etc. But even if these imaginary properties had any inherent correctness, the slightest change of temperament used for them (which can never be accurately done by the tuner of instruments) and even more changes of *Chorton, Kammerton*, French, and the extravagant Venetian tunings would cause continual shipwrecks. In my opinion, the ancient theorists erred in their research of modal characteristics, in the same way as we continue to err today in judging a musical work. If we, for example, find for this or that key (to which a talented composer may usually be more inclined) one or more beautifully tender, plaintive, or serious arias, we prefer to attribute the fine impression of the aria to the key itself and not to the excellent ideas of the composer; and we immediately establish a *proprietas modi*, as if contrary words and affections could not be expressed in this key. This, however, is worse than wrong, as can be proved to the contrary by a thousand beautiful examples. In general, one can say that one key is more suitable than another for expressing [certain] affections. Thus in the practice today using well-tempered scales (we do not speak of old organs), the keys indicated with two and three sharps or flats are particularly beautiful and expressive in the theatrical style; therefore I should not advise the invention of a purely diatonic keyboard, even if it were possible. Yet, to specify this or that key especially for the affection of love, sadness, joy, etc. is not good. Should someone object at this point and say that D, A, B♭ major are much more suited to raging music than the calmer scales of A minor, E minor, and similar ones, then this actually does not prove the *proprietas modorum* even if it were so, but it depends on the inclination of the composer. For we have heard famous composers write the saddest and tenderest music in D, A, and B♭ major, etc., whereas in A minor, E minor, C minor; and in similar scales [we have heard] the most powerful and brilliant music. It remains the case, therefore, that every single key and all keys or musical modes without distinction are suited to expressing many opposing affections. However, the choice of these depends primarily on four basic conditions: (1) As stated previously, purely on the inclination or in physical terms, on the temperament of the composer, for one either a preference in general, or for certain expressions of one or another affection for a certain mode, whereas another [composer] prefers another mode and, so to speak, has certain favorite scales. (2) On the unavoidable changing of a mode in which one has frequently expressed the [same] affection of joy or of sadness. For change is always the soul of music, and who would be so absurd as to state that one must keep a certain scale or mode for the same affection throughout a lengthy theatrical piece or another composition? Why? Just because one of the dear old [theorists] had given this *proprietas* to the mode? (3) On necessity, according to the possibilities of certain instruments which, in order to conform to them, one must frequently use a key against one's will and express in it various contrary affections. (4) Finally, the choice of mode depends frequently on the singer's range: that is, whether he has many or few tones in his throat, and whether his voice is equal throughout, or whether one must treat the upper or lower ranges cautiously. . . . [T]hese four principles prove sufficiently that the choice of musical modes depends partly on our will and preference, partly on the circumstances of the moment. Therefore the old-fashioned and often self-contradictory theory of the *proprietates modorum musicorum* is of as little use as it is in itself unfounded and false.[15]

Many theorists, beginning in the Renaissance with the revived interest in Greek concepts of ethos, had attempted to define keys according to specific affects. Glareanus (*Dodecachordon*, 1547) was one of the first to define the twelve modes according to their affection, and Zarlino (*Istitutioni harmoniche*, 1558) suggested similar affective power for the modes. Mersenne (*Harmonie universelle*, 1636), Kircher (*Mursurgia universalis*, 1650) and Werckmeister (*Harmonologica musica* 1702) all attribute affections to keys, but the most comprehensive catalogue of key affections appears in Johann Mattheson's first published treatise, *Das neu-eröffnete Orchestre* (1713), part III, chapter II. Here we find seventeen keys narrowly delineated according to affection,[16] the very catalogue that Heinichen is attacking, for Mattheson's definition of E♭ major states: "*Es dur hat viel pathetisches an sich; will mit nichts als ernsthafften und dabey plaintiven Sachen gerne zu thun haben.*" The qualifying words *pathetisches* (suffering or sad), *ernsthafften* (serious), and *plaintiven* (plaintive) are exactly those affections repeated in Heinichen's comments as not the only kinds of musical ideas suitable to E♭ major.

Even though Heinichen believes that all music must arouse the affections, he attacks the doctrine of key affections on purely practical grounds. As can be observed in so many of his comments, the composer always rules the theorists. What makes Heinichen's attack on key affections intensely significant is the convincing proof it offers that such ideas as found in Mattheson's treatise were not unique to that composer-theorist-aesthetician, but were prevalent among composers of the early eighteenth century.

Heinichen's concern for the young composer, which he stresses throughout his writing, is specifically related to the following inquiry into the prerequisites for all those wishing to compose. The "modern composer," in Heinichen's words, must posses three basic requirements: (1) talent, (2) knowledge, (3) experience, which in themselves are obvious enough. Heinichen's definition of these three requirements offers more evidence of this very successful composer's insight into the practical problems of musical creation in the early eighteenth century. Talent, he says, "helps its possessor not only to skip lightly over the peaks of musical mountains but also gives him natural, good ideas for the *Arte compositoria* as well as suitable sentiments to promote the expression of the *Finis musices* [i.e., expression of words]. . . . One can as little describe the differences in musical talent as one can describe the differences between all ingenuities. Generally, however, one can say that the good talents of composers differ only in degree. For Nature gives to one an animated, clear, burning spirit, but to another a tempered, modest, or even affective nature. The latter is better suited to the devout church style, the former, however, more to the theatrical. . . ."

Under knowledge Heinichen includes "all important aspects of theoretical and practical music, and in particular, *Musica pœtica*; i.e., he must not only understand thoroughly all the fundamental principles and important rules for music and composition, but also he must be able to use them well and to know how to put together a musical work." The study of counterpoint is not to be excluded if it can be taught without pedantry, "for to be able to employ a theme artistically is surely indispensable to a good composer."

Experience, however, is the most important *requisitum compositoris moderni*, experiences a composer gains after he has learned the regular rules of theory and practice:

If experience is necessary in any art or science, it is certainly necessary in music. In this *Scientia practica*, first of all, we must gain experience . . . either at home, provided opportunities are sufficient, or through traveling. But what is it that one believes one must seek in the experience? I will give a single word defining the three basic *Requisita musices*, i.e., talent, knowledge, and experience, as well as the true *finis musices* as the center: this word is in four letters, *Goût*. Through diligence, talent, and experience, a composer must achieve above all else an exquisite sense of good taste in music. . . . The definition of *Goût*, *Gusto* or *guter Geschmack* is unnecessary for the experienced musician; and it is as difficult to describe in its essentials as the true essence of the soul. One could say that good taste was in itself the soul of music, which so to speak it doubly enlivens and brings pleasure to the senses. The *Proprium 4ti modi* of a composer with good taste is contained solely in the skill with which he makes his music pleasing to and beloved by the general, educated public, or which in the same way pleases our ear by experienced artifices and moves the senses. . . . In general, this can be brought about through a good, well-cultivated, and natural invention or through the beautiful expression of words. In particular, [this is achieved] through an ever dominating *cantabile*, through suitable and affecting accompaniments, through a change of harmonies recommended for the sake of the ears, and through other methods gained from experience and frequently looking poor on paper, which in our times we only label with the obscure name of "rules of experience." . . . An exceptional sense of good taste is so to say the musical *Lapis philisophorum* and the principal key to musical mysteries through which human souls are unlocked and moved and by which the senses are won over. . . . For even the natural gift or talent endowed with most invention resembles only crude gold and silver dross that must be purified first by the fire of experience before it can be shaped into a solid mass — I mean into a finely cultivated and steadfast sense of good taste.[17]

In searching the pages of the two versions of Heinichen's treatise one finds that the earlier work has an almost total absence of references to other composers or theorists that could serve as clues to Heinichen's own sources of knowledge. Despite his close association with Kuhnau, Heinichen includes only a single reference to his teacher at the Leipzig Thomasschule, a citation of the *Biblische Historien*.[18] Considering Kuhnau's widely established fame in North Germany, one might assume that the unknown Heinichen would have drawn attention to this student-teacher friendship, if indeed they were friends in 1711: we know Kuhnau fought a bitter and ceaseless battle against the inroads of opera into the church.[19] Perhaps Heinichen's infatuation with operatic music alienated him from his former teacher. The *General-Bass* omits the reference contained in the first version and includes a new one hardly indicating feelings of increased admiration:

At that time, namely, I received instruction in composition from the then well known Herr Kuhnau, formerly Director of Choruses in Leipzig, while at the same time I studied the *Clavier* and sought to imitate my teacher in this endeavor. . . . My teacher had told me something of the previously reported Circle by Kircher; however, this gave me no satisfaction whenever I was determined to go from a major key to a distantly related minor key and *vice versa*. At that time I still knew nothing of circular modulations in thirds, and neither could I learn more from my teacher. . . .[20]

Except for a reference to Kircher's musical circle, no other theorists are named in the first version.[21] Yet this singular absence of clues to the sources studied by Heinichen cannot be attributed to his ignorance of important treatises. Certainly no student of the profoundly erudite Kuhnau could avoid contact with the significant writings of composers and theorists such as Praetorius, Printz, and Werckmeister. According to Heinichen's own testimony[22] he searched through a number of musical treatises while looking for a better method of modulating through a circle of keys. Undoubtedly he absorbed at the same time the information in these books relating to the thorough-bass and composing in general.

Unlike the first version, the *General-Bass* refers to a small but important group of contemporary musicians; Gasparini and Saint-Lambert have already been mentioned.[23] The foremost name, however, is Johann Mattheson, Hamburg composer, theorist, and journalist, an outspoken and extraordinarily prolific commentator on almost every aspect of eighteenth-century musical practice.[24] While no documentation exists to show that these two great German musicians were personal friends, a tone of familiarity in Heinichen's references to his Hamburg colleague suggests something more than purely professional contacts. For example, some degree of friendship would certainly seem necessary before Heinichen would ask from his deathbed that Mattheson act as his representative in Hamburg, a duty amounting to debt collector for the Heinichen estate.[25]

As early as 1717 Mattheson[26] wrote to Heinichen requesting a biographical sketch intended for publication in the *Ehrenpforte*; unfortunately Heinichen never complied. The *Neu erfundene Anweisung* came from the presses of the Hamburg publisher Benjamin Schiller, who also printed several early works of Mattheson.[27] This leads one to speculate on why Heinichen sent his manuscript to Hamburg for publication when a printer in Leipzig or even Dresden would seem more convenient. Perhaps Mattheson had some role in Heinichen's choice of a printer; in any case Mattheson must have become familiar with the *Neu erfundene Anweisung* almost as soon as the ink was dry.

With the exceptions of the *Grosse General-Bass-Schule* (1731), *Kleine General-Bass-Schule* (1735), and *Der vollkommene Capellmeister* (1739), all of Mattheson's important books appeared during Heinichen's residence in Venice or Dresden. These are cited in Heinichen's second version and include *Das neu-eröffnete Orchestre* (1713), *Das beschützte Orchestre* (1717), *Exemplarische Organisten-Probe* (1719), *Das forschende Orchestre* (1721), and *Critica Musica*, a periodical issued between 1722 and 1725. Heinichen mentions the *Organisten-Probe* no fewer than six times, a statistic of high praise from an author who limited his quotations from other sources to a minimum. Mattheson in turn reaped enormous profit from Heinichen's highly original discussions centering around the thorough-bass and the affections, and Heinichen's spirit haunts both the *Grosse General-Bass-Schule* and *Der vollkommene Capellmeister*.

Other theorists mentioned in the *General-Bass*, Boyvin, Rameau, Werckmeister, and Kircher, all seem to have been admitted solely as targets for criticism. Heinichen mentions Boyvin first in the *Einleitung*,[28] remarking that a Monsieur Boyvin supposedly had written copiously about the thorough-bass, though Heinichen confesses he had not seen the material. Before the printing of the *General-Bass* was completed, however,

Heinichen added a note in the Supplement[29] to the effect that he had seen a small pamphlet by Boyvin, but if this were the extent of Boyvin's efforts it must be judged "trivial and incomplete." Heinichen certainly drew an unfair conclusion for Boyvin's treatise was never intended to be a complete thorough-bass treatise but rather a set of rules to aid in the playing of his music.

In the revised version a few hints exist to help us determine the range of Heinichen's interests in contemporary music or theoretical writing. One clue appears in the reference to Rameau, the great French composer and theoretician who published his revolutionary *Traité de l'harmonie* in 1722. Since Rameau's harmonic theories departed radically from the general practice of the Baroque, Heinichen's[30] lukewarm comments regarding Rameau's *Traité* are not surprising. More curious is the limitation of his remarks to such lesser matters as Rameau's indications of figures for each note of a scale. Heinichen has no comments on Rameau's theories advocating chords built in thirds, a hierarchy of chords related to a tonal center by their harmonic function, or the explanation of dissonant harmonies based on an extension of a series of thirds. One suspects that Heinichen became acquainted with Rameau's treatise only after a considerable portion of the *General-Bass* had been printed. Rameau's name can be found only in the last chapters and in Heinichen's supplementary remarks. Although published in 1728, we know that part of the *General-Bass* had been completed as much as six years earlier in 1722, the publication year of Rameau's treatise.[31]

Heinichen did not restrain himself in criticizing Andreas Werckmeister and his treatise, *Harmonologica musica* (1702). With bitter satire Heinichen attacked Werckmeister's defense of the church modes. As one of the earliest German champions of major and minor scales, Heinichen ridicules the old church modes as forms of foolishness "that no longer apply to our times."[32] He had neither sympathy for nor understanding of Werckmeister's belief that the modes were essential, at least for organ preludes based on modal chorales.

Athanasius Kircher, seventeenth-century philosopher and mathematician, is the only other theorist mentioned in the *General-Bass*. His name had appeared in the first version,[33] where Heinichen credited him with inventing a system of modulations through keys related by a circle of fourths and fifths. In the revised version, Heinichen turns Kircher's honor to dishonor with the opinion that Kircher described "one of the most incomplete"[34] systems of modulating that omits either all major or minor keys. At this point one is not surprised to find Heinichen describing and praising a new method of modulation he had invented.

The pages of the *General-Bass* reflect just as inadequately Heinichen's contemporary musical world, mentioning only the names of Alessandro Scarlatti, Lotti, Vivaldi, Caldara, and D'Astorga. Vivaldi's name receives a single citation in connection with a short example that Heinichen quotes as an unusual modulation in a sequence of fourths.[35] A brief excerpt from a *Salve regina* by Antonio Lotti proves, according to Heinichen, that the harmonic language of even the most recent composers tends to be unduly conservative.[36] A portion of a duet by the same Italian composer serves Heinichen to explain a technical point in accompanying from unfigured basses.[37]

Unquestionably the most significant musical addition to the second version is the solo cantata by Alessandro Scarlatti (1660–1725), *Lascia deh lascia al fine di tormentarmi più*. This bold example of the elder Scarlatti's expressive use of harmony replaces another solo cantata used in the first edition with the title, *Della mia bella Clori*, which Heinichen prints without identifying the composer.[38] In each case a solo cantata with unfigured bass gives students an excellent practical exercise for applying Heinichen's suggestions. Heinichen remarks that he thought Scarlatti's cantatas contained "more extravagant harmonies"[39] than those by any other composer; and certainly the many challenges an accompanist faces in these unfigured basses test fully Heinichen's method of realization.

A comparison of the two versions also aids us in comprehending the impact of the Italian musical experience on Heinichen's harmonic vocabulary. Each version of the treatise contains a table of what Heinichen calls the most common figures. In the *Neu erfundene Anweisung* the table consists of a simple group of symbols (see fig. 3).[40] This table lacks a few figures, however, for in a later section[41] Heinichen gives a supplementary list of chords suited to the recitative style, including in addition to triads:

$$^{+}7 \quad \flat 7 \qquad \quad 6 \quad 6 \quad \sharp \quad 4\flat$$
$$4 \quad \sharp \quad 7 \quad 4 \quad 4$$
$$2 \qquad \qquad 2$$

Only the chords $^{+}7\atop4\atop2$, $6\atop4$, and $6\atop2$ are not found in the preceding table. In 1711, therefore, a set of fourteen figures plus triads comprised all the harmonies Heinichen expected an accompanist to meet in the thorough-bass.

In the *General-Bass* the list of common figures grew to include thirty (not representing, however, variations of chords made by adding certain accidentals or the indication of triads by a single sharp or flat), an increase of sixteen over the earlier table (see fig. 4).[42] Heinichen's purpose in giving this table of figures was to present students with an orderly catalogue, grouping chord indications by the most important interval. The original table printed in 1711 was expanded with the addition of dissonant chords built on minor second, augmented fifth, and various sevenths and ninths, suggesting the difficulties accompanists faced in trying to remember the meaning of the ever-growing list of figures. An end to such complexity, however, was not at hand; a few years later Mattheson[43] published a table of seventy figures, at the same time criticizing Heinichen's list for incompleteness.

No chapter from the *Neu erfundene Anweisung* appears in the *General-Bass* without considerable rewriting. The music examples demonstrate most forcefully Heinichen's concern with practical instruction. For the first time amateurs and students could escape the untold ambiguities of intricate verbal descriptions of thorough-bass accompaniments. Particularly because of its examples, the *General-Bass* is the only entirely practical thorough-bass manual printed in the Baroque.

The first version attempted a new and direct explanation of thorough-bass technique. Its limitations stem largely from the author's still incomplete musical background. The *General-Bass*, on the other hand, impresses one with more than its size, thoroughness, and variety of materials. The writing is infused with the confidence of a successful composer who has practiced the art of accompanying in the opera houses of Italy and Germany and before royal patrons. The interruptions of footnotes and their wide scope of philosophical reflections and practical suggestions, often unrelated to the topic at hand, preserve the immediacy of Heinichen's personality as well as his instruction to this day.

Notes

1. Heinichen, *General-Bass*, 1.

2. Ibid., 23 (footnote).

3. Included in an English translation as Appendix II of the present work

4. Heinichen, *General-Bass*, [vii].

5. The *Neu erfundene Anweisung* contains ten chapters in 284 pages; *General-Bass*, a total of twelve chapters in 960 pages (not counting preface, *errata*, and index sections). The latter has more than 540 pages of music examples as compared to some 153 pages in the first edition. On the basis of this comparison alone it is obviously misleading to equate both editions in the same terms. Lang, *Music in Western Civilization*, for example, refers only to the 1711 edition both in bibliography and footnotes, yet he quotes (pp. 438, 512) passages found only in the *General-Bass*.

6. Heinichen, *General-Bass*, 2 (footnote).

7. Mattheson, *Capellmeister*, 146.

8. Seibel, *Heinichen*, 40–63 lists 119 sacred works.

9. Heinichen, *General-Bass*, 7 (footnote)

10. Ibid., 7–8 (footnote).

11. Ibid., 8 (footnote).

12. See Bukofzer, *Baroque Era*, 360.

13. Heinichen, *General-Bass*, 10 (footnote).

14. Ibid., 47 (footnote).

15. Ibid., 83 (footnote).

16. Rudolf Wustmann compares Mattheson's catalogue of key affections with Bach's use of keys in the *Well-Tempered Clavier*, in *Tonartensymbolik zu Bachs Zeit, BACH-JAHRBUCH* 8 (1911), 60–74.

17. Heinichen, *General-Bass*, 20–24 (footnote i).

18. Heinichen, *Neu erfundene Anweisung*, 6.

19. See above, 5.

20. Heinichen, *General-Bass*, 840–41.

21. Heinichen, *Neu erfundene Anweisung*, 262.

22. Heinichen, *General-Bass*, 841.

23. See above, 17–18.

24. See Hans Turnow, "Mattheson," *MGG* 7, col. 1795–1815.

25. In the *Grosse General-Bass-Schule*, 98, Mattheson quotes Heinichen's letter asking the former to collect money owed him by a Hamburg merchant, money that would help support Heinichen's family after his death.

26. Johann Mattheson, *Das beschützte Orchestre* (Hamburg, 1717), [iv].

27. Schiller printed Mattheson's *Das neu-eröffnete Orchestre* (1713), *Das beschüzte Orchestre* (1717), Niedt's *Musicalische Handleitung dritter und letzter Theil*, with an introduction by Mattheson (1717), and Raupach's *Veritophili deutliche Beweis-Gründe*, also with an introduction by Mattheson (1717).

28. Heinichen, *General-Bass*, 93 (footnote).

29. Ibid., 938.

30. See references to Rameau in the *General-Bass*, 763, 766, 948, 960.

31. Ibid., 938: "Denn es gehet schon in das 6th Jahr, dass die ersten Bogen dieses *Tractates* allbereit im Druck da gelegen."

32. Ibid., 915 (footnote).

33. Heinichen, *Neu erfundene Anweisung*, 262.

34. Heinichen, *General-Bass*, 837.

35. Ibid., 868 (footnote m).

36. Ibid., 955.

37. Ibid., 955.

38. Attempts to identify this cantata have been unsuccessful, though clearly it is not by Alessandro Scarlatti as Denis Stevens incorrectly assumes in his review of the edition by E. C. Hanley of A. Scarlatti's *Passio D. N. Jesu Christi* . . . *JAMS* 9 (1956), 227.

39. Heinichen, *General-Bass*, 797 (footnote **).

40. Heinichen, *Neu erfundene Anweisung*, 65.

41. Ibid., 215.

42. Heinichen, *General-Bass*, 256.

43. Johann Mattheson, *Kleine General-Bass-Schule* (Hamburg, 1735), 136.

Appendix A

Lascia deh lascia al fine di tormentarmi più
Based upon Heinichen's Instructions

The following realization of Heinichen's instructions for the unfigured bass to Alessandro Scarlatti's cantata (see chapter 9) is included with some degree of apprehension. Any published version of a thorough-bass realization implies that this improvisatory art can be captured accurately and completely by musical notation. Yet the very act of representing such an ephemeral art on the printed page destroys much of the spontaneity of performance essential in accompanying from a thorough-bass. This is certainly one reason why Heinichen himself did not give an accompaniment based on his observations. Liberties taken with voice leading, inconsistencies in the number of parts, unconventional doublings in chords — all the freedoms taken with harmonic and contrapuntal practices that might repel an unimaginative theorist — are essential aspects of keyboard extemporization, as long, of course, as the performer stays within the principles of form and style maintained by Heinichen throughout his treatise. The tyranny of the eye trained in the rules of a harmony book confronts every music editor who attempts to give thorough-bass realizations for practical editions of Baroque music; this same tyranny has been met and, it is hoped, routed, in deciding the ultimate form of this appendix.

In adopting Heinichen's directions for Scarlatti's cantata, the author has employed a somewhat free keyboard style, in the spirit of Heinichen's guidance. However, this accompaniment is at best a basis for further extemporization by harpsichordists stimulated by actual performance conditions. Stated in another way, the author urges that the example on succeeding pages be considered only *one possible solution* for this particular unfigured bass. The reader is reminded that Heinichen expected his students to realize each thorough-bass example in three different versions based on the *drei Haupt Accorde*. This would be a most worthwhile exercise to apply to the following accompaniment as well.

di ge - lo - so ti - mo - re in mar' di fie - le   d'un i - dol trop - po in-

(†)   (†)

gra - to   tra gl'in - gan - ni mor - ta - li;   se sco - po all' i - re

(25)   (26)   (†)   (†)

d'un av - ver - so fa - to,   sol per - far - mi mor - ir, mi con - dan-

(†)   (†)   (27)   (28)

na - sti: deh la - scia   deh la - scia a - mor cru - de - le,   non

(†)   (†)   (29)   (30)   (31)

non mi tor—men—tar_____ ch'io vuò mo — ri — —

(33)(34)(†) (35) (36) (†) (37) (38)

re. Quell'

(39) (40) (41)

i — dol'in—fe—de—le ch'ogn' or mi fà__pe—nar, ve —

(†) (†) (42) (43)(44) (†)

de—te ogn'or de—si — a l'a — cer —ba mor—te mi—a, sol

(45) (46) (†)(†) (47)(†) (48) (†)(49)(50)(51)

Appendix B

Heinichen's *Einleitung* to the *General-Bass* Treatise: A Translation

The more than ninety pages encompassing the *Einleitung* to Heinichen's work, though not directly connected to the study of the thorough-bass, have great importance as one of the significant sources of knowledge about various aspects of Baroque music in the early eighteenth century. The range of topics touched upon and at times discussed in considerable detail includes: the general state of music in Heinichen's lifetime, his view of the vices of counterpoint, the essential requirements of a successful composer, the role of good taste (*Goût*) in composing, the concept of the *galant* in musical style, and much more. Of unique value, however, is Heinichen's graphic account of the nature of the affections and their use in music. No other source from the Baroque, not even the extensive writings of Johann Mattheson, is as explicit in its musical definition of various affections. In the *Einleitung* Heinichen incorporates a vivid and exceedingly practical demonstration as to how rhetoric can be applied to music, so that the composer, especially an opera composer, can achieve musical affections for even uninspiring poetry. Employing the oratorical device of the *locus topicus*, Heinichen examines a number of poetic texts in terms of their affective content or lack of it, and in the numerous examples he shows how a composer might express the affections in music.

Therefore, Heinichen's *Einleitung* is a fundamental source of Baroque compositional theory, written it must be emphasized by a gifted, highly honored composer of the German Baroque, schooled in Leipzig, conditioned by the music of Italy, and employed at the Saxon court at Dresden.

It deserves to be familiar to every student of Baroque music,* and it is hoped that this translation will make Heinichen's ideas more readily accessible to those who are unable to decipher the difficult original German text. The translation strives to follow the original without deviation other than for necessary changes of word order and punctuation. However, this aim is not easily reached in many cases where Heinichen himself has raised almost insurmountable barriers. The German in this section of his treatise is often perplexing in its complexity. The author's involuted style seems to thrive on excessively long sentences, including a mixture of several languages and numerous idioms whose meanings have become blurred if not lost by the passage of time. These elements often give rise to ambiguities in details for which approximate interpretation is the only practical solution. However, in no instance does the translation deviate from Heinichen's basic meaning. Since a facsimile reprint of the treatise is now readily available, it is recommended that this translation be used in consultation with the original text.

---

*Even though the importance of Heinichen's *Einleitung* was recognized early in the twentieth century by Hermann Kretzschmar in "Allgemeines und Besonderes zur Affektenlehre," in: *Jahrbuch der Musikbibliothek Peters* 18 (1911), 63–77; 19 (1912), 65–78, no complete translation has ever been published. However, see also the present author's article, "The *Loci Topici* and Affect in Late Baroque Music: Heinichen's Practical Demonstration," in *The Music Review* 27 (1966), 161–76.

Introduction
or
A Musical Discourse on the Thorough-Bass
and
Music in General

No music connoisseur will deny that the *Basso Continuo* or so-called thorough-bass is, next to [the art of] composition, one of the most important and most fundamental of the musical sciences. For from what source other than composition itself does it spring forth? And what actually is the playing of a thorough-bass other than to improvise upon a given bass the remaining parts of a full harmony, or to compose to [the bass]? As noble as the origin of the thorough-bass is, so equally great is the benefit and advantage accruing to all musicians from this knowledge. Even if one does not want to refer to the experience that after having studied the thorough-bass many a singer became more secure in pieces where previously he groped around considerably for a difficult interval or modulation before apprehending the exact tone; but certainly one need only consider that the thorough-bass, like composition itself, leads to the complete investigation of the entire musical edifice. Herein [in the thorough-bass] one learns to recognize precisely the ordinary consonances and dissonances of music, their nature and distinction, and their harmony and alteration. One investigates the nature, digression, and modulation of all keys and modes in such a way that one is capable of proceeding further in all other types of vocal and instrumental music and of attaining greater perfection every day. Indeed, if finally an accomplished thorough-bass performer has such contact with composition that he trusts himself to treat an unfigured bass and that he can see beforehand and guess the composer's idea, then one will easily concede to me that the firm knowledge of the thorough-bass gives each and every musician a true perfection and many-sided advantages in music — whether or not one makes a profession of the keyboard or the thorough-bass. In the end even the musical amateur believes this, and only the imaginary difficulties of the thorough-bass frighten many away from learning it. True, musical knowledge is not an accomplishment one can immediately, so to speak, leap over without wetting one's feet. It contains many complicated, I might say, confusing things. One need not even think of *Musica didactica, poetica, modulatoria* and other *Capita suprema & subalterna* common to music to realize that music has boundaries as wide as all the other sciences, arts, and advanced studies. Music is just as *theoretica & practica* as theology and jurisprudence; music is as *thetic & polemica* as other advanced disciplines, this being particularly evident in our century[a]

(a)   If I may be permitted here to interject incidentally a question: namely, why does our commonwealth of music have so many overwhelming controversies, so many contradictions, and, above all, so many disputes between old and new composers? Answer: the main (though not to say the only) cause for disagreement is the failure of both sides to agree on the first principle on which everything in music depends: whether music and its rules are regulated by the Ear or by the so-called Reason? The old [musicians] side more with Reason, but the new with the Ear; and since both parties do not agree on the first fundamental, it is evident that the conclusions and consequences made from two contrary fundamental principles should breed just as many controversies of inferior rank and thousands of diametrically opposed hypotheses. Musicians of the past, we know, chose two judges in music: Reason and the Ear. The choice would be correct since both are indispensable to music; yet, because of the use of these two concomitants, the present cannot reconcile itself with the past, and in this the past is blamed for two errors. First, it wrongly classed the two judges and placed the Ear, the sovereign of music, below the rank of Reason or would divide its commanding authority with the latter. Whereupon the blameless Ear must immediately cede half of its monarchical domain. In addition, unfortunately, the composers of the past poorly explained the word *ratio*. In those innocent times (in which one knew nothing of present-day good taste and brilliance in music, and every simple harmony seemed beautiful) they thought Reason could be put to no better use than the creation of supposedly learned and speculative artificialities of note writing. Therefore, they began on the one hand to measure out theoretically the innocent notes according to mathematical scales and with the help of the proportioned yardstick, and on the other hand to place these notes in musical practice on the staves (almost as if they were on a rack), and to pull them and stretch them (or in the language of counterpoint, to augment them), to turn them upside down, to repeat and to change their positions, until finally from the latter resulted a practice with an overwhelming number of unnecessary instances of contrapuntal eye-music and from the former resulted a theory with amassed metaphysical contemplations of emotion and reason. Thus, one no longer had cause to ask if music sounded well or pleased the listener, but rather if it looked good on paper. In this way, the visual imperceptibly gained the most in music and used the authority of the imprudent Reason only to cover its own lust for power. Consequently, the suppressed Ear was tyrannized so long that finally it hid behind table

as one tries hard to separate oneself both in music theory and practical music from many principles and preconceived opinions of the past. In short: one can write as many chapters and consequently as many volumes and doctrines for music (just as has been done in part) as exist in theology, jurisprudence, medicine, and philosophy. Nevertheless, no matter how

---

and chairs to await from the distance the condescending, merciful glance of its *usurpatores regni (ratio & visus)*. This grave injustice to the musical sovereign, the Ear, has been reprehended more by present-day musicians than by those of the past. They have begun vigorously to understand the many absurd and preposterous principles of the past and to form completely new ideas about the noble art of music unlike those of the learned ignoramuses. Above all, they return to the oppressed Ear the sovereignty of its realm; they displace Reason from its judicial duties and give it [reason] to the Ear, not as *Domino* or co-regent, but as an intelligent minister and counselor with the absolute mandate to warn its master (the occasionally deceived Ear, if indeed "deceived" can be spoken of) of every false step; but otherwise, and when Reason differs in opinion, it must serve [the Ear] with complete obedience and employ all of its skill to give not the visual appearance of music on paper, but the Ear the satisfaction of an absolute ruler. For this exactly is the true Reason and the greatest art of music. Really! What has the visual to do with music? Could anything more absurd be stated? The [art of] painting is for the eye, music, however, for the ear. Similarly, food is for the [sense of] taste and flowers for the [sense of] smell. Would it not be ridiculous to say the dinner was especially good because it smelled good, even though it was disagreeable to the taste and stomach? It is just as absurd if one should say along with pedants: this is outstanding music because it looks so fine (I mean pedantic) on paper, even though it does not please the ear, for which music solely is made. Now all arts and sciences, indeed all our undertakings and accomplishments tell us: *qui vult finem, vult etiam media ad finem ducentia*. As we must now admit unanimously that our *Finis musices* is to stir the affections and to delight the ear, the true *Objectum musices*, it follows that we must establish all our musical rules according to the Ear. And in this *Frau Vernunfft* (that super-intelligent *ratio*) will have her hands full, even more than we can imagine in our times. Thus the structure of music takes on a very different appearance, and from the previous *Postulata mathematice & demonstrative* one can deduce so much infallible *veritas* that partly transforms and partly overthrows most of the principles of the past. The beginning has already been made in our times; no doubt daily progress will be made in our century to this end for those supposedly paradoxical hypotheses, and finally all the remaining weak and partly-worn pillars of the musical past will be torn completely asunder. One should not take from Herr Capellmeister Mattheson due praise for his tireless and learned efforts in working out such musical matters and in particular his *Dritte Eröffnung der Orchestre, oder der beschirmte Sinnen-Rang* deserves merit, a book that should be required reading for those opposed to the musical Ear, to all pedants, and to Donati's disciples.

vast the art of music appears in general as well as in the particular field of the thorough-bass, these difficulties are not the Pyrenees; and they are not as great as they usually are made by foolish and overzealous individuals, if one will only discard the superfluous from the instruction and will seek a shortcut by disregarding antiquated methods.

Just consider the many clever and abridged methods [of learning] thought up in our times to lead young students many miles closer to Parnassus. Many undoubtedly would rather discard the methods by the learned Scherzer, Mohroff, and by other famous authors who show how a well-guided student can pass by all others and happily climb the highest peak of erudition; however, one should consider, above all, this eternal truth: That the *capable subjectum* who is trained thoroughly, basically, and methodically *inquacumque scientia* will always be several years ahead of any student who, though of the same age and capability of mind, is instructed confusedly and not by a good teacher. It always seems to me that here the same relationship of methods exists as in a situation in which an arithmetician solves a very difficult problem by using common arithmetic rules and thus wastes time and paper, while an experienced algebraist could do the same and even a further problem in a moment. Both finally achieved the same end, but with very different profit and loss of time and effort. If this and other advantages are practiced in other arts and studies, why not apply them to music as well? And furthermore, why should music alone not be seized upon to advantage and not be taught to amateurs of the music-loving world of our age in a shorter time and with fuller comprehension than it was done in the past? This certainly is possible if we think only of the *Finem musices* and above all outlaw from us all the variety of trifling eccentricities [*de lana caprina*] which are disputed,[b] but not ban them to

---

(b)   Also belonging under this heading, in my opinion, are those musical controversies involving the simple little word *Nennen*: (whether to be precise a thing should be called Hanss and not Toffel, little Catherine and not little Sibyl), over which one wastes all too much time and paper, even though there is complete agreement on the *Substantia, natura, & proprietate rei*, and though one knows how to do the thing with mastery. At least we should not burden music with these fruitless controversies, but try to employ our time and talent on something better. It is certainly true: *In verbis simus faciles, modo* etc. Why should we have concern for shells if we are comparing cores? If someone wishes to argue with me simply over the terminology for a thing, I would rather give in to him before he beings to present his quasi-reasoning. What more does he want if he can baptize the thing as he pleases?

those backward people who first had to try what is no longer useful for present-day composers. For these individuals would fight over such musical tomfoolery until they as well as we would achieve something better. One is frequently amazed to see expounded in books *in quarto* on music (not to mention the antique books *in folio*) absurd commonplaces and so-called accuracies of composition that show little significance and soon reveal that their master is one of those musicians who puts down many caprices on paper, but whose music gives less satisfaction to the Ear than that of an organ grinder. The old musical modes,[c] various counterpoints,[d]

(c)   To these we owe the discovery of a musical *ambitus*, or the prescribed modulations of keys. In today's practice, however, they are of little or no use, as will be shown below in various places.

(d)   Once and for all it should be reported that when the word counterpoint is mentioned in this treatise it is not meant *In sensu lato*, nor *Pro compositione in genere*, nor *Quasi punctum contra punctum*, nor *Nota contra notam*, but strictly for those compositions in which themes are used [in a contrapuntal manner]. Therefore, only those musicians can be called contrapuntists and arch-contrapuntists who seek the *Summum bonum* or the entire art of music in the study of counterpoint only. I am very fond of counterpoint, and in my youth I was an ardent adherent of it; as in the past, in the future too I shall continue to demonstrate my willingness to deal with fugues, double fugues, and other artifices of themes on paper in the devout church style. I cannot deny, however, that after many years of experience I have lost my previous enthusiasm for it and absolutely cannot bear our excessive misuse of forced counterpoints, in which for the most part (and I do not say completely) nothing has validity unless it is a pedantic counterpoint, and in which generally the artificial play with notes on paper is given out as the most noble and most artful form of music. This pretext is equally absurd for all reasonable musicians, and whatever the counterpoint-potentates may babble, one can satisfactorily destroy their weak arguments. Counterpoint serves a two-fold good purpose in music if it is cleansed of all useless classifications, sterile devices, and forced pedantries, and if only the true *Inventa* (which tyrannize our Ear the least) are chosen. First, [counterpoint] serves students and beginners in composition. With counterpoint they learn to climb or to spell, and with these given and restricted themes and toilsome exercises they are forced to master skilful progressions or *Passus compositionis*, just as the dancing or fencing master forces students first to make well-formed steps of the dance or a good body posture for fencing before showing them the true art. For such instructions the arch-contrapuntists are the very best suited, but one must not allow students to remain too long in apprenticeship, or else they will become as pedantic as their teachers.

  Second, counterpoint serves church music if it is mixed, according to the style of good church composers, with other techniques of good taste. Here is really its

the monochord, various temperaments, together with other similar musical materials in part should not be completely discarded, as they represent in part — and I repeat in part — what the vowels represent in the 24 letters

---

place, and here the contrapuntist can best show his learned schooling. Because our usual devout church music (more in Germany than in other countries) tolerates neither too much fire, inspiration, nor gay ideas, thus sometimes even a contrapuntist with little taste and invention can slip through at the very first. For after he has a bit of a theme or something of a musical idea captured at the twelfth, then he whips it through all the usual transpositions and common inversions; this then is called erudition, and the man has accomplished Herculean feats. What, however, should I say about the overwhelming amount of stereotyped counterpoint? I will always unpack my Seven Articles of Faith, notwithstanding *praevia protestatione solunni* that I do not speak of discarding all counterpoint but only of *de nimis abuso* of the same. Together with all experienced musicians who believe in the true *Finis musices* in contrast to the essential nature of restricted counterpoint, I can say that: (1) Most of the [contrapuntal] *inventa* (with few exceptions) are based on the visual and lifeless manipulations of notes but not on the actual sound. (2) That the more one sinks into the excesses of such stereotyped artifices, the more one necessarily must depart from the Ear and the true *Finis musices*. (3) That, therefore, those lines of a composition (not the entire piece, for there one can alternate) must be considered *inter casus raros & accidentales* or rare masterpieces, in which considerable sterile art is combined with equal amounts of good taste. (4) That the excessive abuse of too much counterpoint is the shortest path to musical pedantry, ruining many fine talents that otherwise could have been developed into something worthy. (5) That, for the most part, counterpoint in itself is something laborious (like the farmers' work when they must load manure into wheelbarrows) but not artistic once one has learned the routines. (6) That one can make a dull contrapuntist *par force* out of any dumb boy but not a composer with good taste. (7) Finally, to promote the *Finis musices* rather than the forced rules of counterpoint, there are many more beautiful and artistic things in music. "Indeed!" say the embittered contrapuntists, "but one can unite art (paper art) with good taste." Answer: these gentlemen never observe their own watchword, for if one listens to their very best music it sounds as if someone were beating the dust out of an old woman's fur coat, or (as others say) as if an abecedarian were spelling out something, understandable as syllables and words, but not the full sense or connection [of these words in sentences]. In short, when the performance is finished one does not know what the fellow meant to say with it. True, now and then a good composer will show that one can unite counterpoint and good musical taste, *sed non omnes capiunt hoc verbum*. And even if we argue *a po [s] t[er]iori* what can or does happen in nature, it still remains an eternal truth, that the excessive cultivation of counterpoint ruins good music and will ruin many fine natural talents born to music. So much for now concerning the abuses of counterpoint. What remains [to be said] follows in its proper place.

of the alphabet.[e] But one intermixes besides so many useless eccentricities that amount largely to *Ens rationabilibus cujuscunque* and provide music with as much practical advantage as the metaphysical haecceity in studying. And these musical Aristotles consider miraculous the godly things they have created from such nonsense. They mistake the innocent [art of] composition for quite a different creature; and if a composer, who is more concerned with sensitivity, good taste, and brilliance in music than with paper nonsense, writes with reason one little note contrary to their anti-quated, platonic rules, they want to turn him over to the Inquisition to discover whether or not he can be classed among composers. Only it is remarkable how such musical pedants, though they involve themselves so willingly in harmful, authoritative prejudices, do not notice, however, that already in our time not only native but also the most famous foreign[f]

(e)   I.e., he who knew nothing of these materials could never pass for a master either in theory or in practice. On the other hand, the usual abuse of these things certainly makes them more odious, and so it also goes with the monochord. This speculative box is indispensable to a theorist. Indeed, I should almost say that a practical musician can understand this science without harm, in so far as he wishes to be learned in his art and wants to avoid being hoaxed by the antiquitari-ans and super-intelligent theorists. But the unbearable abuse consists in this, that one foolishly tries to draw practical music itself out of this theoretical machine, even though the noble art of music is far removed from all theoretical speculations and can certainly exist without any of them. For who has ever denied it? Who has not seen and heard daily how much outstanding music is being performed by the most famous musicians of our time, certainly without taking the monochord into consideration. Not to mention those many fine musicians who hardly know the name and form, much less the nature of this mathematical touchstone? One distinguishes, therefore, between theory and practice, use and abuse, and thus the argument is resolved.

(f)   Experience teaches that the merchandise, paper music, receives more credit in one nation than in another. One nation is industrious in all endeavors; another laughs over useless school work, and tends to believe skeptically that the "North-erners" [*Tramontani*] (to use their manner of speaking) work like a team of draft horses. One nation believes art is only that which is difficult to compose; another nation, however, seeks a lighter style and correctly states that it is difficult to compose light music or to possess a light style. (Previously I too could not believe it.) One nation seeks its greatest art in nothing but intricate musical "tiff-taff" and elaborate artificialities of note writing. The other nation applies itself more to good taste, and in this way it takes away the former's universal applause; the paper artists, on the contrary, with all their witchcraft remain in obscurity and, in addition, are proclaimed barbarians, even though they could imitate the other

composers have begun to neglect the unnecessary eccentricities in composition and to seek a freer way in music by refining many of the old rules.
To furnish the matter with only some illustrations, I choose from among a
thousand examples by celebrated composers only a few from a first-rate
and otherwise skilled composer, the original for which one can produce if
need be. Observe in the following contrapuntal parts the irregular progressions marked with *:

---

nations blindfolded if they applied themselves more to the good taste and brilliance of music than to fruitless artificialities. An eminent foreign composer once
gave his frank opinion, contrary to the custom of his country, regarding the
differences in music of two nations. "Our nation," he said (since I give his own
words in our language), "is more inclined to *dolcezza* (gracefulness, *tendresse*) in
music, so much so that it must take care not to fall into a kind of indolence. Most
Tramontani on the other hand, are almost too inclined to liveliness in music, so that
they fall too easily into barbarisms. If they would take pains over adapting our
tendresse and would mix it together with their usual *vivacité*, then a third [style]
would result that could not fail to please the whole world, etc." I will not repeat the
comments I made at that time, but will say only that this discourse first brought to
my mind [the thought] that a felicitous mélange of Italian and French taste would
affect the ear most forcefully and must succeed over all other tastes of the world.
For this [conclusion] I imagine not only natural reasons but also actual examples
(though few in number) of the two nations. Nevertheless, the Germans have the
reputation abroad that if they would apply themselves industriously they could
usually surpass other nations in learning. From this principle I [derive my] hope
that some day our composers will try in general (since there is no scarcity of
special instances) to surpass other nations in matters of musical taste as well as
they have succeeded long ago in artful counterpoint and theoretical accuracies.
One more thing: Once I was asked how one can test by oneself whether our music
contains good taste, in case one will not trust *Philautis* or the false flattery of
others? Answer: If your music controlled by much experience, for the most part
and ordinarily pleases (1) both educated and uneducated, (2) individuals of completely different temperaments and humors, (3) in various parts of the world
where tastes are completely different and has the public approval, then you can
trust that you are on the right track. Carry on and think further about the matter.

Example B-1. *General-Bass*, 11–15.

ch' eſſer già non puòmo le - - ſta,

V.V. pizzicati.

raggio di pie tà nella mia mor - - - - te,

pizzicato.

Is it not true [that] many a pedant would become hysterical over such procedures? But one should trust this celebrated man to understand the first rudiments of music and know the nature of [parallel] octaves and the resolution of dissonances.[g] How poor it is actually to attack a skilled

---

(g) One usually acts contrary to the instruction of a fundamental rule for one of three causes: (1) error; (2) ignorance; (3) reason, if one purposely departs from [a rule]. The composer's examples given above belong to the third class. In the first class belong errors with fifths and octaves occurring without reason. And in this regard I should describe as a *Miraculum mundi* that well-known composer who has never made such natural errors during his whole lifetime. (Only if these errors do not occur too frequently and also in one tempo; otherwise they presuppose a most unobserving or inexperienced master.) To the second class, however, belong those real errors whose character prevents them from being considered an oversight or from being saved by rationalizing: these are unpardonable. For example, who would describe it as an oversight if in every piece one frequently proceeds from octaves to ninths in descending motion, ascends from diminished fifths to perfect fifths, makes unusual leaps in parallel motion to perfect consonances, composes three and four intolerable non-harmonic relationships, and a hundred other things contrary to rules and good taste, which even at first sight would shock a well-trained composer? For my part, I know of no excuse for such errors other than the youth of the composer or, in certain cases, the carelessness of the copyist; however, if no one has a better explanation, I will accept this; for to err is human.

master so childishly. Nevertheless, all the previous cases (particularly in this style) are composed with justification, which one would like inexperienced [musicians] to find out, especially (regarding the final example) if they lack familiarity with the vocal style of other nations. If, however, we examine more closely the motives causing famous composers to deviate frequently from the artificial accuracies of pure theorists, then in my judgment they might be: first, [these composers] are ashamed in general of pedantry and forced school book rules, and they search for the *Arcana musica* in much more important things than the easy and frequently irrelevant theories made for students. Second, they have sound practical judgment and know when and where to depart with good reason from theoretical rules. Third, they will not be slaves to the many poorly founded rules from the past, but they would rather agree with the rule, founded on reason itself, though otherwise juristic: *Cessante ratione prohibition is, cessat ipsa prohibitio* — whenever the cause for the prohibition on which a rule is based becomes null and void, the prohibition or the given rule itself becomes null and void. And this judicious practice is ten times more difficult than the frequently prescribed, dry theory. Indeed, for this very reason the unskilled theorists remain so willingly with their dull, antiquated rules, because their judgment is inadequate to allow deviation from them with reason. I cannot continue without inserting the following example from a *Cantata voce sola* by a famous and skilled composer:

Example B-2. *General-Bass*, 17–18.

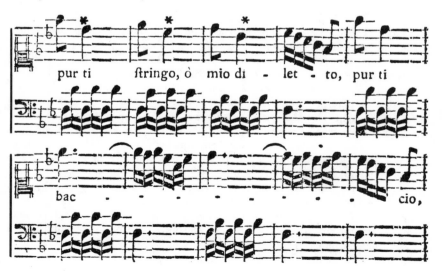

purti ſtringo, ò mio di - - let to, ò mio di-

let to,ò mio di - let - to,

For various reasons, I should not care to confirm this man's achievement, however many a theorist he may have had as tutor, and even though I consider these progressions as the most beautiful expression of the words. In addition, it should be pointed out that the bass begins the aria with no chosen theme but with an ever-changing variation of the single bass note F, as if it were taken extemporaneously. Well-known composers have had good success with similar playful harmonies, particularly in powerful theatrical works. But all such matters beyond the usual circle of things belong only to experienced and judicious composers, not to theoretical antiquitarians and even less to beginners, and these matters are neither recommended nor made a habit of by composers unless they find good reasons to do so. Therefore, whoever knows only how to criticize such supposed liberties does violence to the noble art of composition. [He] clearly shows that either he has not grown out of musical childhood or that he truly belongs to a society of musical pedants (no matter whether he has a Bachelor's, Master's, or Doctor's degree) [whose members] cannot differentiate, or understand what it means to compose either for the eyes or for the ears, even though they see contradictory examples every day, which with all their strength they are not able to imitate. It is true that one must know rules,[h] whether one learns them from experience or from the instruction of

(h)   All arts and sciences have rules and must be learned through rules, if we do not
      wish to remain simple naturalists, i.e., half-ignorant. But we must not err excessively on the side of rules; furthermore, we should not accept so crudely the

equivocal word: Rule, as if we would serve as high sounding rule makers, prescribing laws even to Nature, according to which she must limit herself to *auctoritate nostra*. No! All of our useful rules must be derived from Nature; and we must investigate on all levels the will, preference, and character of this mistress and learn from her *cum submissione*. And from these observations we take our rules that, in accordance with the different characteristics of art, pertain various gradations and (strictly speaking) should be called, on the one hand, rules *par excellence*, permitting few or no exceptions, and on the other hand, *propria tertii, quarti modi, casus ut raro, observationes, adminicula*, etc. Since all these observations of nature and art are aimed at the same goal, namely, teaching the student the *essentiam, qualitatem, & accidentia rei* of all arts, they will generally be labeled (in order not to multiply technical terms in a fruitless way) with the word "rule" without any regard for the metaphysical contemplation defining a rule. Similar rules of varied types and gradations are found in all the arts, sciences, and studies of higher learning (one should just look around a little). Music has the same rules of all types and levels from the ground up. Of a similar kind are the thousands of rules for composition that have been given to the world. Also similar (speaking *à propos* in this case) are those rules that German, French, and Italian authors began to formulate long ago for the unfigured thorough-bass, partly having been brought to maturity by them in recent times. Since all these authors have carefully considered the numerous things brought to our attention daily within many scores in the *stylo theatrali* (even here one cannot on first intuition pick out figures from all the parts), and in the *stylo camerali*, the many thousands of cantatas and instrumental pieces with a single part [over the thorough-bass] without figures; and since not all accompanists are, at the same time, experienced composers able to judge the figures from the art of composition, therefore all these writers have made *excerpta, observationes*, rules, or *adminicula* from the most useful sections of compositions with which the accompanist can almost predict immediately the nature and changes of the harmony and the intention of the composer. As long as we do not proclaim a general mandate in all countries against producing these unfigured thorough-basses in private or public, we cannot reprove the profitable attempts of all these writers who ventured to give rules for the unfigured thorough-bass. For a zealous student will want to learn everything about accompanying; however, he will not have good teachers at all times. Indeed, even if the student had good teachers, the latter could not discuss this material differently than is shown in the whole Part II of this treatise, and particularly in the fourth chapter, discussing two cantatas. If one would take his students through a dozen or even a half-dozen cantatas in this manner, one would see how much they profited in a short time. But here someone might say: the rules that one can give for the unfigured thorough-bass are too changeable; and one must frequently add the words "naturally," "generally," "for the most part," or "seldom." The answer would be: Certainly. Since the nature of the source from which one must derive thorough-bass rules, namely the composition itself, is changeable, therefore the rules and observations taken from it, in order to fit into the picture, must also be variable. But what does this mean? Examine the thousands of composition rules written in *octavo, quarto*, and *folio* and see if only very few should add the word others. Without them, a composer will certainly commit many a folly in music, which frequently occurs with those who are versed in one extreme — I mean whose entire musical knowledge and background consist merely of a little natural disposition and invention,(i) in so far as the latter is

---

"always," whereas most of them should add such words as "generally," "naturally," "mostly," or "seldom." But should we discard composition itself because of the changeable nature of its rules? Both [sets of] rules must stand or fall together; there is no third choice, or if there were I should like to see this miraculous creature. Besides, I should not generally advise one to think about discarding all the variable rules; because in many cases we should do no slight harm to ourselves if the opposite were proved.

(i)   I.e. Those who do not possess all of a composer's *Requisita essentialia*. Many requirements actually belong to a composer's perfection, which one could specify in great numbers theoretically, practically, even politically, as has occurred to some extent in [the works of] other authors. Here, however, we will examine only three essential *Requisita compositoris moderni* by which one can place himself or others on the scales and easily discover the principal defect of a composer. Accordingly, I say that three basic *requisita* establish a good, modern composer: (1) talent, (2) knowledge, (3) experience. And these three *requisita* (which in the following explanation are somewhat different from the usual understanding of the words) must stand in mutual support, if not already the weakness in one of them produces a major deficiency in the composer. (1) As far as the musical talent or natural personality is concerned, it consists generally of a natural, good disposition, spirit, and skill in relation to music in general, and specifically in relation to composition. It helps its possessor not only to skip lightly over the peaks of musical mountains, but also gives him natural, good ideas for the *Arte compositoria*, as well as suitable sentiments to promote the *Finis musices* in all possible ways. In a word, it facilitates all other *requisita* contributing to the completeness of a composer's training. One can as little describe the differences in musical talent as one can describe the differences between all ingenuities. Generally, however, one can say that the good talents of composers differ only in degree. For Nature gives to one an animated, clear, burning spirit, but to another a tempered, modest, or even affective nature. The latter is better suited to the devout church style, the former, however, more to the theatrical, if [the composer] does not know how to modify his natural fire (which, however, in itself is certainly possible). Yet, if Nature denies musical talent to an individual, he had better leave composing alone, for he will remain a pale glimmer from under a basket. And even if he learns all the rules, and studies every writer since Jubal's time, and travels through Germany, Italy, France, and Spain, his composition will still turn out a botched work, or (depending on how much he tortures himself and imitates *par force* the works of other virtuosos) a beggar's cloak bordered with velvet patches. (2) Knowledge was the second *Requisitum essentiale*. A composer must possess all the important aspects of theoretical and practical music and, in particular, *Musica poetica*; i.e., he must not only understand thoroughly all the fundamental principles and important rules for music and composition, but also he must be able to use them well and to put together nicely a musical work. Herein the often cited counterpoint is not excluded, provided one will only avoid the *nimium abusum* and pedantry. For to be able to employ a theme suitably is surely indispensable to a good composer. If one wishes, however, to pursue theory further and to learn also the principles of physics and mathematics applied to music, this actually will do no harm. However, to the circumnavigation of the ocean in the musical world belong, above all, good fortune and a good wind in the sails (i.e., a good teacher and, for the student, talent and also judgment) to avoid Scylla and Charybdis, I mean the two extremes of theory in order that we neither become pedants — from whose music everyone flees — through too many superfluous eccentricities in music made for the ear, overly pure naturalists who cannot give reasons for their works from all too superficial learnedness. And the latter in all honesty belong among the ignorant.

The third and most important *Requisitum compositoris moderni* was experience. We refer to that experience a composer has to achieve after going through the regular rules of art in theory and practice. For if an artist dismisses his student from taking lessons, this means the latter must go out now into the world and look around to see what others are doing in his profession. In other words: he must gain experience and seek to refine his theoretical and practical knowledge. If experience is necessary in any art or science, it is certainly necessary in music. In this *Scientia practica*, first of all, we must gain experience (which by nature abhors all theoretical superfluities based purely on speculation), either at home, provided opportunities are sufficient, or through traveling. But what is it that one believes one must seek in the experience? I will give a single word, defining the three basic *Requisita musices*, i.e., talent, knowledge, and experience, as well as the true *finis musices*, as the center: this word is in four letters, *Goût* [good taste]. Through diligence, talent, and experience, a composer must achieve above all else an exquisite sense of good taste in music. Therefore, I am particularly pleased with certain foreign nations, whose first question or consideration of a musical performance usually results in asking: does the music have *Goût* [good taste], or a *bon gusto*? The definition of *Goût, Gusto,* or *guter Geschmack* is unnecessary for the experienced musician; and it is as difficult to describe in its essentials as the true essence of the soul. One could say that good taste was in itself the soul of music, which so to speak it doubly enlivens and brings pleasure to the senses. The *Proprium 4ti modi* of a composer with good taste is contained solely in the skill with which he makes his music pleasing to and beloved by the general, educated public, or which in the same way pleases our ear by experienced artifices and moves the senses (the internal senses, the physical senses of sight, smell, hearing that are not concerned here). In general, this can be brought about through a good, well-cultivated, and natural invention or through the beautiful expression of words. In particular, [this is achieved] through an ever dominating *cantabile*, through suitable and affecting accompaniments, through a change of harmonies recommended for the sake of the ears, and through other methods gained from experience and frequently looking poor on paper, which in our times we only label with the obscure name of "rules of experience." In summary, everything is good taste or stems from it that contributes to the real progress of the true *Finis musices*. An exceptional sense of good taste is so to say the musical *Lapis philosophorum* and the principal key to musical mysteries through which human souls are unlocked and moved and by which the senses are won over. Indeed, if one has achieved a place through music in the world and emerges [successfully], it is certainly achieved by music with good taste (and never by eye-music). Good taste is not only the most useful but also the rarest jewel, which one must seek with the greater effort, the less it can be given to one who has not found it by his own experience. Here I recall that some authors have said that we need to profit in certain circumstances from other nations. What shall we adopt for our own profit? Or, better formulated, why do we go through effort, danger, and expense to travel around from nation to nation where music has more supporters than with us (at the same time also more amateurs as well as professionals)? Is it, perhaps, to seek musical knowledge? Oh no! We have that at home as good if not better, and he who does not bring something along will most certainly not take something away. Perhaps then we travel to capture musical talent? This would in itself be impossible even if talent would not be as native to our country as to others. What then do we lack as a *Requisitum compositoris*, or in a word: why do we travel? Answer: Simply and solely to develop our good taste. By this we tacitly admit that we consider *Goût* as having the greatest importance in music. For even the natural gift or talent endowed with most invention resembles only crude gold and silver dross that must be purified first by the fire of experience before it can be shaped into a solid mass—I mean into a finely cultivated and steadfast sense of good taste. Which proves, contrary to the beliefs of many half-experienced [people], that invention and good taste (consequently also personality or talent and *Goût*) are two totally different things. For invention is innate to us and can be either good or bad; good taste, however, must control it [invention], and remains to be accomplished by us by work and experience, and, of course, through a great number of and frequently difficult rules of experience. In this connection many otherwise good subjects can serve as an example, subjects that do not lack two of the *Requisita compositoris* (i.e., knowledge and natural talents); but, because fortune denied them the third requisite, namely the opportunity to listen continuously to good music in order to gain sufficient experience (I shall not speak of those ignorant pedants who through their own over-presumptuousness do not want to acquire more knowledge), they remain with all their invention-rich pieces composers without good taste. This means they compose constantly more that is poor than good; they have no consistent style; and they do not know what they are doing, except now and then their inborn talent leads them quasi-blindly into the right path. Therefore, none of our three basic requisites is unnecessary to the composer of integrity; he must have a combination of talent, knowledge, and experience on a high level, otherwise his music will always stand on weak feet.

not borrowed legally or illegally from other writers. On the other hand, one also must not stumble into the opposite extreme of such useless and often incorrectly founded rules of composition, in which the proud art of music is enchained and the shortest way to its true purpose is obstructed. For truly the soul and gracefulness of a composition do not consist of a few hundred antiquated and unnecessary rules, which if they were necessary any country bumpkin could learn to understand and to observe. One can really find superior, more artistic, and necessary things on which to spend better one's energy for one's own good, provided only that one studies hard and ponders further each day the *Arcana musica*. What a bottomless ocean we still have before us merely in the expression of words (**) and the affections in music. And how delighted is the ear, if we perceive in a refined church composition[(k)] or other music how a skilled virtuoso has

---

(**)   To express words with naturalness, ease, and in good taste, in such places where it occurs *à propos*, is a fine as well as difficult art. Otherwise [these attempts] sound mannered, and one can easily make oneself ridiculous with such expressions. Thus, one can find printed pieces, written by pretentious *practici* (I wish they were *theoretici*) that could make a whole company of friends laugh without special effort. Yet it astonishes one, how such pieces without heartfelt emotion can be recited. One not only has to know good *principia practica*, but also has to be able to realize them. A mighty chasm stretches between knowledge and ability.

(k)   We speak here of those worthy church music composers who have learned something besides counterpoint and who lack neither good taste nor invention. Since in the church style we do not want to specialize in one extreme or the other, or (better said) since we will have to deal in this devout style with themes and counterpoint and at the same time our ears also demand their satisfaction (which need not consist of merry dance music), therefore, we must modify the wooden counterpoints and vary them with music of good taste. Thus, the composers of today usually leave behind the unsalted character of the antiquated church style. Those contrapuntists, however, who are not endowed with good taste and who stick to a common repertory of notes are pursued by the natural punishment, resembling the original sin: their music is not liked by a single living soul. It would be better, therefore, to burn immediately their all too artificial compositions before they cool down, and to scatter the ashes into their eyes. Then at least one of the senses would gain something from it, for otherwise neither the eye nor the ear profits from such a paper art. Still more: I have seen examples abroad: after formerly renowned theatrical composers, in their old age, had lost all their creative fire and invention, they became for the first time good church composers, working contrary to former habit as good contrapuntists. From this arise various arguments.

attempted here and there to move the feelings of an audience through his *galanterie* and other devices that express the text, and in this way to find successfully the true purpose of music. Nevertheless, no one wants to search deeper into this beautiful musical *Rhetorica* and to invent good rules. What could one not write about musical taste, invention, accompaniment, and their nature, differences, and effects? But no one wants to investigate the matters aiming at this lofty practice or to give even the slightest introduction to it. On the other hand, for other frequently pedantic subjects cartloads of rules are devised. Yes, since nowadays we do not even want to believe that instructions and rules could be given in matters which are like those still strange to our thinking, we blindly orient most of our studies to mere eye-music and value as the most beautiful only those compositions in which this paper art holds the scepter; but we falsely condemn those works displaying taste, brilliance, and numerous difficult controls gained by experience. To the latter category mainly belongs the theatrical style and, given permission, I shall contribute to its defense with a few observations at this place.

This blameless style, unknown to antiquity, is frequently considered very easy and almost unimportant, because the inexperienced believe one is much freer in it and need not observe the rules of composition (many of them) as carefully as in church music or other affective music. But with such reasoning these individuals reveal on the one hand their ignorance in not understanding that this style in many pieces has far more and stricter rules than other styles.[(1)] On the other hand, they clearly indicate that they

---

(1)   This will certainly be clarified by the following reply to the three common objections that the ignorant usually make against this style. Their first argument: the theatrical style observes no suspensions and resolutions, which are certainly the most beautiful and legitimate [aspects] of music. Answer: *si tacuisses, poëta mansisses*. Chapter 1, Part II [of the *General-Bass*] will show extensively that this blameless style contains more beautiful and artistic ways of treating and resolving dissonances than other styles. Second, they say: the theatrical style observes none of the *ambitus modi* that the old theorists so thoughtfully established, but one proceeds with modulations of keys according to one's taste. Answer: *plus artis, minus simplicitatis*. It no longer is something new today for even our most illustrious and highly trained church composers to move back and forth from the remotest of keys at the proper opportunity and for good reason, without giving the slightest disturbance to our ears — an art in which not every poor imitator will succeed. On the other hand, it is not hard for any average student to keep his compositions moving around the usual *ambitus modorum* (which is fully described in Chapter 2, Part II). Which of the two is the more difficult? Theorists of the past already called cadences on notes only one step outside the tones of the triad on the first degree of

are musicians of little taste, stupidly valuing only the notes on paper as the most artistic aspect of music. Because now and then the theatrical style allows free thoughts and unconstrained ideas, one must certainly not think it easier and without artistry. For not to mention that such arbitrary things frequently add the best seasoning and are often three times more difficult to invent than conventional harmony or a double counterpoint, one need only consider carefully where we have the greatest need today for these

---

the fundamental scale (*Triade harmonica*) *peregrinae*, or alien cadences. Today it is no longer strange for a well-trained composer to move through a circle of all the keys or modes at one time. Which then is the more artistic, the old or the new? Third and last, these opponents say with particular gravity: The theatrical style has no counterpoint. Answer: This would be an excellent misfortune, but in this case this also means, *mentiris Cain*. Not to mention the good theatrical composer's need to know his counterpoint, if he is not to betray occasional weaknesses in this style. But who can tell me the particular power of the eminent word *Contrapunct*? What does counterpoint really mean? Nothing more than the frequent repetition of thematic materials in various ways. What is a theme? The retention of certain intervals following each other in a special order or a continuation of a certain pattern [*clausul*]. But does one not exercise the same art in the theatrical style; and after all is it enough only to begin a theme, an imitation, a pattern, or an invention, without correctly developing it? It seems to me that this is pure counterpoint according to the correct meaning of the word. And who can really be prevented from trying to use themes and counter-themes also in a theatrical aria, duet, trio, etc., as long as the great number of counterpoints do not tear apart the body? Thus, one cannot blame the theatrical style for anything but lacking opportunities to employ a number of laborious tuttis, full-voiced fugues, counterfugues, the *allabreve* [style], and similar devout things. Why are those devices excluded from the *galant* theatrical style? Was it not the opinion of the best contrapuntists in the past that one recognizes a learned composer easier by his 2, 3, and 4 voiced compositions than by his excessive [use of] overladen contrapuntal combinations, where it is impossible by their nature to observe any rules of composition? Why should the noble music encompass only laborious school craft? Yes, if one wants to work and work, one can do this in different ways in theatrical music as well as in the strictest church style. I recall that in my previous Leipzig operas I used arias in 6, 7, and up to 8 real parts which needed a great deal of work; however, today I would write over most of them: *sed cui bono*. True art is found elsewhere than on paper. Whoever then wants to compare all the prerogatives in which our tasteful, inventive, and brilliant theatrical style exceeds all the other styles in good taste and invention with the above objections, should draw conclusions according to his reason and should solve this question for me: How does it happen that now and then in this and other countries there are so many good church composers, yet everywhere so few good composers for the theatre?

scorned, difficult and, for the most part, still uncultivated skills in music, if not in the theatrical style, or in operas? How many otherwise unusual effects are customarily invented in those works in order constantly to amuse the ear in extended theatrical works and to achieve successfully the basic purpose of music, I mean giving pleasure to our ears? An experienced composer always has to search for constant changing of keys, instruments, meter, the various forms of invention (in order that arias will not be largely brothers and sisters), especially since in an opera the same affection, according to circumstance, will be repeated ten or more times and therefore should be expressed in different ways. What more must he seek in changes of meter, which in poetry, the various types of verses, often appear unvaried, as well as other judicious aids? Yes, there is still more to be considered in the theatrical style. It is not ever enough that a composer writes down a naturally occurring, good invention expressing the words and pleasing the good taste of intelligent listeners. It also requires an artist to work out [these inventions] at the right occasion according to the rules and to prove that he possesses knowledge and good taste. If we think further [and include] the recitative style, this practice demands much more experience than the novices believe. And though once I, too, thought that this style could not have either rules or methodical instruction, a more exact examination of it has changed my mind; and I am certain that one can give the finest rules for it, particularly concerning the sudden shifts to remote keys and the artistic application of unusual consonances and dissonances. (I confess I still desire to delve further into this, and perhaps some day another kind of musical circle will be found than the one appearing at the end of Chapter 5, Part II, or at least a new method for using the same.) In summary, whoever gives mature thought to all this will be convinced that in itself the *galant* and refined theatrical style possesses much individual artistry with which it can stand in perfect balance with all other styles; one might even say it surpasses them in certain pieces. And, certainly, to be able to distinguish oneself in it from others requires more experience than can be imagined; indeed, it even requires a special talent. If one could but experiment, and let this [type of composer] set something for the theatre who at other times composes the most beautiful church pieces embellished with ten thousand counterpoints, then one will see that if the composer is not already trained to some degree in the theatrical style (which could occur, though these individuals are rare), just how much bad taste will slip through — as greatly amused me once when one of the most artistic and famed contrapuntists of our time showed me his theatrical ideas or *Contrapuncto florido* (as he called it). Should I give one undisputed characteristic of the *stylo theatralis*, showing its superiority to all other styles, I should say that it needs a much greater amount of invention than all other forms of composing. Actually, in the strictest church style one can use a single passable theme of a few measures to fill up two, three, or more sheets of paper, once one has learned the usual school lessons *ex fundamento*. But in the theatrical style one must forget such things, for in it invention, good taste, and brilliance must always be evident. Indeed, even nowadays one has to avoid the misfortune to include in so many large theatrical works a single aria or even a melodic pattern of a few notes seeming to have the slightest similarity with a former work. For even if these [similarities] are only approximations and occur contrary to the composer's intention, or the inventions are barely similar *in tertio, quarto*, comparable to women who resemble each other *in sexu feminino*; there will be those who will in stupidity and passion take the opportunity to rebuke the composer for plagiarism (because he who could not write instead of such a little formula twenty others extemporaneously must be considered a poor composer). And for this very reason, no composer could succeed nowadays if he simply sought and thought of his invention in the otherwise useful *Arte combinatoria*, because by means of this art one can vary 4 notes 24 times and 5 notes 120, etc. according to the usual arithmetical progression. Thus, he could derive from 5 notes 120 *inventiones*, of which only 10 would be useful and dissimilar. In this a composer may succeed once; I am sure it does not happen too often, even though he might change the quantity of the notes at will. Because it is impossible to find the tenderness of the soul of music with mere numeric changes of dead notes and, on the other hand, it is most necessary in certain cases to stimulate the soul, therefore one ought rather to think of such *Modi inveniendi* that exert the vivid imagination of the composer. In truth, only half the effort is required for a musical invention, if the composer can derive a good musical idea from the given (but frequently unfruitful) text. But to lead our thoughts to good ideas and to encourage our natural imagination cannot, I believe, be better accomplished than through the oratorical *Loci topici*. Even with the most uninspired text one can take just the three principal sources, namely, *antecedentia, concomitantia*, and *consequentia textus* and examine them according to the *locus topicus* by weighing carefully the purpose of the words, including the related circumstances of persons, things, conditions, the origins, the means, purpose, time, place, etc. Thus, the inborn natural imagination (we speak not of stupid dispositions) never lacks for the expression of pleasing ideas or, to speak more clearly, skillful inventions.[m] It will be worthwhile to spend the effort illustrating this useful material (in which particularly the composers born ungifted are usually lacking) with copious examples. Therefore we take some shallow texts and examine them

---

(m)   It has been several years since I came upon these thoughts because of certain uninspiring texts, though otherwise I probably did not need such an aid, in that ordinarily I do not need the use of the *loci topici*. But I cannot deny that at times I should not have known how to write a single note in those hours when I faced an uninspiring text or also when I did not feel disposed to writing (which is a common feeling for all composers), if this craft had not served me. I think that with this craft one assists natural imagination in the same way as one assists the memory with the well-known *Arte mnemonica*, or mnemonics. Actually, we know that there are individuals who can, with certain techniques, repeat 30, 40 or even 100 and more names, numbers, or other things in a certain accurate order, forward and backward or mixed in order, after they had been slowly recited to them. Once I tested a good friend who had inscribed on his mind the entire Bible by using this very same skill; and I, going through all the books without special order and while he looked elsewhere, cited a certain versicle here and there or even only single words; this man knew immediately the book [of the citation], chapter, verse, and often the section where to find the right page, even though in other things he had a poor memory. Such things could not be accomplished by the normal mind without the support given by profitable aids. In just this sense we want the natural good imagination of a composer to be supported and incited with the excellent assistance of the *loci topici*. I also realize that actually there are other means to be made use of to create ideas, and in this regard: *chacun à son goût*. But one must take care in some places that the method does not become so ingrained that a real plague results; similarly in the case of some nations where young, wild musicians frequently say: *bisogna farsi idea*, with which they run off to other music and copy down the kernel of the best ideas of other composers and, scarcely restirring the brew, pour it into their own work. Respectable and wise composers, however, shun opportunities to listen to great music shortly before they are going to compose, fearing that as it usually happens something of it will remain in their memory and that they might include it in their own work, innocently thinking it was their own thought and bringing suspicion of injudicious censors upon him. In such doubtful situations I look somewhat to the *Arte combinatoria*. That such an art could give someone true mastery (and not be used merely as an aid, as some writers in the learned sciences suggest) is as unlikely as

according to their inspiration as *fontes*. For example, Metilde enters in an opera and has the following aria to sing after a preceding recitative:

Non è sola, non è straniera	[The motive is not unique,
la causa, ch'e vera;	it is not strange, that is true;
non dubito, nò.	I do not doubt, no.
scoprire si sà	Very often the truth is
spesso meglio de se la verità.	better uncovered by iself.]
D.C.	D.C.

What should a composer make of this? And where should he find the source of his invention? For not once in the entire aria, not to mention the *da capo* or first section of the same (where every time the force of a poem as well as of the music should really be found), is there a single word that gives the slightest opportunity for expressing a single affection.

But if one looks at the antecedent of the text (in order to take up our three principal sources in the right order), [one sees that] Metilde fully discovers her affection in the preceding recitative, if she answers Adolpho's question: *che machini, che pensi?* [What are you planning, what are you thinking?] with: *alti dissegni, e precipizii immensi; accusare, gridare, chieder raggione etc., e con nove d'amor fatto animoso liberare il mio sposo, etc.* [Lofty plans and great destructions; to accuse, to cry out, to ask reasons, etc., and made bold with the renewal of love, free my husband, etc.]. Only now the composer can derive from Metilde's intentions that this in itself dry aria can be represented in the most furious of affections, which should fire invention-rich composers to transform their formerly suspended thoughts into beautiful musical ideas. But should the natural fantasy require still more help, one can proceed to special expressions of the recitative such as: *alti dissegni, e precipizii immensi*, and these could give something like the following expression (or ten other inventions of this type):

---

that the *loci topici* are apt to endow someone with true invention when by nature the individual has no talent for music. Finally, I believe that the well-known school rhyme, *quis, quid, ubi*, etc. tells about as much of the oratorical *loci topici* as the tail tells about the whole dog. However, whoever knows nothing of the *loci topici* will gain from this verse (since it is in itself derived from the L.T.) only incomplete assistance. But if one examines thoroughly the above examples, one will find comprehension in the matter.

Example B-3. *General-Bass*, 32–35.

If we are not pleased with this manner of invention, we can go further and consider the words: *accusare, gridere, chieder raggione.* Here the imagination has the best opportunity for a "quarrelsome" or, better said, many-voiced, concerted invention. For brevity, the following will suffice:

Example B-4. *General-Bass*, 36–38.

(n) In order to save space in this and all following examples, we have not only reduced the accompaniment as much as possible, but also have brought the voice part to the first cadence without elaborations. Otherwise, it is understood as in good Greek that one can begin and develop all of these examples more elaborately and with greater completeness.

nò, nò, nò, non   du - bì - to, nò.

Should we still be dissatisfied, we could try to represent the heroic resolution of Metilde in some sort of pompous manner, by association with the final words: *con novo d'amor fatto animoso liberare il mio sposo.*

Example B-5. *General-Bass*, 39–41.

Vivace.

Non è sola, non è   straniera la cau · sa ch'è ve · ra, la

cau - sa, ch'è ve · ra, ch'è ve - - -

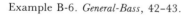

These represent three types of invention from the antecedent of this most uninspiring aria, all of which are perfectly suited to the text. We continue further and seek invention in the concomitant, I mean in the different words of the *da capo*, or first part of the aria itself which could, for example, begin:

chi hà nemica la fortuna   [He who has fortune as an enemy
si vedrà sempre penar.   will always see himself in want.]

This moralistic text, like most moralistic arias, is not particularly gratifying to the composer. However, if one observes the qualities of Fortune, one could express it in various ways, for example: its constant pursuit; or its fickleness and inconsistency, the raging and fleeing, the obstinacy and contrariness and, above all, the sorrow that fortune brings. This can be accomplished through a strongly concerted harmony in the form of violin and bass themes or through solo instruments chosen *à propos*. We shall again discuss only three of the various possibilities; first we shall try to express in the following bass theme fortune's eternal pursuit of us:

Example B-6. *General-Bass*, 42–43.

Chi hà ne   mi · ca la for - tu - na, fi ve drà fem pre fempre pe·

nar,   fi ve drà fem - - pre penar,   (*o*)

(o)   More than certain other nations, we tend to cultivate a greater number of bass themes. In the past seven or eight years I cannot recall hearing in their music more than a dozen formal, obbligato bass themes among the quantity of so many pieces. For the rest, there exist at the most in their music *badinanten* little trifling patterns of notes that all the violins and violas double in octaves, in the belief that this emphasizes and at the same time distinguishes their less-penetrating low tones. By the way, since they profess to be admirers of the *cantabile*, they think that the more one attempts to bind the dominating vocal or instrumental part to a given bass theme, the more one is forced to depart from the natural *cantabile*, except as it is achieved accidentally or through much work of good taste. Since

Fugitive or raging fortune could be expressed by various strongly concerted harmonies. The following invention will suffice:

Example B-7. *General-Bass*, 43–45.

---

they will not leave themselves to chance, but also according to their nature they will not perform drudgery, they push these laborious crafts into the background more than we do. For the same reasons, they do not uphold to any extent the many-faceted elaboration of instrumental parts in individual vocal pieces, with the pretext that this would only hinder the singer, a remark calling for an apology to [those possessing] good, resolute voices. Otherwise, instrumental parts in music of other countries are considered artistic as long as they are not overdone and are appropriate to the music. Nevertheless, a clever composer certainly can write arias that do not appear laborious on paper and can still achieve all the effects when performed in public, even if a great singer energetically performs them too slowly or the poorest [singer] distorts them. For whatever impresses the ear favorably still cannot be concealed by a mediocre performance; and the ear distinguishes at any time the value of a composition, without the composer having to depend on the singer's performance to show its value. For the flow of melody or *cantabile* that the singer ought to create can be written into the music by the composer; additional trimmings have little worth, and I have a poor conception of those composers whose music is only impressive if it is worked out with special effort by the most excellent singers. For this reason, good singers used to say of a good composition: *Canta da se stesso* — it sings by itself, and one cannot add much to it.

Chi hà ne - mi - ca la for-

tu - na   fi   ve drà fem - pre,   fi   ve drà

fempre fempre pe nar   .   .   .   .   .

The impression of ever-changing or calamity-bearing fortune, refer-ring to the word *penare* found in the *da capo*, can be represented in various ways completely different from the preceding, for example:

Example B-8. *General-Bass*, 46–47.

(p)   I would never suggest to anyone to fill up the theatrical style with too many
serious inventions like these. For pathetic, melancholic, and phlegmatic music (in
so far as it is based on tenderness and good taste) is effective in the church and
chamber styles; but it is not well suited to the theatrical style, and one uses serious
pieces simply for judicious changes. And if their lordships, the poets, overload us
with pathetic and sorrowful arias, we must try to sweeten these either with mixed
inventions or effective accompaniments; or in those arias containing a double
affection, one turns the invention more generally to the lively element rather than

We proceed to the third *fons* and ask how the composer can derive the invention for the following *da capo* of [another] aria (which begins immediately with a person's appearance on the scene and without a preceding recitative)?

Non lo dirò col labro   [I will not say it with my lips
che tanto ardir non hà.   which have not so much boldness.]

From this one does not know if the affection should be expressed in a sad or gay, amorous or serious way. Also, in these two lines not a single word offers an opportunity for an invention. Since we cannot use either the antecedent [recitative] or the concomitant (*da capo*) itself, we shall see what the consequence, namely the second section of the aria (in other cases it might be the following recitative, if both sections of the aria were useless) has to offer, in which the reciting person says:

forse con le faville   [Perhaps my glance with its
dell' avide pupille   sparkling, eager eyes,
per dirche già tutt' ardo,   will show that I am really
lo squardo   most ardent.]
parlerà.

---

the serious one. Thus, e.g., with the melancholy of love, one should rather express the pleasantness of love and not the blackness of melancholy. With the petition of a lover for a reciprocation of love, one should rather express more the tenderness of his affection than the seriousness of his plea or sad sighs. With death-like despondency, one should pay more attention to the fury or at least a blend of affections than solely to that of dying, etc. In summary, the theatrical style for the most part requires something moving or adroit, though I should not call it simply merry. For merry music in itself can easily degenerate into barbarism and is unpleasant to sensitive ears. But if its noble vivaciousness is combined with good taste, tenderness, and an effective or brilliant style, this will always please the ear, even if all the world should become saturated with melancholic, phlegmatic, and sullen humor contrary to Nature. *Contraria contrariis medicantur.* In musically famous places where serious taste usually dominates, I have seen the most curious and persistent example of the latter by celebrated composers. By the way, it is, of course, part of the *Requisita politica boni compositoris* to adjust ourselves to the circumstances of time, place, and the audience, which is no minor craft and presupposes much experience, provided each talented individual will reconcile himself to it.

Here we see that the *da capo* [first section] requires an amorous invention, and one can use all kinds of *aimable* melodies such as those in this
example:

Example B-9. *General-Bass*, 49–51.

Should one wish to try special expressions, the words *faville, pupille, l'ardore, lo squardo* give our imagination much opportunity for pleasant and almost playful inventions. For example, one could represent the burning fire of love in the following invention:

Example B-10. *General-Bass*, 52–53.

For the remaining ideas, such as amorous glances, burning eyes, etc., it would be easy to find examples in a flirtatious style. The following *da capo* will serve as the usual third example:

Example B-11. *General-Bass*, 54–59.

la - bro, non lo dirò col la -

- bro, che tan - to ar dir, che tan - -

(q)   Here perhaps there is opportunity to chat about unisons. Therefore, I gave the entire first half of the aria in order to have a little example (which requires nothing further) of the way composers today make use of the unison in certain instances. Namely: they join the string instruments (rarely the wind instruments) in unison or perhaps at the octave with the voice part in a distinct piano, which brings out the dominating voice part composed in a spirited manner in a special way (particularly if the obstructing basses are replaced by a gentle cello), almost augments it, and, speaking in terms of physics, spreads its substance through the

surrounding air so that it seems to the ear as if the voice is further extended: the strings no longer seem as if they are accompanying, but as if the harmony of the general unison (if one can speak of a unison in this way) comes solely from the voice part. Those who have not observed from experience that arias composed in a similar way by famous composers frequently have the greatest effect on the public and that famous singers actually prefer to display their artistry in this free and unencumbered way, can make the following two tests: First, take away the instrumental unison from such a universally applauded aria, and throughout replace the gentle cellos with the full accompaniment of the thorough-bass. In this form, again perform the aria in public with the same good or poor singer and all the same details, and you will undoubtedly find that the aria no longer has its previous effectiveness and that sixty percent of public approbation is lost. Why? The dominating or singing melody no longer is emphasized by the previous accompaniment; the penetrating basses give the Ear more to do; and lastly, the incidental though always pleasing alternations cease between the forte of the ritornellos and the piano of the unison accompaniment, between the tutti of the former and the repeated solo, duet, or trio of the latter, which always gives the Ear something new to do. In summary, the entire aria is metamorphosed and must necessarily lose its previous effectiveness. If this test is difficult or inconvenient for some, they may try the following easier method: Take a *pièce*, a ritornello, an aria, etc., with one or two recorders playing in unison or *a 2* (the remaining parts can be used as accompaniment in proportion). They will immediately notice what little effect this incomplete harmony has in *pleno auditorio*. Then use this same piece with a distinct, soft accompaniment of many strings in unison; thus the former inadequate harmony of recorders will suddenly be brought out so that it seems to be no longer violins, but a full recorder choir, which is quite a different effect. One could give extensive examples here (especially as to the result of unison of many different instruments); however, the previous [explanation] shows fully that if unisons are applied correctly according to the circum-

I believe it is quite clear now how one can find a variety of inventions from apparently unfruitful texts with the help of the antecedent, concomitant, and consequent *loci topici*. Now it is easy to imagine just how much more diversity these sources could give us from fruitful texts in which the rich poetry had already supplied good ideas to our imagination. This needs no further proof, but rather than spare a few pages, we will fully illustrate the matter; and we take the following aria that has been skilfully set to music in which Aminta looks for his shepherdess under the shade of trees [speaking] these words:

Vò cercando il vero Nume	[I seek the true Deity,
che sospira la mia fè.	for whom my faith eagerly sighs.
Qual farfaletta intorno al lume	Like a tiny butterfly encircling the light
fra quest' ombre aggiro il piè. D.C.	I walk around among these Shadows.] D.C.

This text, beautiful in itself, on first inspiration creates in our imagination six, eight, or more entirely different inventions, if one will give some consideration to the words and circumstances or, as I would say, the *loci topici*. In general, one could seize upon the tenderness of the affection; and with this in mind, a *Siciliana* (a form of composition willingly expressing languid thoughts) might suggest the following invention among others:

---

stances, they contain something beautiful and effective, as long as they are not abused by setting all music in unison. I admit that I frequently thought in terms of speculations in physics with regard to the former, as well as many other seemingly poor practical experiments that could be deduced, should this be appropriate here. Such things, however, are as strange to the pure theorists as Chinese is to Thuringian farmers. For most [of these theorists] (though not all) are so slow, stubborn, and insensitive, that they will never catch by reason what they cannot touch or grasp on paper with their five fingers. Sometimes they like to imitate such so-called bagatelles, but if it comes to producing them, the sound is not there, and then they do not know what is wrong. One could phrase it, according to the well-known axiom: *Due cum faciunt idem, non est idem.*

Example B-12. *General-Bass*, 62–64.

If we wish to proceed to special expressions, we could consider first of all the "sighs of love," and the following invention might allude to this:

Example B-13. *General-Bass*, 64–66.

Third, one could try to portray Aminta, who anxiously seeks after his love, according to the text, by a bizarre theme filled with suspensions and chromatic notes. Here a double opportunity arises for expression, and the following might serve as an example:

Example B-14. *General-Bass*, 67–69.

pian.

Vò cer - cando il ve ro Nu me, che ſo -

ſpi - ra ſo - ſpira la mia te - - -

Fourth, we could represent the result or the consequences of the search and believe that now Aminta had found his love; then in this case the imagination takes the opportunity to portray the playful looks of love:

Example B-15. *General-Bass*, 69–71.

Vo cer - cando   il ve ro Nu   me

che fo - - fpi - ra   la - mia

Finally the second result follows, namely the corresponding emotions of his beloved; and one could, for example, try to represent through the use of two well-chosen instruments alternating in pleasant consonances and dissonances: Portraying mutual love, almost quarrelsome but always reuniting the spirits of the two lovers. Here the following can be an example:

Example B-16. *General-Bass*, 72–75.

la mia fë che fo - fpira la mia fë.

These should be sufficient inventions for the *da capo* of this aria; and as it is done frequently, one could begin the second section of the same [aria] with a completely new invention, according to the succeeding beautiful words. Assuming that the previous inventions of the *da capo* did not come easily to our mind, or assuming that our imagination finds more expressive and more agreeable ideas in the second section of the aria, then one can compose the entire aria with an idea taken from the second section as shown above. Here the *farfaletta* gives particular opportunities for various bantering ideas:

Example B-17. *General-Bass*, 76–83.

Vò · cer -

ve - ro Nume, il ve - ro Nume -

vò cer - cando - - che ſo - - - ſpi - ra

la mia fè.   (r)

(r) In this aria there is no embellishing of notes, but in a complete elaboration it may
be so embellished with good taste, brilliance, and accompaniment that it necessarily will encounter complete success in public. Further to be observed: [the aria]
begins in D-sharp [E-flat]; for this reason, however, the invention need not be
sad, serious, or plaintive, for brilliant concertos as well as joyous arias in certain
cases can be composed with the greatest effect in this beautiful key. Furthermore,
the previous examples given in reference to the *loci topici* clearly show that one can
express the same words and affections in various and, according to the old theory,
opposing keys. For that reason, what previous theorists have written and re-
written about the properties of the modes are nothing but trifles, as if one mode
could be merry, another sad, a third pious, heroic, war-like, etc. But even if these
imaginary properties had any inherent correctness, the slightest change of temperament used for them (which can never be accurately done by the tuners of
instruments) and even more changes of *Chorton, Kammerton*, French, and the
extravagant Venetian tunings would cause continual shipwrecks. In my opinion,
the ancient theorists erred in their research of modal characteristics in the same
way as we continue to err today in judging a musical work. If we, for example,
find for this or that key (to which a talented composer may usually be more
inclined) one or more beautifully tender, plaintive, or serious arias, we prefer to
attribute the fine impression of the aria to the key itself and not to the excellent

ideas of the composer; and we immediately establish a *proprietas modi*, as if contrary words and affections could not be expressed in this key. This, however, is worse than wrong, as can be proved to the contrary by a thousand beautiful examples. In general, one can say that one key is more suitable than another for expressing [certain] affections. Thus in the practice today using well-tempered scales (we do not speak of old organs), the keys indicated with two and three sharps or flats are particularly beautiful and expressive in the theatrical style; therefore I should not advise the invention of a purely diatonic keyboard, even if it were possible. Yet, to specify this or that key especially for the affection of love, sadness, joy, etc. is not good. Should someone object at this point and say that D, A, B-flat major are much more suited to raging music than the calmer scales of A minor, E minor, and similar ones, then this actually does not prove the *proprietas modorum*, even if it were so, but it depends on the inclination of the composer. For we have heard famous composers write the saddest and tenderest music in D, A, and B-flat major, etc., whereas in A minor, E minor, C minor, and in similar scales [we have heard] the most powerful and brilliant music. It remains the case, therefore, that every single key and all keys or musical modes without distinction are suited to expressing many opposing affections. However, the choice of these depends primarily on four basic conditions: (1) As stated previously, purely on the inclination or in physical terms, on the temperament of the composer, for one either has a preference in general or, for certain expressions of one or another affection for a certain mode, whereas another [composer] prefers another mode and, so to speak, has certain favorite scales. (2) On the unavoidable changing of a mode in which one has frequently expressed the [same] affection of joy or of sadness. For change is always the soul of music, and who would be so absurd as to state that one must keep a certain scale or mode for the same affection throughout a lengthy theatrical piece or another composition? Why? Just because one of the dear old [theorists] had given this *proprietas* to the mode? (3) On necessity, according to the possibilities of certain instruments which, in order to conform to them, one must frequently use a key against one's will and express in it various contrary affections. (4) Finally, the choice of mode depends frequently on the singer's range: that is, whether he has many or few tones in his throat, and whether his voice is equal throughout, or whether one must treat the upper or lower ranges cautiously. Composers often find a case here that makes the use of all musical modes impossible without being overly artificial (which would be easy to prove by the inequality of certain notes of some singers). The composer must often think more of the singer than of the modal properties, particularly in countries where everything applies to singing and many poorly endowed creatures, with hardly three or four good notes in their throats, thus force the composer to martyr his composition so that Monsieur or Madame is not embarrassed. For these special cases, it is true, fundamental rules are not usually needed; but these four principles prove sufficiently that the choice of musical modes depends partly on our will and preference, partly on the circumstances of the moment. Therefore, the old-fashioned and often self-contradictory theory of *proprietates modorum musicorum* is of as little use as it is in itself unfounded and false.

Finally we could express according to time and place Aminta who is wandering surrounded by shades. The expression of these dark shadows can give rise in our imagination to many ideas. One might be the following:

Example B-18. *General-Bass*, 84–88.

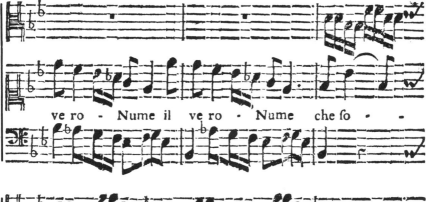

It would be easy to extract additional, completely different inventions from the last part of this aria, but for now this will suffice. Whoever has not studied these examples [merely] superficially will readily concede that if an experienced master were challenged, he could obligate himself to

compose whatever kind of aria and therefore also an entire opera in this
manner, five or six times over in a different way, according to the possibilities of the text, and without a single aria having the slightest element in
common, which is another strong proof that the *loci topici* offer us the best
path to invention and are as useful in music as in oratory. The facts are
there; one may think about them as much as one wishes. For with the same
reason that makes one believe that all possible topics of argumentation
existing in nature for a philosophical or oratorical thesis can be found in
the *loci topici*, with this very same reason one can find all the *genera* of
musical invention and expression existing in nature for a given text or
musical thesis. And I believe that a hundred composers could not find a
single invention for the same words whose nature, form, and essence (not
the individual invention in itself) could not be found beforehand in these
sources, if one would first make the effort to work out this text according to
the *loci topici*. There could be other discussions in these arbitrary matters, if
we had not already digressed too far from our basic purpose. But enough
has been shown by the hitherto useful digressions to prove by examples
how much good and beautiful material exists in music for study, and how
important it is not to waste time with useless, pedantic eccentricities, but
to strive to give the amateur a shorter road to the art of music than usually
occurs. I recall that often skilled virtuosos agreed with me in my belief that
a work of reform in composition and music would be as useful as it would
be necessary (even the critics would not deny this). And it seems to me that
this important, but surmountable, and certainly useful effort would not be
ill-spent if a well-schooled, unprejudiced composer would take composition in hand and separate the chaff from the grain by abolishing all musical
quackery, metaphysical contemplations, barbaric nomenclatures, ridiculous classifications, antiquated, abolished rules, and similar fruitless nonsense, while choosing only the useful rules truly applicable to the real
practice. By bringing these [rules] into a correct and accurate classification, a well-founded, orderly, and useful method could finally be chosen
[to determine] how and in what manner similar excellent principles could
be given to a naturally-talented student and how to put them into practice.
In this way, the innocent art of composition would be cleansed of all
sophistry, prejudice, and especially of the blind faith with which many
rules were held for good and true up to now, only because the ancient
musical Christian church had held them for true. Indeed, it would then be
very easy for naturally gifted individuals to combine music with other
studies or to make even greater gains and daily growth in music. We have
said, however, that first a correct method must be employed; otherwise it
is like the carpenter who lays all the boards, beams, and other building

materials before his apprentice, teaches him how to prepare these things, yet does not show him how to put and fit the pieces together into a house. Is it not true that the lad is lacking yet the most important knowledge? The dispassionate composer should only realize that many hundreds of rules for composing lie in bundles still untouched, as the *Leges corpore juris* did for quite a while. For the most part, these were also studied and explained impractically. Thus, the musical rules as well as the *Leges* lack nothing but the best to be brought into correct order and into systems applicable to current usage, as has been done for the old precepts[s] of advanced studies, which nowadays have been cleansed from their old-fashioned characteristics. In this way, learning and teaching composition may proceed quickly, practically, and methodically (and therefore in an orderly fashion). What seems to be missing in composition and in music generally [we] sought to supply in this treatise through the necessary and useful knowledge of the thorough-bass. Many years ago I had the opportunity to recognize by my own experience that the greatest hindrance to the ambitious student in this knowledge lies purely in the confused leadership of the teacher. Thus I wondered whether it would not be possible to find a shorter way to acquiring this solid knowledge; and finally it seemed to me that the method in these pages would not be without value, especially the first part of the book which is written particularly for beginners. One must not be deterred by the usual difficulties of the thorough-bass, but only believe that good instruction and order at least constitute two parts of the troublesome effort. Therefore, in this currently enlarged work I have vigorously excised those rules of little value and not pertaining to the basic subject; I have included only useful rules and explained everything at its proper place

---

(s)   In former times persons had beards before they learned half of the Latin language from the *Grammatica* by Schmid. Today one finds boys of fourteen and fifteen who speak it with mastery. Formerly one studied only philosophy until one was twenty-four or twenty-five before advancing to higher studies. Today they leave the university at twenty with more knowledge. Formerly it took five years to finish the law course, and even then one did not know how in practice to dispute in order to regain a stolen egg from a farmer. Today three years is sufficient to complete the entire philosophical and law courses. What is the reason for such great changes in the times? Answer: The changing of old, pedantic methods, since today one usually studies all things more completely, more briefly, and with greater vigor, for which a good order or a good, applicable method is absolutely necessary. *Ordo docet omnia*, etc.

with practical examples. The complete work (in two parts) gives instruction in the *basso continuo* for both sacred as well as theatrical music. In the first part, following the valuable theory of intervals, I have sought to include all the chords and figures found in the thorough-bass together with their alterations, and to show short, clear examples of these. Also I have pointed out how to employ them in exercises with help of the three basic forms of a chord. This is followed by a general example in which separate, learned principles are joined together and are applied to all practical tonalities in order to show students that these few principles remain unchanged and that nothing new arises other than that one has to become accustomed to indications of sharps or flats for each key. Finally, a separate chapter gives additional advice [on] how an individual or his student each day can make greater progress toward perfection. The second part discusses the unfigured[(t)] thorough-bass in which, according to the nature of this mate-

---

(t)   Ten to twelve years previous, when I first gave this treatise to the printer, I did not think that another author had issued an extensive study about these matters; and therefore I ventured forth at that time, since I am more a friend of one's own efforts than of materials borrowed from other authors. Nevertheless, since there are things in these newly appearing matters that could be contradicted more easily than the divine word, I avow that (according to the common manner of speaking) I was struck with secret joy when, quite by accident as I spent the last years in Italy, I came upon a little treatise of the upright and in that country widely-celebrated Gasparini, in which he also ventures to establish new and extensive rules for the unfigured bass. The treatise is *in quarto*, with approximately fifteen sheets, and is entitled: *L'Armonico prattico al Cembalo* [sic] *Di Francesco Gasparini Lucchese, In Venice M. DCC. VIII. appresso Antonio Bartoli.* The author's fundamental approach gives many rules more important to the skilled composer than to the thorough-bass player (who should really play only the previously composed thorough-bass). However, these are general principles of composition, and in this case one could say: *Superflua non nocent*. In addition to these, the author has some truly good things that I shall deal with separately below to his praise. And though we both aim for the same goal, we agree in neither principle nor method, except for two general concepts (which I shall give later), which at first glance I had almost confused with my supposedly own thoughts until I traced a noteworthy difference in them. Whoever [wants to] compare both treatises will do me a special favor. That author [Gasparini] has also christened all the precepts of the unfigured thorough-bass as *regulas* or *regole, osservationi* or *avertimenti*, which strengthens my own opinion about the varying nature of rules given above. And finally, what would have been the good if he had given them names according to their rank in value, either as common examples or rare examples (as they are in fact)? The matter would neither have lost nor won anything important. In addition to this still living and famous author [Gasparini], there are various authors of

rial, I extracted certain brief principles illustrated with many examples; and finally in which the ambitious student is presented in turn with various tricky aspects of the craft for his further consideration, all of which will be clearer after he reads through the pages. It is sufficient to say that nothing has been written without reason or experience, and on every page of this book, order and advantage have been sought. Moreover, this work can serve those who think of instructing others according to such a method; on the other hand, [the treatise] has been written largely for the advantage of beginners. And the latter, if they gain only a little advancement in this art, can practice the given examples and see how far they have been led by their teacher. They can note the rules and help themselves little by little in the fundamental [rules], until finally [they are] capable of reading the second part of this work with profit. While the first part is written for beginners only, the second part is for the adult and widely-experienced; thus I have completely changed the method of the latter part, proceeding more arbitrarily and discursively, which should not be done differently according to the material and the purpose, and the intelligent reader will find the reason by himself.

Finally, I must request my favorably inclined reader not to expound the preceding general discourse on music contrary to my intentions. Each person knows his own excellent reasons why he believes this or that. Should he have another opinion in some cases, he is free to keep his knowledge to himself and leave others untouched; or to bring his reasons out into public according to the reasonable form of *disputatorum modeste* & *debito modo*, in which case one will answer him in a similar way. In addition, the honest world would pardon him if he was compelled to give tit for tat and sought to make known his *contra lectiones*. Everything can be disputed if one twists the thing a little. I consider this no art for those established in a profession and with a talent for writing, since those matters impress only ignorant and half-educated individuals; intelligent people recognize the truth through the gauze of obscurity. Yet I am not the only

---

renown in France and Germany who have sought some time ago to establish the rudiments of this art. Saint-Lambert's treatise compares in some particular examples and rules with Gasparini's. Above all others, a Frenchman, Monsieur Boivin [sic], is supposed to have written an extensive [study] about this subject, of which I have not seen anything. Indeed, it pleases me that there are authors from three nations who all together think about extensive writings on these matters and who give rules for the unfigured bass as being good, basic, and useful, although they undoubtedly have foreseen all the objections one could make against this material. The rest will be carefully passed over this time.

one in the world of music today with such thoughts on music. Should anyone find things in these pages to his taste, he is endeared to me; if not, then he should work out something better. New ideas in all sciences have always found heavy criticisms in their process of growth until finally time itself has overthrown all obstacles such as jealousy, ambition, ignorance, and obsolete prejudices only based on authorities. So it has been in previous times, so it will be in the future. What seems still paradoxical in our century will perhaps be venerated as an unalterable truth in the future. And how can I be opposed if I believe that the passage of time could well make as much difference for music as it did previously for the sciences; in the past those believing that there were antipodes and that the earth was round were excommunicated — but today almost every farmer believes it! *Cum Deo & Dei*, more later about these various materials.

Appendix C

Heinichen's Treatment of Dissonances

Heinichen's fascinating study of dissonances and their resolution in the theatrical style remains one of his most original contributions to the history of Baroque music theory. The principles that he derived for an understanding of the often complex and remarkably free treatment of dissonances in operatic music are exceedingly instructive. They are indeed essential guidelines for every accompanist of thorough-basses for the often aggressively vertical and powerfully dissonant music of the Italian-influenced Baroque which Heinichen knew intimately. Especially the harmonic freedoms occurring in recitatives in the theatrical style are often only comprehensible when viewed from the theoretical perspective found in this section of the treatise.

This material had appeared as a separate article in the Yale *Journal of Music Theory* for 1962. A number of reviews of the first edition of this book lamented the fact that this article had been omitted. The opportunity of the second edition allows it to be reprinted with the permission of the editor of the Yale *Journal of Music Theory*.

* * *

Der General-Bass in der Composition not only surpasses other Baroque treatises in the exhaustive nature of its explanations concerning thorough-bass techniques, but it establishes specific characteristics of the *stylus theatralis* as it affects the art of accompanying from a thorough-bass.

Heinichen's treatise, comprising about 1000 pages of text and music examples, is divided into two *Abtheilungen*: Part One, for the beginner in thorough-bass training; Part Two, for the more advanced accompanist as well as the student of composition. This latter half is devoted to training in the *stylus theatralis*. Heinichen provides an explicit analysis of this style; and the significance of this material becomes imposing when we realize how incomplete our knowledge remains for the elements of the trinity governing Baroque music: the church, chamber, and theatrical (or operatic) styles. Our concern here is with just one segment of Heinichen's style-doctrine, contained in the first chapter of this second part and entitled: *Von Theatralischen Resolutionibus der Dissonantien.*

What is the theatrical style? According to Heinichen its primary distinction rests almost entirely on a free dissonance treatment. This freedom, however, implies neither disorder nor lack of resolutions, for

> nothing is more common than to accuse the *stylus theatralis* of not observing rules and of permitting one to proceed in dissonances and their beautiful resolutions contrary to fundamentals. We shall, however, show here the ignorance of those individuals and prove that this style is absolutely fundamental and, in addition, [that it] has far more artful and beautiful resolutions of consonances and dissonances than the most regular, antique [church] style. And since this material currently is *inter terra incognitas* . . . for most [musicians], even [which is surprising] for otherwise famous composers and great contrapuntists — though at the same time all the fundamentals of the theatrical style depend on it — one hopes that many will consider it a favor if we try to give a basic study of this most useful material (for which one knows of no predecessors).[1]

Heinichen believes that gradual changes in the handling of dissonances occurred as composers modified the rules pertaining to the *stylus gravis* (or *allabreve* style). More and more efforts were made to liberate music from the monotonous regularity of preparing dissonances and resolving them down by step until

> finally one began to change the style, to invert chords more freely, and particularly to alter in various ways suspensions and resolutions of dissonances according to Nature's guidance (she is the best teacher in all the arts) and to exchange the parts both before and after the resolution. . . . After the invention of the theatrical style this inversion of parts — or of harmonies (to speak in the accepted fashion) — has been advanced to perfection but at the same time to excess, because one will always try to outdo others in new things and imaginary freedoms without knowing why or the fundamental principle on which such things are based.[2]

To purify the theatrical style Heinichen proposes a reëxamination of its harmonies based on the following principle:

> Normally [in the theatrical style] no chord or progression can be considered correct that is not followed by a correct resolution of the dissonance, whether it occurs before or after the inversion of harmonies, in the upper, middle, or lowest part. If the chord passes this test, it is fundamental; when it does not, it is incorrect and without a very important reason to the contrary cannot be allowed.[3]

Heinichen divides theatrical resolutions of dissonances into eight major categories; and though all of them observe his fundamental rule, they suggest at the same time harmonic freedom far beyond the discipline of academic counterpoint. In addition to the variety of factual information Heinichen offers, a bonus value lies in the opportunity for us to understand how an important Baroque composer viewed his musical language. Heinichen attempts to systematize a vast amount of harmonic material that previously had no real organization such as had existed for counterpoint for centuries. Unlike his contemporary, Rameau (whose *Traité de l'harmonie* he knew), Heinichen avoids evolving theoretical premises such as the *basse fondamentale* or the construction of all chords in thirds. Rather he attempts to codify by seeking basic principles of harmonic procedures underlying the current practice in the theatrical style of music. He freely admits that exceptions exist which fit no convenient category but which need to be recognized as part of the harmonic freedom of his day. This refreshing open-mindedness makes it possible for us to learn much from Heinichen about the late Baroque composer's métier.

I. The Variation of Dissonances before the Resolution

a. The basic parts of a suspension, the note of preparation and the suspended tone itself, must never be omitted; they can be varied, however, by inserting notes between them and the resolution.

For example, the following illustrations give several variations of a suspended second in the bass part:

Example C-1. *General-Bass*, 588–89.

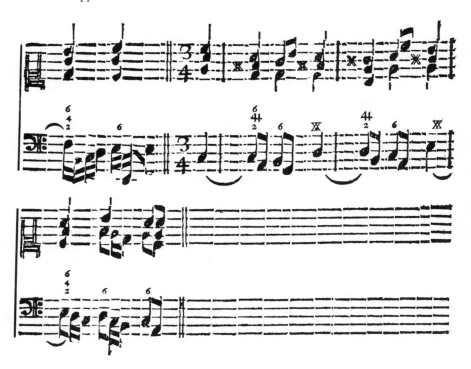

Who would say that the seconds in this example do not resolve according to rule, because the resolution [of each] does not immediately follow the suspended tone? The notes coming in between are only a variation (as can be seen) that also is ignored by the accompaniment. The resolution of the second, therefore, is correct in all cases, as one can see best from the fundamental notes of this example.[4]

Example C-2. *General-Bass*, 590.

Heinichen demonstrates similar variations for suspensions of fourths and diminished fifths employed in the right hand of an accompaniment.[5] Suspended sevenths offer even more numerous possibilities for varying their resolutions. The final section of example C-3 is particularly unusual, because the melodic variation begins even before the suspended note is played (for the harmonic basis of this as well as the entire example, see the "fundamental notes" immediately below the example).

Example C-3. *General-Bass*, 593–95.

The fundamental notes:

Example C-4 illustrates a deceptive variation of the seventh, since the dissonance appears to resolve up by step. This results from a simple embellishment of the note (or, in Heinichen's words, *eine blosse Bewegung der Stimme*), and the part always returns to the dissonance before resolving down.

Example C-4. *General-Bass*, 596.

b. Unbound (i.e., unprepared) dissonances may be varied in the same way as suspensions in previous examples.

To demonstrate this point Heinichen offers an example in recitative style because, as he says, "the elaborate variations and inversions of harmonies occur nowhere as frequently as in the recitative.[6]

Example C-5. *General-Bass*, 599.

The fundamental notes:

This example provides an important clue to the practicality of Heinichen's codification of dissonances and their resolutions. Much of the skill involved in accompanying recitatives depends on a trained eye capable of distinguishing the basic substance of dissonances from the surrounding melodic enrichment. This analytical training is also indispensable for accompanying unfigured thorough-basses, which make up the great majority of continuo parts in late Baroque operas and cantatas.

To complete the explanation for the first type of resolutions in the theatrical style, Heinichen illustrates several incorrect uses of dissonances, typical errors found in works of composers unskilled in this style:

Example C-6. *General-Bass*, 600–601.

In the first two examples the diminished fifths have absolutely no resolution, even though the parts move along very naturally. In the third and fourth examples the sevenths also lack a proper resolution. The ninth in the fifth example does not resolve; and in the last example the second lacks the same thing, for the rapidly moving passing tone B cannot be considered a resolution of the preceding C, and also it is not observed in the accompaniment. Now all of these examples could be defended either as incorrectly inverted voices or in some other way, but they are and remain false.[7]

II. How to Leap to and from Dissonances

How has the use of unprepared dissonances come about, Heinichen ponders, when composers of the *stylus gravis* disliked such freedom and required preparation for all dissonances? In searching through other treatises he found the only answer implied was *sic volo, sic jubeo.* Heinichen[8] suggests, however, that all unprepared dissonances actually result from anticipated passing tones. He argues that since dissonances may be formed without preparation by a descending passing note in the bass or an upper part, for example:

Example C-7. *General-Bass*, 603.

therefore, composers found they could refine their style by writing similar passages without the first fundamental note and by forming a passing note anticipated *per ellipsis.* In this way, one could alter the previous example to:

Example C-8. *General-Bass*, 604–5.

In addition to these common forms of unprepared dissonances:

a. One can leap into any dissonance that has been prepared in another part.

As the figures indicate in the next example, the dissonances between bass and melody all have been prepared regularly in a part other than the one leaping into the dissonant note. The fundamental notes illustrate these preparations.

Example C-9. *General-Bass*, 606–7.

The fundamental notes:

b. Also one can leap into any dissonance that occurs in another part as a passing tone (*transitus*).

In example C-10 the thorough-bass figures indicate the chord tones of the third part; in each case the dissonance in the melodic line occurs on a "weak" beat as a passing tone, although the note from which it descends is found only in the accompanying harmony:

Example C-10. *General-Bass*, 609.

c. Similarly, one can leap into any dissonance that occurs as a quick passing note in another part.

Unlike the dissonances in the previous example, those formed from quick passing notes do not become an integral part of the harmony and consequently are not indicated by the thorough-bass figures.

Example C-11. *General-Bass*, 610, 612.

The fundamental notes:

d. One can leap into any dissonance that results from a simple step-wise embellishment of another part.

These dissonances also remain unconnected to the thorough-bass accompaniment.

Example C-12. *General-Bass*, 613–14.

The fundamental notes:

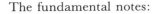

e. One can leap into a dissonance and leap away again if the resolution occurs in another part. The accompanist must be careful not to omit the resolution, even if it is not found in the concerted part.

The fundamental notes (limited to the bass clef by Heinichen to conserve space) demonstrate the correct resolution of each dissonance.

Example C-13. *General-Bass*, 615–16.

The fundamental notes:

A special type of melodic variation allows the same part to resolve a dissonance even after leaping to and from it. In each of the following examples the top part returns to the resolving note after leaping away from the dissonance note:

Example C-14. *General-Bass*, 617–18.

III. Inversions of Harmonies before Resolution

While Heinichen fully understands the principle of chord inversion (which he discusses at some length,[9] more important to his classification of resolutions in the theatrical style are the harmonic implications of various two-part inversions:

> This is indeed an extensive but also a very important subject that makes up the considerable part of the chamber and theatrical styles in which one continually finds two-part lines [of music]. Also to be remembered [is] the special recitative style where usually two-part inversions of harmony reign.[10]

In cantatas and operas accompanists frequently perform from unfigured basses; in lieu of figures one must depend largely on a single melodic line for help in extemporizing the correct harmonization. The problem becomes specially acute when a composer employs inversions of dissonant chords; for example, a suspended F in the melodic part against a D in the thorough-bass may not simply represent the third in a D minor triad, but can belong to the second inversion of the 7th chord on G. Heinichen developed an elaborate method of analysis to assist accompanists to divine chord inversions and, more important, to recognize inversions of dissonances before resolution. The basis of his method is formed from dividing the diminished seventh chord into all possible inversions formed by an exchange of the bass and upper chord-tone with the remaining parts of the chord (i.e., for each of the three inversions there are three two-part inversions). These twelve two-part inversions are reduced to six fundamental types. (Each of the following inversions is based on a diminished seventh chord constructed on G♯; the "×" in each instance means "recombined into.")

Inversion type 1   The inversion of the dissonant seventh itself:

f   g♯
    ×
G♯   F

Inversion type 2   Two cases in which the bass G♯ is inverted against an upper part of the chord:

f   g♯   f   g♯
    ×   and   ×
G♯   D   G♯   B

Inversion type 3   Two cases in which the concert part f only is inverted against an upper part of the chord:

f   b   f   d
    ×   and   ×
G♯   F   G♯   F

Inversion type 4   Two cases in which neither the concert part f nor the bass G♯ is retained in the inversion:

f   d   f   b
    ×   and   ×
G♯   B   G♯   D

Inversion type 5   Two cases in which the bass only is exchanged for an upper part of the chord while the concert part F is retained and correctly resolved:

<pre>
f   f   e   f   f   e
   ×   and   ×
G♯   B   C   G♯   D   C
</pre>

Inversion type 6   Three cases in which both parts come together on an octave:

<pre>
f   b   f   d   f   f
   ×   ,   ×   , and   ×
G♯   B   G♯   D   G♯   F
</pre>

Since these six types (or six-fold *casus*) for a two-part inversion of a harmony occur naturally with the two-part inversions of all remaining dissonances . . . we shall, therefore, apply them in turn to various other dissonances and illustrate each type of inversion with particularly varied examples. I say with varied examples, because in practice two-part inversions of harmony either happen rarely in simple, fundamental notes, or in such cases they are so clear and distinct that no additional examples are needed for clarification. In contrast, these continually different variations frequently hide or obscure the inversion of the harmony. For, so to speak, there are as many variations and [new] ideas for these [inversions] as there are composers.[11]

A selection from Heinichen's numerous examples will be sufficient to demonstrate how a composer can invert the dissonances found in a diminished (and also dominant) seventh chord to conform with the six basic types. In each instance the original dissonance remains unresolved until after the inversion.

Inversion Type 1

Seconds become sevenths, for example:

<pre>
c   b♭   e   d
   ×   or   ×
B♭   C   D   E
</pre>

Example C-15. *General-Bass*, 630.

Augmented fourths become diminished fifths:

$$g^{\sharp} \quad d \qquad a^{\sharp} \quad e$$
$$\times \quad \text{or} \quad \times$$
$$D \quad G^{\sharp} \qquad E \quad A^{\sharp}$$

Example C-16. *General-Bass*, 630–31.

Following the same procedure diminished fifths become augmented fourths and sevenths become seconds.

Inversion Type 2

Seconds become thirds or augmented fourths:

$$
\begin{array}{cccc}
\text{g} & \text{f} & \text{g} & \text{f} \\
\times & \text{or} & \times & \\
\text{F} & \text{D} & \text{F} & \text{B}
\end{array}
$$

Augmented fourths become thirds or sevenths:

$$
\begin{array}{cccc}
\text{g}\sharp & \text{d} & \text{g}\sharp & \text{d} \\
\times & \text{or} & \times & \\
\text{D} & \text{B} & \text{D} & \text{E}
\end{array}
$$

Example C-17. *General-Bass*, 634.

The doubled notes in the basses of these and subsequent examples illustrate the alternate inversions for each interval; either may be chosen as the bass. The inversion, however, forming a dissonance is preferable to a consonance, for in the latter case the interval "does not appear to be a true inversion of the previous harmony when the dissonances are exchanged for consonances."[12] Diminished fifths become thirds or sixths:

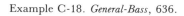

$$
\begin{array}{cccc}
b\flat & e & b\flat & e \\
\times & & \times & \\
E & C & E & G
\end{array}
$$

To avoid progressing from a dissonance to a consonance Heinichen suggests that the dissonances belonging to the chord be worked into the melodic variation of either part.

Example C-18. *General-Bass*, 636.

Sevenths become fourths or sixths:

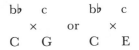

According to Heinichen[13] the former inversion is impractical because the lower tone of the fourth cannot serve as the root of the chord (since the fourth appears between outer voice parts and is not prepared) and the fourth cannot resolve. The inversion of the sixth needs the addition of a diminished fifth in the melodic or chordal figuration:

Example C-19. *General Bass*, 637.

A diminished seventh inverted according to the second type of inversion becomes either an augmented fourth or a major sixth:

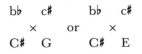

The latter also needs the addition of the diminished fifth in the variation of one of the parts, or the minor third combined with the diminished fifth. When the augmented fourth is used, an exceptional chord $_2^{4+}$ may be substituted for $_3^4$ (the remaining tones of the diminished seventh chord).

Inversion Type 3

Seconds become thirds or fifths:

a   c#   a   e

×   or   ×

G   A   G   A

Again a dissonance is worked into the melodic part to avoid the impression of progression from dissonance to consonance.

Example C-20. *General-Bass*, 640.

Augmented fourths become thirds or sixths:

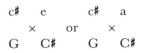

requiring the addition of a dissonance in the accompanying parts. When the minor third accompanies the augmented fourth (i.e., in the diminished seventh chord), an inversion of the latter may also form the diminished seventh:

Example C-21 illustrates two types of variations based on this last inversion:

Example C-21. *General-Bass*, 642.

Finally, according to type three, diminished fifths become seconds or sixths:

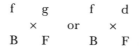

and sevenths become augmented fourths or sixths when combined with a major third:

$$
\begin{array}{cccc}
e\flat & a & e\flat & c \\
\times & & \text{or} & \times \\
F & E\flat & F & E\flat
\end{array}
$$

The diminished seventh becomes either an augmented fourth or sixth:

$$
\begin{array}{cccc}
f & b & f & d \\
\times & & \text{or} & \times \\
G\sharp & F & G\sharp & F
\end{array}
$$

Example C-22 illustrates the last inversion:

Example C-22. *General-Bass*, 645.

Inversion Type 4

In this type, one replaces both parts of each dissonance, making every inversion consonant. Therefore, dissonant notes should be included in the accompaniment, especially if they are not present in the melodic line. In this type of inversion seconds become thirds or sixths:

$$
\begin{array}{cccc}
g & d & g & b \\
\times & & \text{or} & \times \\
F & B & F & D
\end{array}
$$

Augmented fourths become perfect fourths or fifths:

$$
\begin{array}{cccc}
c\sharp & a & c\sharp & e \\
\times & & \text{or} & \times \\
G & E & G & A
\end{array}
$$

Heinichen discards this inversion of the fourth as impractical for the same reason offered earlier. Diminished fifths become perfect fourths

$$
\begin{array}{cc}
e\flat & f \\
& \times \\
A & C
\end{array}
$$

(again discarded) or perfect fifths

$$
\begin{array}{cc}
e\flat & c \\
& \times \\
A & F
\end{array}
$$

(see first section of ex. C-23). Sevenths joined with major thirds become thirds or sixths:

$$
\begin{array}{ccccc}
c & a & & c & f\sharp \\
& \times & or & & \times \\
D & F\sharp & & D & A
\end{array}
$$

(see last two sections of ex. C-23).

Example C-23. *General-Bass*, 648–49.

Diminished sevenths also form thirds or sixths:

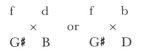

Unlike the previous example for the minor seventh in which the diminished fifth occurs only in the inversion, in example C-24 the diminished fifth appears only as part of the chord before inversion, a distinction Heinichen stresses.

Example C-24. *General-Bass*, 649–50.

Inversion Type 5

This type retains the upper part of the interval while the bass is exchanged for another chord-tone. Heinichen suggests these inversions are largely familiar from daily occurrences; and since their application includes no difficulties a single example will be sufficient:

Example C-25. *General-Bass*, 650–651.

Inversion Type 6

In two parts the final type of inversion always consists of octaves. Since these offer no special problems, Heinichen concludes the discussion, satisfied that he has "established the true fundamentals of all inversions existing in nature."[14]

IV. The Inversion of the Resolution Itself

Now we shall want to know how to invert the resolution of a dissonance, or what actually is an inversion of a resolution? On the whole and in a general sense, the inversion of a resolution occurs if one part of a chord (it can be the upper, middle, or lowest part) does not resolve its own dissonance, but rather the note where the dissonance should resolve is given over to another part against which is taken another note of the same chord. In this procedure, therefore, the resolution is thrown to another part and thus exchanges or inverts the parts.[15]

Inverted resolutions take place either (1) between upper parts only, or (2) between an upper part and the bass of the chord. Although the chords in the first group are not true inversions (since their bass notes remain unchanged), nevertheless, this first class frequently appears in music, and Heinichen is prompted to explain it with the following example:

Example C-26. *General-Bass*, 663.

Each resolution in example C-26 comes in a part not containing the preparation of the dissonance. This same characteristic occurs widely in two parts (i.e., between the thorough-bass and a solo part), in which the solo line does not resolve its dissonances but leaves vacant each time the *locus resolutionis*. The accompanist, therefore, has the responsibility of locating these dissonances in the solo part and then resolving them in his realization. The following excerpt gives a typical example of this kind of problem.

Example C-27. *General-Bass*, 664.

There are two procedures for playing true inversions of resolutions. In the first, the composer exchanges the notes of the resolving interval so that the bass takes the upper tone and the upper part the lower tone. For example, a tritone normally resolving to a sixth $_{F\ E}^{b\ c}$ proceeds instead to a third: $_{F\ C}^{b\ e}$. Example C-28 illustrates the resolution of a $_{2}^{4+}$ chord according to this first type of inverted resolution:

Example C-28. *General-Bass*, 668–69.

Inverted resolutions of the diminished fifth and minor seventh might occur in the following form:

Example C-29. *General-Bass*, 670.

In the second type of inverted resolution the composer exchanges the bass note for the upper note of the resolution: the latter part, however, does not reciprocate, but rather takes another note from the chord of resolution. The following example illustrates the inverted resolution of a $\frac{4+}{2}$ chord according to this second procedure:

Example C-30. *General-Bass*, 673.

The final sections in example C-29 include cadences that, Heinichen points out, "constantly appear" in the recitative. In these there seems to be

a complete lack of resolution for the chord (+). . . . The figure of the third example [section] might retain its name as an inverted resolution (as long as the accompanist plays distinctly the figures $\begin{smallmatrix}6&5\\4&\#\end{smallmatrix}$ over the E), because in this way the C to which the bass should naturally resolve is displaced to the sixth in the upper part. One cannot, however, expect the accompanist always to maintain the accuracy exhibited by this third example with similar rapidly occurring cadences. Therefore, one must accept the fourth and fifth examples as exceptions contrary to the general rule, retaining them as liberties that have gained citizenship through long usage.[16]

Further, concerning these resolutions, Heinichen supplies the following footnote comment, particularly interesting for anyone endeavoring to trace the evolution of harmonic practices:

Naturally this recitative cadence should always, and I repeat, always resolve in the following way, as one finds now and then in practice:

But because similar tedious and constantly appearing cadences in theatrical pieces would finally become oppressive to hear [and] indeed not infrequently seem to hold fruitlessly the acting singer, it could be that one has taken the opportunity to shorten the matter by going straight to the cadence, as in the fourth and fifth examples above [ex. C-29].[17]

The inverted resolutions in Nos. 1 and 2 (ex. C-31) result from a procedure opposite to the one just examined. In these resolutions the bass note takes instead of the upper part another note from the chord of resolution. The upper part, on the contrary, borrows the note normally found in the bass. Nos. 3 and 4 illustrate the fundamental notes of the natural resolutions while Nos. 5 and 6 give the fundamental notes for Nos. 1 and 2.

Example C-31. *General-Bass*, 677.

No. 3.   No. 4.

No. 5.   No. 6.

All of the inverted resolutions included in the previous examples have been consonant, and Heinichen suggests the possibility of interspersing dissonances within these chords:

> The latter is more practical in full-voiced pieces [i.e., music such as orchestral works with several parts] than in two parts, and on reflection two possible cases occur to me. The first would be this: just as in place of the following natural resolutions

the sixth can be retarded by inserting a seventh in the first example, and the octave can be retarded by inserting a ninth in the three remaining examples:

Therefore, this would also occur with the correct inversions of these chords. For from the sevenths, ninths are formed, and from the ninths, sevenths:

As a consonant inversion of the resolution, this example would appear . . .:

In comparing both the consonant and dissonant inversion of the resolutions, one sees that the basses are identical and that the inserted dissonances are nothing more than pure delays of the triad and chords of the sixth.[18]

The second case in which the chords of an inverted resolution can be interspersed with dissonances would be this: if with many chords of the sixth one includes the diminished seventh and with major triads, the minor seventh, so that all the notes of the triad as well as the equivalent sixth chord are retained before as well as after [the inversion]. For example, in place of the following natural consonant resolution

the [resolutions] can be made dissonant:

With the correct inversion of the resolution the diminished fifth always becomes a seventh, and the seventh, a diminished fifth:

As a consonant inversion of the resolution this example would appear as. . . .[19]

V. Anticipated Passing Tones in the Bass

Earlier we referred to the *anticipatio transitus*, a device Heinichen identifies as one of the most notable means for creating expressive harmonies. "Hardly a line of the recitative passes by without the frequent appearance of these anticipations,[20] and they often occur amidst the notes of inverted harmonies.

A composer may employ the anticipated passing tone whenever he finds the following elements: a group of three bass notes descending a major or minor third; the second note descends a whole tone to form an augmented fourth (but never a perfect fourth) with the preceding chord. For example, the progressions

Example C-32. *General-Bass*, 686.

become anticipated passing tones simply by omitting the bass notes before the $\frac{6}{4+}$ chords. The following two examples (Nos. 1 and 2) of anticipated passing tones result from the inversion of the chord. Rather than resolving naturally to the chord of the sixth on E (No. 3) and to the $\frac{6^+}{4}$ on E (No. 4), the bass exchanges its note for G in such a way that the notes for the inversions $\frac{6}{4+}$ match those of the natural resolution 6^+_e or $\frac{4}{3}$. According to Heinichen these anticipated passing tones possess particular qualities for expressing harsh words in recitatives:

Example C-33. *General-Bass*, 688.

The next examples of anticipated passing tones at first glance seem to lack resolution for the diminished sevenths:

Example C-34. *General-Bass*, 689.

This is nothing moe than an excessive delay of the diminished seventh so that the following sixth is omitted completely by ellipsis, a freedom composers employ at times for the expression of harsh words. This ellipsis, therefore, is not only permissible but also makes the chord more beautiful; at the same time the *locus resolutionis* is not lacking in which [the diminished seventh] could and should have resolved, as in No. 3 [of ex. C-34].[21]

Example C-35 also gives an illustration of anticipated passing tones apparently lacking resolution:

Example C-35. *General-Bass*, 690.

One inverts the resolution of the diminished seventh as shown in No. 2 and follows it by a passing tone as in No. 3. By anticipating this passing tone, one arrives at the same harmony found in No. 1 (see No. 4).

Closely related to these anticipations of passing tones is the technique permitting a dissonance to "resolve" to another dissonance. Both rely on the deliberate omission of a bass note and the anticipation of an ensuing dissonance. The omission occurs in one of two ways:

1. Rather than holding a bass note while the dissonance resolves and then permitting it to move on to another dissonance, one can anticipate the second dissonance by omitting part or all of the preceding bass note. The following resolutions of dissonances to dissonances (which Heinichen describes as "well-known"),

Example C-36. *General-Bass*, 691.

should resolve as in example C-37 to conform with the *antiquen Fundament*:[22]

Example C-37. *General-Bass*, 692.

2. The bass note to which a dissonance should resolve can be omitted while the upper note of the resolution is retained; the bass anticipates the dissonance properly belonging to the next beat. These chords, too, have special effectiveness in the recitative or in other contexts requiring an expression of harsh words:

Example C-38. *General-Bass*, 693.

According to the old rules of dissonance resolution, example C-38 would have to be written as:

Example C-39. *General-Bass*, 694.

To summarize the various kinds of harmonic inversions and the anticipated passing tone, Heinichen combines some of the most common examples into a recitative passage to which he adds an expansive analysis:

Example C-40. *General-Bass*, 696.

Note 1 is an anticipated passing tone, because it should have been preceded by the $^{6}_{e}$ chord. On Note 2 the anticipated passing tone inverts its harmony in such a way that the chord-tones of 1 and 2 remain identical. Instead of Note 2 resolving to A as it should, it anticipates the [following] passing tone, [Note] 3. This passing tone should resolve naturally to the sixth chord $^{d}_{a}$; instead it inverts its resolution for the equally valid (or the identical) notes of the triad $^{F}_{f}$ ^{a}. In the following example Note 5 again shows an anticipated passing tone, because it should have been preceded by the chord [on] C. In place of Note 5 resolving naturally to the sixth chord $^{d}_{c}$ ^{f}, it inverts the resolution on Note 6 for the equally valid triad $^{c}_{a}$, which in this form ^{A} immediately becomes an anticipated passing note: $^{c}_{f}$ $^{f}_{a}$. Thus an anticipated passing tone and an inverted resolution converge on this one Note 6. In place of all these artistic and harmonically effective inversions, the above examples would have sounded in their simple harmonies as:[23]

VI. Retardations and Anticipations of the Upper Part

According to Heinichen[24] a retardation is a "dissonance resulting from holding too long the previous note that does not belong to the following chord and will not be able to resolve." For example:

Example C-41. *General-Bass*, 702.

Here we see that by his phrase "will not be able to resolve," Heinichen means the dissonance will not resolve down. The dissonances formed by retardations are not represented in the thorough-bass figures; therefore, the correct accompaniment for the preceding example would follow the fundamental notes of example C-42:

Example C-42. *General-Bass*, 703.

The anticipation of an upper part reverses the principle of retardations: a part hurries on to the next chord ahead of time and forcefully anticipates a note of that chord. For example:

Example C-43. *General-Bass*, 704.

Anticipations generally occur as quick notes and are not considered an integral part of the chordal accompaniment. Consequently the correct accompaniment of example C-43 would rely on the harmony as indicated by the bass notes and their figures.

In three or more parts the composer can join both retardations and anticipations with the inversion of a resolution. In these formations the accompanist need be concerned only with beginning the invention of the suspension, for "it does not matter to him if the continuation of the same results in a retardation, anticipation, inverted resolution, or even an ordinary resolution of a dissonance."[25] For example:

Example C-44. *General-Bass*, 704–5.

On Note 1 the progression of the upper part from A to B should actually be considered an inverted resolution, because this A could easily have resolved to G, which, however, was given over to the middle part. Yet, the lower part with Note 1 is a retardation that does not belong to this chord, which lacks a resolution and, therefore, will not be observed in an accompaniment with a rapid tempo. On Note 2 a correct inversion of the resolution occurs in the upper part. On Note 3 the resolution is usual, and with Notes 4, 5, 6 one finds simple anticipations of the next chords. The second example of [Ex. C-44] consists throughout of the often employed anticipation of the upper part. Since both examples have a rapid tempo, it does not matter if the accompanist skips over all these retardations, anticipations, inverted resolutions, and ordinary resolutions, and proceeds with the fundamental notes of the thorough-bass as if [the accompaniment] were formed as:[26]

VII. Resolution of Dissonances with Changing Musical Genders

When identical notes appear successively in different, enharmonic notation (i.e., F to E♯), Heinichen would describe this as a change of musical
gender; for example:

Example C-45. *General-Bass*, 706–7.

Composers occasionally make use of these harsh progressions with the expression
of such harsh words as pain, despair, terror, etc.; in these cases they attend as
much as possible to the *cantabile* of the vocal part and leave the playing of unexpected as well as unnatural harmonies to the accompaniment. Also, the same
thing is practiced now and then in music of many parts; however, this must be
done with particular care so that at least the vocal part does not have unnatural
intervals. Therefore, . . . that seems proper in which one keeps the vocal part,
where the two differently notated semitones follow one after the other, in the first
notation until the remaining [instrumental] parts actually change gender and
until the singer grows accustomed to the metamorphosis, as the following example
shows:[27]

The composer employs these changes of gender in the recitative, and the accompanist must be prepared to solve the special problems they create for resolving dissonances. In the following example each change of gender alters the dissonance and its accompaniment; in addition, one finds harmonic inversions occurring between the gender alterations.

Example C-46. *General-Bass*, 708.

We see in the first example that the augmented fourth (1) becomes a diminished fifth on the next chord (2) according to the step [of the note] on the staff; and therefore [it] receives a completely different accompaniment and resolution, even though the F forms the bass of both chords. In the second example we see the B♭ minor given in the voice part over (3) is inverted with the following bass (4) transforming [the harmony] to B♭ major and again altering the accompaniment and the resolution, even though the root of both chords is B♭. In the third example, the same thing happens again, only the final B♭ major harmony has a somewhat altered accompaniment, as the figures show. In all three examples, however, the notes of the main chord and those of the following one with which the gender is changed could be identical, if one seeks accuracy and would give both chords the same accompaniment, as the following illustrates:[28]

The next examples show dissonances transformed into consonances by the change of gender; consequently the need for their resolution disappears.

Example C-47. *General-Bass*, 710–11.

Heinichen warns us, however, that these enharmonic changes will not always appear in music; rather some well-known composers (whom he does not name) prefer to write passages such as the first part of example C-46 and example C-47 as:

Example C-48. *General-Bass*, 713.

With justification Heinichen disapproves of hiding enharmonic changes in this way, since the notation obviously misleads the accompanist. For example, the notation of the first full measure in example C-48 would lead an accompanist to play a $\frac{6}{4}$ chord, even though it cannot resolve on the F♯. The correct resolution demands an E♯ for the second half of the measure, as example C-46 has shown.

VIII. Some Ambiguous and Doubtful Cases

Heinichen concludes his investigation of dissonances in the theatrical style with four sets of examples and analyses, each containing three exceptional progressions of harmony typical of music written by Heinchen's contemporaries. Such obscurities, Heinichen believes, result from composers' attempts to hide resolutions of dissonances. One hardly need emphasize at this point the significance of these analyses. They demonstrate that an important part of Heinichen's legacy to us, in addition to the exhaustive account of the thorough-bass, includes his codification of harmony as it was practiced in the final decades of the Baroque. As the preceding material has shown, his account of the theatrical style is in fact a comprehensive harmony course.

Example C-49. *General-Bass*, 714–15.

In the first example the bass B♭ should resolve naturally down to A, as is shown in No. 1 below. This single resolving tone, however, is thrown to the upper parts while the entirely foreign chord $\overset{d}{a}$ is chosen, which has no relationship to the natural chord of resolution $\overset{e}{\underset{f}{c\sharp}}$ and, therefore, is not derived from the inversion of the resolution. In the second $\overset{a}{\text{example}}$ the diminished seventh and diminished fifth have absolutely no resolution, but notwithstanding this chord is used today by good composers. If we want to defend it with a plausible reason, then I would say that the three upper parts $(\overset{b\flat}{\underset{e}{g}})$ over the bass c♯ are played as the following chord with alterations of a natural and a sharp $(\overset{b}{g\sharp})$; and only with the third chord does it resolve after a fashion in the following way: $\overset{e}{4}\overset{6}{\underset{\sharp}{5}}$, as is clearly shown in No. 2 below. In the third example it seems as if the fourth F would not resolve; one can say, however, that it is suspended into the next chord D as a third and then resolves to the next chord on E, as No. 3 shows [below], though this is not one of the best resolutions:[29]

Example C-50. *General-Bass*, 716.

The first example seems to resolve irregularly. If, however, one compares this with No. 1 below to see how it would resolve naturally, one finds no difference other than the natural sign before the bass in the last half of the measure and the frequently used anticipation of the diminished seventh in the upper part. In the second example the augmented fourth appears to lack a resolution; and since each accompanist would normally use the harmony $\frac{6^+}{4+}$ with this chord, therefore these notes do not form an inverted harmony with the following chord. If, however, over the first chord on E one plays in place of the second, a third $\overset{6}{\underset{3}{4+}}$ and correctly inverts these notes for the following chord on c♯, then the latter chord can resolve according to rule as No. 2 shows. Or one can also exchange the 6♯ for the 6♮ over the bass c♯; then the scale structure [*ambitus*] will lie correctly for the singer, as No. 3 shows. In the third example the resolution of the $\overset{+7}{\underset{5}{4}}$ chord should return naturally to the $\overset{2}{3}$. The two fundamental tones of this chord are $\overset{b}{g}$, because the diminished fifth $\overset{c\sharp}{f}$ in the chord $\overset{+7}{\underset{2}{4}}$ resolves naturally to these two notes: $\overset{c}{f\sharp}\;\overset{b}{g}$. Now these two main notes $\overset{b}{g}$ are retained with the resolving chord by adding a sharp $(\overset{b}{g\sharp})$; however, a new tone E is played, a procedure that should not be criticized and [which] amounts to that form of an inverted resolution as we have seen it previously with the resolution of a dissonance to a dissonance:[30]

Example C-51. *General-Bass*, 718.

With the first example the diminished seventh appears to have no resolution, and the accompanist undoubtedly would play the natural sixth F over the bass note Ab. Yet this chord is based on the obscured inversion of the harmony. For instead of resolving naturally as No. 1 shows below, it exchanges its bass F♯ with the third of the chord, as No. 2 shows. However, a flat is placed before the inverted bass A as No. 3 indicates; and this is the correct inversion and the proper accompaniment of this chord, after which the resolution of the diminished seventh first takes place on the following chord. Since, however, in the usual number of parts two fifths would arise between the upper part and the bass, as No. 4 shows, one tries to bury them in a full-voiced accompaniment; or one can play the major sixth without the fifth on the bass Ab as No. 5 shows, [since] such omissions of inverted extra parts do not affect the accompaniment:

The second example above [Ex. C-51] has the chord $\overset{6}{\underset{2}{4♮}}$ over the bass F. At first glance this [chord] also seems to lack a resolution. This matter also depends on the obscured inversion of the harmony. For the resolution of the chord [on] F should occur as No. 1 below shows. Instead, the bass exchanges its note F♯ with the third of the chord; thus the correctly inverted chord of No. 2 would result. A flat is placed before this new note; and again one can retain or omit the extra augmented fourth found over this note; in the latter case arises the natural accompaniment [shown] in No. 3:[31]

The third example above [ex. C-51] . . . also should resolve as No. 1 below shows. Now the resolving bass note D has the following parts over it as No. 2 shows. This chord, however, is inverted so that the Bb in the upper part is placed in the bass. However, a natural is placed before this bass note, and in this way results the inverted chord No. 3 as found in the third example above [of ex. C-51]. This chord, however, again inverts its harmony on the following bass note F in a way already familiar to us from other examples in this chapter:[32]

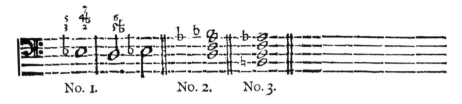

The last trio of examples presents variations of the $\frac{7}{4}$ chord which frequently appear in recitatives:

Example C-52. *General-Bass*, 720–21.

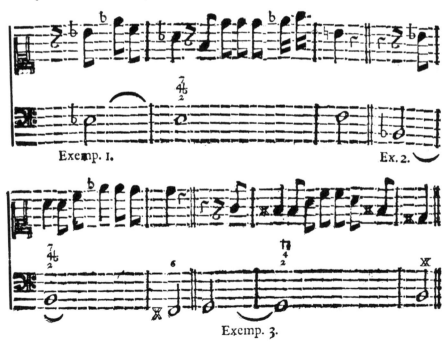

In the first example the last half of the bar should resolve naturally to D, as No. 1 below shows. If one places a natural before the sixth of this note, as No. 2 shows, and inverts the bass with the third of the chord, i.e., the F, then the result is the first chord above with the accompaniment $\frac{6}{4\natural}$ as No. 3 [below] shows. Should the accompanist not guess the minor third of this chord and play the second instead, namely $\frac{6}{4\natural}$, then one must consider this a liberty of no importance here:[33]

No. 1.   No. 2.   No. 3.

The second example above [ex. C-52] should resolve as is shown in No. 1 below, because the diminished fifth $\frac{e\flat}{a}$ concealed in the $\frac{7}{4}$ chord usually resolves naturally to the third, as No. 2 shows. However, because in unusual cases the diminished fifth can also resolve to the sixth as No. 3 shows, thus one sees that the bass of the second example above [ex. C-52] achieves this very resolution:[34]

No. 1.   No. 2.   No. 3.

The third example above [ex. C-52] is again the same case as the second example except for the difference that the parts of the resolution are inverted. For instead of the diminished fifth $\frac{c}{f\sharp}$ concealed in the $\frac{+7}{4}$ resolving according to the second example above [and] shown in No. 1 below, it inverts its resolution as in No. 2, in which the bass moves as in the third example above:[35]

No. 1.   No. 2.

One could hardly formulate a better conclusion to this material than Heinichen's own words:

Now these would be the ambiguous and doubtful cases of the current practice that we wished to illustrate, particularly with recitative examples, because the greatest misuses of theatrical fundamentals occur in this very style. As we do not intend that someone should accustom himself to these independent chords and should imitate them indiscriminately, therefore, music students profit at least this advantage from [this study]: they can use [these chords] to train their own practical judgment and to learn the distinction between black and white—I mean the gradations of good, passable, bad, better, and less good theatrical harmony. Above all, this entire chapter illustrates how extensive and also how refined is the study of the theatrical [style of] harmony. It certainly is not enough to invert indiscriminately every harmony before or with the resolution of dissonances according to ordinary principles, for practice and experience also are needed if such efforts are not to result in awkwardness. One chord permits this practice, another does not and runs contrary either to good taste or other rules of harmony that stand in our way. In this [materia], therefore, as in the learning of composition in general, one needs to look at examples and the practice of good composers.[36]

Notes

1. Johann David Heinichen, *Der General-Bass in der Composition* (Dresden, 1728), 536.

2. Ibid., 587.

3. Ibid.

4. Ibid., 589.

5. A unique aspect of Heinichen's work is the exceptional number of music examples. The reader is urged to consult the treatise for additional examples omitted here.

6. Heinichen, *General-Bass*, 598.

7. Ibid., 601.

8. Ibid., 602 (footnote d).

9. Cf. Ibid., 624.

10. Ibid., 626 (footnote o).

11. Ibid., 629–30.

12. Ibid., 635.

13. Ibid., 636.

14. Ibid., 651.

15. Ibid., 662.

16. Ibid., 674.

17. Ibid., 674 (footnote dd).

18. Ibid., 682–83.

19. Ibid., 683.

20. Ibid., 686.

21. Ibid., 688–89.

22. Ibid., 692.

23. Ibid., 696–97.

24. Ibid., 702.

25. Ibid., 704.

26. Ibid., 705.

27. Ibid., 707–9 (footnote).

28. Ibid., 709–10.

29. Ibid., 715.

30. Ibid., 717.

31. Ibid., 719.

32. Ibid., 720.

33. Ibid., 721.

34. Ibid.

35. Ibid., 722.

36. Ibid., 722–23.

Bibliography

Asterisks indicate sources of special significance for the present study.
Anonymi are entered alphabetically by title.

I. Sources before 1800

ADLUNG, JACOB. *Anleitung zu der musikalischen Gelahrtheit* (Erfurt, 1758); facs. ed. H. J. MOSER (Kassel, 1953).

*AGAZZARI, AGOSTINO. *Del sonare sopra'l basso con tutti li stromenti* (Siena, 1607); facs. ed. *Bollettino bibliografico musicale* (Milan, 1933).

*ALBERT, HEINRICH. *Ander Theil der Arien oder Melodien* (Königsberg, 1640); new ed. DENKMÄLER DEUTSCHER TONKUNST 13 (Leipzig, 1903, repr. Wiesbaden, 1958).

ALBRECHTSBERGER, JOHANN G. *Kurzgefasste Methode den Generalbass zu erlernen* (Vienna & Mainz, 1792).

D'ALEMBERT, JEAN. *Elémens de musique théorique et pratique suivant les principes de M. Rameau* (Paris, 1752).

D'ANGLEBERT, JEAN H. *Principes de l'accompagnement* (Paris, 1689); new ed. M. ROESGEN-CHAMPION (Paris, 1934).

AVISON, CHARLES. *An Essay on Musical Expression* (London, 1752).

*BACH, C.P.E. *Versuch über die wahre Art das Clavier zu spielen* (2 vols. Berlin, 1753–62); tr. & ed. W. MITCHELL (New York, 1949).

BACH, JOHANN M. *Kurze und systematische Anleitung zum General-Bass und der Tonkunst überhaupt* (Kassel, 1780).

*BANCHIERI, ADRIANO. *Conclusioni nel suono dell' organo* (Bologna, 1609); facs. ed. *Bollettino bibliografico musicale* (Milan, 1934).

BARTOLOMI, ANGELO M. *Table pour apprendre facilement à toucher le théorbe sur la basse-continue* (Paris, 1669).

[BAYNE, ALEXANDER]. *An Introduction to the Knowledge and Practice of the Thoro'-Bass* (Edinburgh, 1717).

BEMETZRIEDER, ANTON. *Méthode et réflexions sur les leçons de musique* (Paris, 1778).

BIANCIARDI, FRANCESCO. *Breve regola per imparar' a sonare sopra il basso con ogni sorte d'istrumento* (Siena, 1607).

BLANKENBURG, QUIRINUS VAN. *Elementa Musica, of niew Licht tot het Welverstaan van de Musiec en de Bas-Continuo* (The Hague, 1739).

BLOW, JOHN. *Rules for Playing a Thorough Bass* (MS British Library Add. 34072); new ed. F. T. ARNOLD, *Thorough-bass*, pp. 163–72.

BÖDDECKER, PHILIPP. *Manductio nova methodico-practica ad bassum generalem* (Stuttgart, 1701).

BOUTMY, JEAN-BAPTISTE. *Traité abrégé sur la basse continuë* (The Hague, 1760).

*BOYVIN, JACQUES. *Traité abrégé de l'accompagnement* (2d ed. Paris, 1705) [1st ed. Paris, 1700 unavailable].

BURMAN, ERIK. *Dissertatio musica. De basso fundamentali* (Uppsala, 1728).

BURNEY, CHARLES. *A General History of Music* (4 vols. London, 1776–89); new ed. F. MERCER (London, 1932, repr. New York, 1957).

CACCINI, GIULIO. *Euridice* (Florence, 1600).

————. *Le nuove musiche* (Florence, 1601–2 n.s.); facs. ed. F. Mantica (Rome, 1934).

*CAMPION, FRANÇOIS. *Traité d'accompagnement et de composition selon la règle des octaves de musique. Oeuvre second* (Paris, 1716).

*————. *Addition au traité d'accompagnement et de composition* (Paris, 1730).

CAVALIERI, EMILIO DE. *Rappresentazione di anima e di corpo.* (Rome, 1600); facs. ed. F. MANTICA (Rome, 1912).

CLEMENT, CHARLES. *Essai sur l'accompagnement du clavecin* (Paris, 1758).

————. *Essai sur la basse fondamentale; pour servir de supplément à l'essai sur l'accompagnement* (Paris, 1762).

CORRETTE, MICHEL. *Le maître de clavecin pour l'accompagnement* (Paris, 1753).

COUPERIN, FRANÇOIS. *Règles pour l'accompagnement* (MS Paris, ca. 1698); new ed. P. BRUNOLD, *Oeuvres Complètes* 1 (Paris, 1933).

*————. *L'art de toucher le clavecin* (Paris, 1717); tr. into German and English, A. LINDE & M. ROBERTS (Wiesbaden, 1933).

DANDRIEU, JEAN F. *Principes de l'acompagnement [sic] du clavecin* (Paris, 1718).

*DAUBE, JOHANN. *General-Bass in drey Accorden* (Leipzig, 1756).

*DELAIR, ETIENNE D. *Traité d'acompagnement [sic] pour le théorbe et le clavessin [sic]* (Paris, 1690).

DIRUTA, GIROLAMO. *Il transilvano* (pt. 2 Venice, 1609).

EBNER, WOLFANG. *Eine kurtze Instruction und Anleitung zum General-Bass* [In: Herbst, *Arte prattica & poëtica* (Frankfurt/Main, 1653)].

FALKENER, ROBERT. *Instructions for Playing the Harpsichord* (2d ed. London, 1774) [1st ed. London, 1764 unavailable].

*FISCHER, J. P. A. *Korte en noodigste Grondregelen van de Bassus-Continuus* (Utrecht, 1731).

FLEURY, NICHOLAS. *Méthode pour apprendre facilement à toucher le théorbe sur la basse-continuë* (Paris, 1660).

FORKEL, JOHANN. *Allgemeine Geschichte der Musik* (Leipzig, 1788).

————. *Allgemeine Litteratur der Musik* (Leipzig, 1792).

FRICK [FRIKE], PHILIPP. *A Treatise on Thorough Bass* (London, 1786).

*GASPARINI, FRANCESCO. *L'armonico pratico al cimbalo* (Venice, 1708); tr. F. STILLINGS (New Haven, Conn., 1963).

GEMINIANI, FRANCESCO. *Rules for Playing in a True Taste on the Violin and Harpsichord, Particularly the Thorough-Bass* (London, 1739).

————. *The Art of Accompaniament [sic]* (London, 1755).

*GERBER, ERNEST L., *Historisch-biographisches Lexicon der Tonkünstler* (2 vols. Leipzig, 1790–92).

GERVAIS, LAURENT. *Méthode pour l'accompagnement du clavecin* (Paris, 1734).

GRAAF, CHRISTIAAN E. *Proeve over de Natur der Harmonie in de Generaal Bas* (The Hague, 1782).

GUGL, MATTHAEUS. *Fundamenta partiturae in compendio data* (Augsburg & Innsbruck, 1727).

HAHN, GEORG J. *Clavierübung, welcher eine Erklärung der Ziffern nebst praktischen Exempeln beigefügt sind* (Nürnberg, 1750).

————. *Der nach der neuern Art wohl unterwiesene General-Bass-Schüler* (Augsburg, 1751).

HALTMEIER, CARL J. *Anleitung: wie man einen General-Bass . . . in alle Töne transponieren könne* (Hamburg, 1737).

HECK, JOHANN. *The Art of Playing Thorough Bass* (London, ca. 1780).

*HEINICHEN, JOHANN D. *Neu erfundene und gründliche Anweisung . . . zu vollkommener Erlernung des General-Basses* (Hamburg, 1711).

*————. *Der General-Bass in der Composition* (Dresden, 1728).

HERBST, JOHANN. *Arte prattica & poëtica* (Frankfurt/Main, 1653).

HESSE, JOHANN H. *Kurz, Doch hinlängliche Anweisung zum General-Basse* (Hamburg, 1776).

*HILLER, JOHANN A. *Lebensbeschreibungen berühmter Musikgelehrten und Tonkünstler, neuerer Zeit* (Leipzig, 1784).

HOLDER, WILLIAM. *A Treatise of the Natural Grounds and Principles of Harmony* (2d ed. London, 1731) [1st ed. London, 1694 unavailable].

KELLER, GODFRY. *A Compleat Method, for Attaining to Play a Thorough Bass* (London, 1707).

*KELLNER, DAVID. *Treulicher Unterricht im General-Bass* (Hamburg, 1732).

KELLNER, JOHANN C. *Grundriss des Generalbasses* (Kassel, 1783).

KIRNBERGER, JOHANN P. *Grundsätze des Generalbasses* (Berlin, 1781).

KNECHT JUSTIN H. *Gemeinnützliches Elementarwerk der Harmonie und des General-Basses* (Augsburg, 1792–98).

KUHNAU, JOHANN. *Der musikalische Quacksalber* (Dresden, 1700); new ed. K. BENNDORF (Berlin, 1900).

Kurtze Anführung zum General-Bass (Leipzig, 1728).

LAAG, HEINRICH. *Anfangsgründe zum Clavierspielen und Generalbass* (Osnabrück, 1774).

L'AFFILARD, MICHEL. *Principes très-faciles pour bien apprendre la musique* (Paris, 1694).

LAMPE, JOHN. *A Plain and Compendious Method of Teaching Thorough-Bass* (London, 1737).

LANGLÉ, HONORÉ. *Traité de la basse sous le chant* (Paris, 1798).

LAPORTE, NICHOLAS DE. *Traité théorique et pratique de l'accompagnement du clavecin* (Paris, ca. 1750).

*LOCKE, MATTHEW. *Melothesia: or, Certain General Rules for Playing upon a Continued-Bass* (London, 1673).

LOEHLEIN, GEORG S. *Clavier-Schule oder kurze und gründliche Anweisung zur Melodie und Harmonie* (Leipzig, 1765).

MAJER, JOSEPH. *Museum musicum theoretico practicum* (Schwäbisch-Hall, 1732); facs. ed. H. BECKER (Kassel, 1954).

MANFREDINI, VINCENZO. *Regole armoniche, o sieno precetti ragionati per apprendere i principj della musica* (Venice, 1775).

MARPURG, FRIEDRICH W. *Handbuch bey dem Generalbasse und der Composition* (3 vols. Berlin, 1755–58.).

————. *Historisch-kritische Beyträge zur Aufnahme der Musik* (5 vols. Berlin, 1758–78).

————. *Herrn Georg Andreas Sorgens Anleitung zum Generalbass . . . mit Anmerkungen von Friedrich Wilhelm Marpurg* (Berlin, 1760).

[MARPURG, FRIEDRICH W.] *Kritische Briefe über die Tonkunst* (Berlin, 1763).

MASSON, CHARLES. *Nouveau traité des règles pour la composition de la musique* (Paris, 1705).

MATTHESON, JOHANN. *Das neu-eröffnete Orchestre* (Hamburg, 1713).

————. *Das beschützte Orchestre* (Hamburg, 1717).

*————. *Exemplarische Organisten-Probe* (Hamburg, 1719).

————. *Das forschende Orchestre* (Hamburg, 1721).

————. *Critica musica* (2 vols. Hamburg, 1722–25).

————. *Der musicalische Patriot* (Hamburg, 1728).

*————. *Grosse General-Bass-Schule* (Hamburg, 1731).

*————. *Kleine General-Bass-Schule* (Hamburg, 1735).

*————. *Der vollkommene Capellmeister* (Hamburg, 1739); facs. ed. M. REIMANN (Kassel, 1954).

————. *Grundlage einer Ehrenpforte* (Hamburg, 1740); new ed. M. SCHNEIDER (Berlin, 1910).

MIZLER [VON KOLOF], LORENZ. *Neu eröffnete musikalische Bibliothek* (4 vols. Leipzig, 1736–54).

————. *Anfangs-Gründe des Generalbasses* (Leipzig, 1739).

MORLEY, THOMAS. *A Plaine and Easie Introduction to Practicall Musicke* (London, 1597); facs. ed. E. FELLOWES (London, 1937); new ed. R. HARMAN (New York, [1952]).

MUFFAT, GEORG. *An Essay on Thoroughbass* (MS Vienna, 1699); new ed. H. FEDERHOFER (Tübingen, 1961).

NAUSS, JOHANN X. *Gründlicher Unterricht den General-Bass recht zu erlernen* (Augsburg, 1769).

*NIEDT, FRIEDRICH E. *Musicalische Handleitung* (Hamburg, 1700).

————. *Handleitung zur Variation* (Hamburg, 1706).

NIVERS, GUILLAUME-GABRIEL. *Motets à voix seule . . . avec l'art d'accompagner sur la basse continuë* (Paris, 1689).

PAISIELLO, GIOVANNI. *Regole per bene accompagnare il partimento* (St. Petersburg, 1782).

PASQUALI, NICCOLO. *Thorough-bass Made Easy* (Edinburgh, 1757).

PENNA, LORENZO. *Li primi albori musicali* (Bologna, 1672).

PERI, JACOPO. *Euridice* (Florence, 1600–1601 n.s.); facs. ed. E. MAGNI DUFFLOCQ (Rome, 1934).

PORTMANN, JOHANN G. *Leichtes Lehrbuch der Harmonie, Composition und des Generalbass* (Darmstadt, 1789).

*PRAETORIUS, MICHAEL. *Syntagma musicum* (vol. 3 Wolfenbüttel, 1619); facs. ed. W. GURLITT (Kassel, 1958).

————. *Gesamtausgabe*, ed. F. BLUME (21 vols. Berlin, 1928–61).

*PRINTZ, WOLFFGANG C. *Phrynis Mitilenaeus oder Satyrischer Componist* (Leipzig & Dresden, 1696).

*QUANTZ, JOHANN J. *Versuch einer Anweisung die Flöte traversiere zu spielen* (Berlin, 1752); facs. ed. H.-P. SCHMITZ (Kassel, 1953); Eng. tr. E. REILLY (London, 1966).

RAMEAU, JEAN-PHILIPPE. *Traité de l'harmonie* (Paris, 1722).

————. *Nouveau système de musique théorique* (Paris, 1726).

————. *Dissertation sur les différentes méthodes d'accompagnement* (Paris, 1732).

————. *Génération harmonique* (Paris, 1737).

REINHARD, LEONHARD. *Kurzer und deutlicher Unterricht von dem General-Bass* (Augsburg, 1750).

RODOLPHE, JEAN. *Théorie d'accompagnement et de composition* (Paris, ca. 1785).

ROUSSEAU, JEAN-JACQUES. *Dictionnaire de musique* (Amsterdam, 1768); new ed. *Oeuvres Complètes* vol. 13–14 (Paris, 1825).

SABBATINI, GALEAZZO. *Regola facile e breve per sonare sopra il basso continuo* (Venice, 1628).

*SAINT-LAMBERT, [MICHEL] DE. *Nouveau traité de l'accompagnement du clavecin* (Amsterdam, ca. 1710) [1st ed. Paris, 1707 unavailable].

SCARLATTI, ALESSANDRO. *Principj* (MS British Library Add. 14244).

———. *Regole per cembalo* (MS British Library Add. 31517).

SCHEIBE, JOHANN A. *Der critische musikus* (Leipzig, 1740).

SCHEIN, JOHANN. *Sämtliche Werke*, ed. A. PRUFER (7 vols. Leipzig, 1901–23).

SCHROETER, CHRISTOPH G. *Deutliche Anweisung zum General-Bass* (Halberstadt, 1772).

SCHÜTZ, HEINRICH. *Sämmtliche Werke*, ed. P. SPITTA (18 vols. Leipzig, 1885–1927).

SOLANO, FRANCISCO. *Novo tratado de musica metrica e rythmica* (Lisbon, 1779).

*SORGE, GEORG A. *Vorgemach der musicalischen Composition* (3 vols. Lobenstein, 1745–47).

SPEER, DANIEL. *Grundrichtiger, kurtz- leicht- und nöthiger, jetzt wol-vermehrter Unterricht der musicalischen Kunst* (Ulm, 1697) [1st ed. Ulm, 1687 unavailable].

STADEN, JOHANN. *Kurzer und einfältiger Bericht für diejenigen so im Basso ad Organum unerfahren* (Nürnberg, 1626); new ed. ALLGEMEINE MUSIKALISCHE ZEITUNG 12(1877), 99–103, 119–23.

TELEMANN, GEORG M. *Unterricht im General-Bass-Spielen* (Hamburg, 1773).

*TELEMANN, GEORG P. *Singe-, Spiel-, und Generalbass-Übungen* (Hamburg, 1733); new ed. M. SEIFFERT (Berlin, 1927).

TOMEONI, PELLEGRINO. *Regole pratiche per accompagnare basso continuo* (Florence, 1795).

TORRES, JOSÉ DE. *Reglas generales de acompañar* (Madrid, 1702).

TREIBER, JOHANN. *Der accurate Organist* (Jena, 1704).

TÜRK, DANIEL. *Kurze Anweisung zum Generalbass-Spielen* (Leipzig & Halle, 1791).

Vermehrter und nun zum zweytenmal in Druck beförderter kurtzer jedoch gründlicher Wegweiser (Augsburg, 1693).

*VIADANA, LODOVICO DA. *Cento concerti ecclesiastici* (Venice, 1602).

*WALTHER, JOHANN G. *Praecepta der musicalischen Composition* (MS Weimar, 1708); ed. P. BENARY (Leipzig, 1955).

*———. *Musicalisches Lexicon* (Leipzig, 1732); facs. ed. R. SCHAAL (Kassel, 1953).

*WERCKMEISTER, ANDREAS. *Die nothwendigsten Anmerckungen und Regeln wie der Bassus Continuus oder General-Bass wohl könne tractiret werden* (Aschersleben, 1698).

———. *Cribrum musicum, oder musicalisches Sieb* (Quedlinburg & Leipzig, 1700).

*———. *Harmonologica musica, oder kurtze Anleitung zur musicalischen Composition* (Frankfurt/Main & Leipzig, 1702).

WIEDEBURG, MICHAEL. *Anderer Teil des sich selbst informierenden Clavierspielers* (Halle & Leipzig, 1765–75).

WOLF, GEORG. *Kurzer Unterricht im Klavierspielen* (Halle, 1784).

ZUMBAG DE KOESFELT, COENRAAD. *Institutiones Musicae, of Korte Onderwyzinger* (Leiden, 1743).

II. Sources after 1800[1]

ABERT, HERMANN. *Gesammelte Schriften und Vorträge* (Halle, 1929).

ABRAHAM, LARS U. *Der Generalbass im Schaffen des Michael Praetorius und seine harmonischen Voraussetzungen* (Berlin, 1961).

ALDRICH, PUTNAM. *Ornamentation in J. S. Bach's Organ Works* (New York, 1950).

APEL, WILLI. *Harvard Dictionary of Music* (Cambridge, Mass., 1944).

*ARNOLD, FRANK T. *The Art of Accompaniment from a Thorough-Bass* (London, 1931); repr. (London, 1961).

Baker's Biographical Dictionary, ed. N. SLONIMSKY (5th ed. New York, 1958).

*BECKER-GLAUGH, IRMGARD. *Dis Bedeutung der Music für die Dresdener Hoffeste . . .* (Kassel, 1951).

*BEREND, FRITZ. *Nicolaus Adam Strungk, sein Leben und seine Werke . . .* (Hannover, 1913).

BOHN, EMIL. *Bibliographie der Musik-Druckwerke bis 1700, welche in der Univ.-Bibl., Stadtbibl. und der Bibl. des Akademischen Instituts für Kirchenmusik zu Breslau aufbewahrt werden* (Berlin, 1883).

*BORGIR, THARALD. *The Performance of Basso Continuo in Italy during the Seventeenth Century* (Ph.D. Dissertation, University of California, Berkeley, 1971).

The British Union-Catalogue of Early Music, ed. E. SCHNAPPER (London, 1957).

*BUELOW, GEORGE J. *The Full-Voiced Style of Thorough-Bass Realization*, ACTA MUSICOLOGICA 35 (1963), 216–73.

*———. *The "Loci Topici" and Affect in Late Baroque Music*, THE MUSIC REVIEW (August 1966), 161–76.

———. *Figured Bass as Improvisation* (with R. Donington), ACTA MUSICOLOGICA 40 (1968), 178–79.

———. *German Music Theory of the 17th Century*, JOURNAL OF MUSIC THEORY 16 (1972), 36–49.

———. *Music, Rhetoric, and the Concept of the Affections: A Selective Bibliography*, MLA NOTES 30 (1973), 250–59.

———. *A Lesson in Operatic Performance Practice by Madame Faustina Bordoni*, A MUSICAL OFFERING, ESSAYS IN HONOR OF MARTIN BERNSTEIN (New York, 1976).

———. *Johann Mattheson and the Invention of the "Affektenlehre,"* NEW MATTHESON STUDIES (Cambridge, 1983).

*BUKOFZER, MANFRED. *Music in the Baroque Era* (New York, 1947).

CANNON, BEEKMAN, *Johann Mattheson: Spectator in Music* (New Haven, Conn., 1947).

---

[1]Note to the revised edition: Surprisingly few new, major studies of Baroque thorough-bass practice have appeared since this book was first published. The bibliography has included them as well as a few significant works on other aspects of Baroque performance practices. Although the *New Grove Dictionary of Music and Musicians* is cited, it has not been possible to incorporate all of the invaluable new information appearing in this great scholarly research tool in the body of the text or in the bibliography. Especially for more recent biographical data the reader is urged to consult the *New Grove*.

CARPENTER, NAN C. *Music in the Medieval and Renaissance Universities* (Norman, Okla., 1958).

Catalogue critique et descriptif des imprimés de musique des XVIe et XVIIe siècles, conservés à la Bibliothèque de l'Université Royale d'Upsala, vol. 1, ed. R. MITJANA (Uppsala, 1911); vol. 2–3, ed. A. DAVIDSSON (Uppsala, 1951).

Cataloque della biblioteca del Liceo Musicale di Bologna, ed. G. GASPARI (4 vols. Bologna, 1890–1905).

*CLERCX, SUZANNE. *Le baroque et la musique* (Brussels, 1948).

CROCE, BENEDETTO. *I teatri di Napoli, secolo XV–XVIII* (Naples, 1891).

DAHMS, WALTER. *The "Gallant" Style of Music*, MUSICAL QUARTERLY 11 (1925), 356–72.

DAVID, HANS T. *J. S. Bach's Musical Offering* (New York, 1945).

DAVID, HANS T. & ARTHUR MENDEL. *The Bach Reader* (New York, 1945).

DENT, EDWARD. *Alessandro Scarlatti: His Life and Works* (London, 1905); repr. with preface and additional notes by J. WALKER (London, 1960).

DOLMETSCH, ARNOLD. *The Interpretation of the Music of the XVIIth and XVIIIth Centuries* (London, 1915).

DOMMER, ARREY VON. *Handbuch der Musikgeschichte* . . . (Leipzig, 1878).

DONINGTON, ROBERT. *The Interpretation of Early Music* (new ed. London, 1974).

*———. *A Performer's Guide to Baroque Music* (New York, 1973).

ECORCHEVILLE, JULES. *De Lulli à Rameau, 1690–1730* (Paris, 1906).

*EGGEBRECHT, HANS H. *Arten des Generalbasses im frühen und mittleren 17. Jahrhundert*, ARCHIV FÜR MUSIKWISSENSCHAFT 14 (1957), 61–82.

EITNER, ROBERT. *Biographisch-Bibliographisches Quellen-Lexikon* . . . (10 vols. Leipzig, 1899–1904).

*———. *Der Generalbass des 18. Jahrhunderts*, MONATSHEFTE FÜR MUSIKGESCHICHTE 12 (1880), 151–54.

ENGEL, HANS. *Deutschland und Italien in ihren musikgeschichtlichen Beziehungen* (Regensburg, 1944).

ENGELKE, BERNARD. *J. F. Fasch, Versuch einer Biographie*, SAMMELBÄNDE DER IMG 10 (1909), 263–83.

ENGLÄNDER, RICHARD. *Zur Edition von J. D. Heinichen Concerto G Dur*, SVENSK TIDSKRIFT FOER MUSIKFORSKNING 36 (1954), 94–98.

FERAND, ERNEST T. *Die Improvisation in der Musik* (Zürich, 1938).

FÉTIS, FRANÇOIS-JOSEPH. *Biographie universelle des musiciens* . . . (2d ed. 8 vols. Paris, 1860–67).

———. *Traité complet de la théorie et de la pratique de l'harmonie* (Paris, 1844).

FORTUNE, NIGEL. *Continuo Instruments in Italian Monodies*, THE GALPIN SOCIETY JOURNAL 6 (1953), 10–13.

*FREY, MAX W. *Georg Philipp Telemanns Singe-, Spiel- und Generalbass-Übungen* (Zürich, 1922).

FROTSCHER, GOTTHOLD. *Geschichte des Orgelspiels und der Orgelkomposition* (2 vols. Berlin, 1935–36).

*FÜRSTENAU, MORITZ. *Beiträge zur Geschichte der königlich sächsischen musikalischen Kapelle* (Dresden, 1849).

*———. *Zur Geschichte der Musik und des Theaters am Hofe der Kurfürsten von Sachsen* . . . (Dresden, 1861/1862).

GERBER, ERNST L. *Neues historisch-biographisches Lexikon der Tonkünstler* . . . (2d ed. 4 vols. Leipzig, 1812–14).

GERSTENBERG, WALTER. *Generalbasslehre und Kompositionstechnik in Niedts "Musikalischen Handleitung,"* KONGRESS-BERICHT, GESELLSCHAFT FÜR MUSIKFORSCHUNG (Bamberg, 1953), 152–55.

GIRDLESTONE, CUTHBERT. *Jean-Philippe Rameau, His Life and Work* (London, 1957).

GOLDSCHMIDT, HUGO. *Das Cembalo im Orchester der italienischen Oper der zweiten Hälfte des 18. Jahrhunderts,* FESTSCHRIFT LILIENCRON (Leipzig, 1910), 87–92.

————. *Die Musikästhetik des 18. Jahrhunderts und ihre Beziehungen zu seinem Kunstschaffen* (Zürich & Leipzig, 1915).

GROUT, DONALD J. *A Short History of Opera* (2 vols. New York, 1947).

Grove's Dictionary of Music and Musicians, ed. E. BLOM (5th ed. 9 vols. New York, 1954).

GURLITT, WILIBALD. *Die Kompositionslehre des deutschen 16. and 17. Jahrhunderts,* KONGRESS-BERICHT, GESELLSCHAFT FÜR MUSIKFORSCHUNG (Hamburg, 1953), 103–13.

HAAS, ROBERT. *Aufführungspraxis der Musik* (Potsdam, 1931).

*————. *Das Generalbassflugblatt Francesco Bianciardis,* FESTSCHRIFT JOHANNES WOLF (Berlin, 1929), 48–56.

————. *Die Musik des Barocks* (Potsdam, 1928).

HARICH-SCHNEIDER, ETA. *The Harpsichord, An Introduction to Technique, Style, and the Historical Sources* (St. Louis, Mo., 1954).

*HAUSSWALD, GUENTER. *Johann David Heinichens Instrumentalwerke* (Leipzig, 1937).

HAYDON, GLEN. *The Evolution of the Six-Four Chord* (Berkeley, Calif., 1933).

HÜSCHEN, HEINRICH. *Die Musik im Kreise der artes liberales,* KONGRESS-BERICHT, GESELLSCHAFT FÜR MUSIKFORSCHUNG (Hamburg, 1956), 117–23.

JEPPESEN, KNUD. *The Style of Palestrina and the Dissonance* (London, 1927).

*KELLER, HERMANN. *Schule der Generalbass-Spiele* (Kassel, 1931); tr. C. PARRISH (New York, 1965).

*KINKELDEY, OTTO. *Orgel und Klavier in der Musik des 16. Jahrhunderts* (Leipzig, 1910).

KIRCHNER, GERHARD. *Der Generalbass bie Heinrich Schütz* (Kassel, 1960).

KIRKPATRICK, RALPH. *Johann Sebastian Bach, The "Goldberg" Variations* (New York, 1938).

KITTEL, JOHANN C. *Der angehende praktische Organist* (Erfurt, 1808).

KREBS, CARL. *Girolamo Diruta's Transilvano* . . . , VIERTEL JAHRSSCHRIFT FÜR MUSIKWISSENSCHAFT 13 (1892), 307–88.

*KRETZSCHMAR, HERMANN. *Allgemeines und Besonderes zur Affektenlehre,* JAHRBUCH DER MUSIKBIBLIOTHEK PETERS 18 (1911), 63–77; 19 (1912) 65–78.

————. *Das erste Jahrhundert der deutschen Oper,* SAMMELBÄNDE DER IMG 3 (1901–2), 270–93.

KROYER, THEODOR. *Zwischen Renaissance und Barock,* JAHRBUCH DER MUSIKBIBLIOTHEK PETERS 34 (1927), 45–54.

KRÜGER, WALTHER. *Das Concerto Grosso in Deutschland* (Wolfenbüttel, 1932).

LA MARA [IDA MARIA LIPSIUS]. *Musikerbriefe aus fünf Jahrhunderten* (Leipzig, 1886).

*LANDSHOFF, LUDWIG. *Über das vielstimmige Akkompagnement und andere Fragen des Generalbassspiels,* FESTSCHRIFT ADOLF SANDBERGER (Munich, 1918), 189–208.

LANG, PAUL H. *Music in Western Civilization* (New York, 1941).

LEPEL, FELIX VON. *Die Geschichte der sächsischen Hof- und Staatskapelle zu Dresden* (Dresden, 1948).

LOEWENBERG, ALFRED. *Annals of Opera, 1597–1940* (2d ed. Geneva, 1955).

LOWINSKY, EDWARD. *Early Scores in Manuscript*, JOURNAL OF THE AMERICAN MUSICOLOGICAL SOCIETY 13 (1960), 126–73.

MELLERS, WILFRID. *François Couperin and the French Classical Tradition* (London, 1950).

MENDEL, HERMANN. *Musikalisches Conversations-Lexikon* (Berlin, 1878).

MORGENSTERN, SAM (ed.). *Composers on Music* (New York, 1956).

MUELLER, ERICH (ed.). *Heinirich Schütz: Gesammelte Briefe und Schriften* (Regensburg, 1931).

MÜLLER-BLATTAU, JOSEPH. *Die Kompositionslehre Heinrich Schützens in der Fassung seines Schülers Christoph Bernhard* (Leipzig, 1926).

MÜNNICH, RICHARD. *Kuhnaus Leben*, SAMMELBÄNDE DER IMG 3 (1901–2), 473–527.

*Die Musik in Geschichte und Gegenwart, ed. F. BLUME (16 vols. Kassel 1949–79).

NAGEL, WILLIBALD. *Das Leben Christoph Graupners*, SAMMERBÄNDE DER IMG 10 (1908–9), 568–612.

─────. *Gottfried Grünewald*, SAMMELBÄNDE DER IMG 12 (1910–11), 99–107.

NEUMANN, FREDERICK. *Ornamentation in Baroque and Post-Baroque Music* (Princeton, 1978).

New Grove Dictionary of Music and Musicians, ed. S. Sadie (20 vols. London, 1980).

NEWMAN, WILLIAM S. *The Sonata in the Baroque Era* (Chapel Hill, N.C., 1959).

*OBERDÖRFFER, FRITZ. *Der Generalbass in der Instrumentalmusik des ausgehenden 18. Jahrunderts* (Kassel, 1939).

*─────. *Über die Generalbassbegleitung zu Kammermusikwerken Bachs und des Spätbarock*, DIE MUSIKFORSCHUNG 10 (1957), 61–74.

*─────. *Über die Generalbassbegleitung zu Kammermusikwerken Bachs, Schlusswort*, DIE MUSIKFORSCHUNG 11 (1958), 79–82.

*PIETZSCH, GERHARD. *Dresdner Hoffesste vom 16.–18. Jahrhundert*, MUSIK UND BILD: FESTSCHRIFT MAX SEIFFERT (Kassel, 1938), 83–86.

PINCHERLE, MARC. *Antonio Vivaldi et la musique instrumentale* (Paris, 1948).

*REDDICK, HARVEY. *Johann Mattheson's 48 Thorough-Bass Test-Pieces: Translation and Commentary* (Diss., University of Michigan, 1956).

REESE, GUSTAVE. *Music in the Renaissance* (New York, 1954).

*RICHTER, BERNHARD F. *Eine Abhandlung Johann Kuhnaus*, MONATSHEFTE FÜR MUSIKGESCHICHTE 24 (1902), 147–54.

RIEMANN, HUGO. *Geschichte der Musiktheorie im IX. -XIX. Jahrhundert* (Leipzig, 1898).

─────. *Handbuch der Musikgeschichte* vol. 2, pt. 2: *Das Generalbasszeitalter* (Leipzig, 1922).

RIEMANN, HUGO. *Musik-Lexikon*, ed. A. EINSTEIN (11th ed. Berlin, 1929).

SACHS, CURT. *Barockmusik*, JAHRBUCH DER MUSIKBIBLIOTHEK PETERS 26 (1919), 7–15.

─────. *History of Musical Instruments* (New York, 1940).

─────. *Rhythm and Tempo* (New York, 1953).

*SARTORI, CLAUDIO. *Bibliografia della musica strumentale italiana stampata in Italia fino al 1700* (Florence, 1952).

SCHÄFKE, RUDOLF. *Geschichte der Musikästhetik in Umrissen* (Berlin, 1934).

─────. *Quantz als Ästhetiker*, ARCHIV FÜR MUSIKWISSENSCHAFT 6 (1924), 213–42.

SCHERING, ARNOLD (ed.). *Geschichte der Musik in Beispielen* (Leipzig, 1931).

─────. *Geschichte des Instrumental-Konzerts* (Leipzig, 1905).

─────. *Die Musikästhetik der deutschen Aukflärung*, ZEITSCHRIFT DER IMG 8 (1907), 263–71, 316–22.

*————. *Musikgeschichte Leipzigs von 1650 bis 1723* (Leipzig, 1926).

*SCHMIDT, GUSTAV F. *Die älteste deutsche Oper in Leipzig am Ende des 17. und Anfang des 18. Jahrhunderts*, FESTSCHRIFT ADOLF SANDBERGER (Munich, 1918), 209–57.

*————. *Die frühdeutsche Oper und die musikdramatische Kunst Georg Caspar Schürmanns* (2 vols. Regensburg, 1933–34).

SCHMITZ, EUGEN. *Geschichte der weltlichen Solokantate* (2d ed. Leipzig, 1955).

SCHMITZ, HANS-PETER. *Die Kunst der Verzierung im 18. Jahrhundert* (Kassel, 1955).

*SCHNEIDER, MAX. *Die Anfänge des Basso Continuo* (Leipzig, 1918).

*SCHNOOR, HANS. *Dresden. Vierhundert Jahre deutsche[r] Musikkultur* (Dresden, 1948).

*SEIBEL, GUSTAV. *Das Leben des königl. polnischen und kurfürstl. sächs. Hofkapellmeisters Johann David Heinichen . . .* (Leipzig, 1913).

SEIFFERT, MAX. *Geschichte der Klaviermusik* (Leipzig, 1899).

SERAUKY, WALTER. *Die musikalische Nachahmungsästhetik im Zeitraum von 1700 bis 1850* (Münster/Westfalen, 1929).

SPITTA, PHILIPP. *Heinichen*, ALLGEMEINE DEUTSCHE BIOGRAPHIE 11 (1880), 367–69.

————. *Johann Sebastian Bach* (2 vols. 1873–80); tr. C. BELL & J. A. FULLER-MAITLAND (3 vols. London, 1884–85).

*STEGLICH, RUDOLF. *Nochmals: Über die Generalbassbegleitung zu Kammermusikwerken Bachs*, DIE MUSIKFORSCHUNG 10 (1957), 422–23.

STEVENS, DENIS. *Problems of Editing and Publishing Old Music*, REPORT OF THE EIGHTH CONGRESS OF THE IMS (New York, 1961), 150–58.

STRUNK, OLIVER. *Source Readings in Music History* (New York, 1950).

*TANNER, RICHARD. *Heinichen als Dramatischer Komponist* (Leipzig, 1916).

TERRY, CHARLES S. *Bach, A Biography* (London, 1928).

*TIRABASSI, ANTONIO. *Histoire de l'harmonisation à partir de 1600 à 1750*, KONGRESS-BERICHT, NEUE SCHWEIZERISCHE MUSIKGESELLSCHAFT (Basel, 1924), 328–33.

TORCHI, LUIGI. *L'accompagnamento degli istrumenti nei melodrammi italiani della prima metà del seicento*, RIVISTA MUSICALE ITALIANA 1 (1894), 7–38; 2 (1895), 666–71.

*ULRICH, ERNST. *Studien zur deutschen Generalbass-Praxis in der ersten Hälfte des 18. Jahrhunderts* (Kassel, 1932).

United States Library of Congress, Division of Music. *Catalogue of Opera Librettos Printed before 1800*, ed. O. SONNECK (Washington, D.C., 1914).

*VINQUIST, MARY & NEAL ZASLAW (eds.). *Performance Practice: A Bibliography* (New York, 1971).

VOIGHT, FR. A. *Reinhard Keiser*, VIERTELJAHRSSCHRIFT FÜR MUSIKWISSENSCHAFT 6 (1890), 151–203.

WELLESZ, EGON. *Die Aussetzung des Basso Continuo in der italienischen Oper*, REPORT OF THE FOURTH CONGRESS OF THE IMS (London, 1921), 282–85.

*WERNER, ARNO. *Sachsen-Thüringen in der Musikgeschichte*, ARCHIV FÜR MUSIKWISSENSCHAFT 4 (1922), 322–35.

————. *Städtische und fürstliche Musikpflege in Weissenfels bis zum Ende des 18. Jahrhunderts* (Leipzig, 1911).

WIEL, TADDEO. *I teatri musicali veneziani del settecento . . .* (Venice, 1897).

*WIENANDT, ELWYN. *David Kellner's "Lautenstücke,"* JOURNAL OF THE AMERICAN MUSICOLOGICAL SOCIETY 10 (1957), 29–38.

*WILLIAMS, PETER. *Figured Bass Accompaniment* (2 vols. Edinburgh, 1970).

WOLF, JOHANNES. *Handbuch der Notationskunde* (2 vols. Leipzig, 1913–19).
———— (ed). *Music of Earlier Times* (New York, 1946).
WOLFF, HELLMUTH C. *Die Barockoper in Hamburg* (Wolfenbüttel, 1957).
WORSTHORNE, SIMON. *Venetian Opera in the Seventeenth Century* (Oxford, 1954).

Index

An asterisk (*) is used to designate the pages containing the most significant discussions among the index entries.

Page numbers in quotation marks refer to statements quoted verbatim from the persons indexed.